VIA Folios 86

Strangers in a Strange Land

A Survey of Italian-language American Books (1830-1945)

James J. Periconi

BORDIGHERA PRESS

Library of Congress Control Number: 2013931866

First published in hardback edition by
The Grolier Club, New York
2012

Set in Bodoni Types and designed by
Jerry Kelly

Printed in the United States.

Published by
BORDIGHERA PRESS
John D. Calandra Italian American Institute
25 West 43rd Street, 17th Floor
New York, NY 10036

VIA FOLIOS 86
ISBN 978-1-59954-057-3

Preface

I am very grateful to Bordighera Press, especially Anthony Tamburri, Dean of the John D. Calandra Italian American Institute of the City University of New York, for bringing out this edition of *Strangers in a Strange Land*. Thanks to Lisa Cecchetti for her terrific book design, and to Robert Viscusi for his constant encouragement.

Originally conceived of as the companion work to an exhibition of Italian-language American imprints at the Grolier Club in the Fall of 2012, the first *Strangers* was a beautifully wrought, hardcover work of art, designed by one of the country's great book designers, Jerry Kelly. Bordighera Press has now produced an equally beautiful paperback edition. It arrives just in time for the remounting of the same exhibition at the Brooklyn College Library in the spring of 2013 and at Westchester Community College in the fall of 2013, and for the students who I hope to attract to the exhibition.

I thank Bordighera Press for giving a great push to my modest goal, set out in the "Introduction" to this work, of curing the historical amnesia that I believe still besets Italian Americans.

New York, New York
January 30, 2013

For two great readers and writers of Italian,
Joseph F. Periconi, Sr. and Benedetto Rosario Scovotti
And to the son and daughter of each, respectively, my parents
Joseph F. Periconi, Jr. and Rosemary Scovotti Periconi,
to whom I owe everything.

Contents

ACKNOWLEDGEMENTS

The list of those who encouraged and assisted in the undertaking of this exhibition (and this catalogue) is long, and it starts with the beginnings of this project, with Grolier Club members: first, Jean Ashton, for encouraging and enriching my early research about ten years ago on Lorenzo Da Ponte, and Victor Basile, who heard me give a lecture, based on that research, at an academic conference in 2004 about Da Ponte's Italian book collecting and selling in and around New York, and who suggested that the time might be right for an exhibition of Italian books at the Club, slyly adding that it would be better if I first became a member. Mary Young, then Members' Exhibition Committee chair, saw promise in an exhibition like this with my participation in the New Members' Exhibition in 2006. Szilvia Szmuk-Tanenbaum, current chair of the Members' Exhibition Committee, and Mark Tomasko, a member of that Committee, have been very supportive and encouraging throughout the life of this project. More than anyone I have to thank for the realization of this catalogue and bibliography, I thank George Ong, whose meticulous professional editing, as chair of the Publications Committee, and incisive questions about both bibliographic information and how I told my story in this work improved my manuscript and the exhibition – immeasurably. The enthusiastic support and encouragement of Michael Suarez and Michael Ryan were sustaining. I thank in advance Jean Stephenson and other Club volunteers for mounting the exhibition with flair and understanding. Director Eric Holzenberg, Maev Brennan and Exhibitions Coordinator Megan Smith were, as always, indispensable.

Numerous Italian Americanists have encouraged and supported this project, and prevented me from making too many mistakes from beginning to end: starting with Francesco Durante and Martino Marazzi, who inspired my collecting and research passions and cheered every new "find" I made, to Robert Viscusi, the editor-in-chief of the parallel Fordham University translation project of Francesco's monumental *Italoamericana* (vol. II) and fellow Grolier Club member, whose constant personal as well as professional support in the bad as well as good times in the life of this project put me in his debt forever. Emelise Aleandri was enormously helpful in thinking through parts of the project as well as loaning materials from her superb library. Richard Mattiaccio's excellent translation of Francesco Durante's essay was a life-saver. Marcella Bencivenni, Alexandra DeLuise, Bénédicte Deschamps, Donna Gabaccia, Fred Gardaphé, Charles Killinger, Gail Levin, Frank Lentricchia, Federico Mennella, Gerald Meyer, Ernie Rossi, Anthony Julian Tamburri, Michael Miller Topp and Mary Anne Trasciatti have all contributed to my education and understanding of the materials before me. Current or former book dealers and friends (virtually all Grolier Club members), including Lorne Bair, Dan DeSimone, Rodger Friedman and Will Monie, were helpful in developing my interest, my collection or my understanding of materials. Jerry Kelly's expert eye in book design and layout, not to speak of his ability to calm a nervous client, made the production of this book a pleasure. At a critical early stage, Jordan DeButts, formerly of Lorne Bair Rare Books, and currently in the library program at Pratt, enabled me to complete the first draft of the manuscript. God bless Nancy Tomasko, who rescued me from chaos in the preparation of the index and bibliography. Needless to say, despite my very good fortune in friends and colleagues, there will be mistakes, and they will be entirely my own doing and my responsibility.

My family's encouragement kept me going throughout: my brother, Paul and his wife, Ann, my children, Francesca, Justin, Alicia and Regina, and their spouses, cheered me throughout. Above all, I thank my long-suffering, usually patient but occasionally and understandably impatient wife, Alice McCarthy, who excused my many sins of omission and commission, not the least of which was emptying the family coffers frequently to buy yet another work, and who also gifted me with her brilliant and timely *aperçus* about many aspects of this project.

James J. Periconi Introduction

I am often asked by collectors and others about the origins of my collecting works written in Italian, published in this country (or if published abroad, reflecting experiences here). After all, there has not traditionally been, even since the expansion of the possibilities of book collecting that began between the two World Wars,[1] a well-recognized field of collecting Italian American books.

The simple answer is that this collecting activity unites two core passions in my life: my deep interest in the history and role of books in the human experience, and the perplexity that I share with every Italian American intellectual about the peculiar place that Italians have had, and continue to have, in American culture — most simply put, deeply admired but more deeply reviled.

One answer to this perplexity is to understand the book history of Italians better, especially since Italian Americans are often beset with a deep amnesia about their origins, and the Italian American experience has more often begun with the understandable desire to learn and live in the language of their country of adoption, not their country of origin. As the significance of language in identity formation is all too obvious,[2] a fresh examination of an extensive Italian-language publishing history, in newspapers and in books, seems like an excellent starting point to understanding the place of Italians in American history. It is how the identity of those living in an almost forbidden language — the prevailing pedagogic and political theory had public school teachers in the first half of the 20th century instruct Italian children like my mother in the 1920s to "tell your parents to stop speaking Italian at home, so you'll learn English more quickly" — plays out in any particular instance that makes the story meaningful. (The experience of Italian immigrants to Argentina was an utterly different one from that of immigrants to the United States, for example.) The United States, a land of immigrants, has a tortured history of how it received any particular immigrant group. In the case of the Italians, the reception accorded to this group was and remains deeply ambivalent.

To get to the heart of it: my examination of this publishing history led to the conclusion that Italian-language American book publishing before World War II created and reflected a vibrant literary and political culture among a broad spectrum of Italians living and working in the United States for lengthy periods and, in many cases, as permanent immigrants. This conclusion need not clash with statistics showing high rates (as high as 53%) of illiteracy among Italian immigrants. By 1910, in a population in the U.S. of perhaps five million Italian immigrants, there remained perhaps 2.35 million immigrants literate in Italian, for whom reading was an important activity outside of work and family, as the flourishing of a thousand or more Italian-language newspapers in the first half of the 20th century suggests. In addition, of those illiterate upon entry to the U.S., Italians, more than any immigrant group other than Jews, used public libraries extensively to learn to read and write in Italian (as they had not in Italy), as well as to learn to read and write in English.[3]

The first reason for my conclusion is that many of the immigrant book authors reflected in this exhibition were already accomplished writers, usually journalists by trade, most of them educated and trained in Italy. In addition to the literary and political culture that they created or found themselves involved in, the overall quality of their written work was not an amateurish literature (more on that later) that might not be worth our time and attention. If it were, it would perhaps be less of literary interest, than of historical or anthropological interest to us now.

Secondly, I hope the catalogue that follows the essays will make clear that there was a broad cross-pollination of these sophisticated imaginative writers of fiction, poetry and politics between and among publishing houses, in fact, so great as to suggest the existence of a real, mostly urban literary culture that reached across the nation, among obvious centers like New York, Chicago and San Francisco, but also in seemingly unlikely locales for literary activity, such as Scranton. Cordiferro's *Ode alla Calabria* (cat. 72), in addition to the poem itself, here published in Argentina (which was reprinted from a January 1931 issue of his family's brilliant literary review, *La Follia di New York*) contains copies of appreciations of the poem in the

Italian-language immigrant press, ranging from *La Sentinella* of Bridgeport, Connecticut, to *Colombo*, a weekly journal in Houston, Texas, to *La Tribuna del New Jersey*, in Jersey City, to a writer from Westerly, Rhode Island, to a reader of *La Follia*, to *La Follia*'s own reviewer. These notices provide evidence of a widespread common literary culture among Italian immigrants in the United States. Moreover, the notice or review published in a Calabrian newspaper shows that interest in Cordiferro reached back to the mother country.

One must conclude that these were not solitary scribblers whose works were dutifully published by their friends, having no real impact. Average people, as well as the *literati*, read these works. Besides the readers of poetry who thrilled to the latest work of Cordiferro, Italians waited patiently for the latest episode of, say, a novel by Bernardino Ciambelli to appear as an "appendix" in one or another newspaper, or in issues of *La Follia*, much like the more familiar phenomenon of English and American middle class readers awaiting the latest episode of a Dickens novel to be released in parts. Writers of Ciambelli's stature could then, and did, sell the rights to a publisher to release the serialized work in a single volume (cat. 135b).

To better understand how widespread not merely the praise but the very genuine interest was in works like Cordiferro's poem, to take that example again, one need only look at the vivid and dramatic literary life of Riccardo Cordiferro himself, first in Italy and then in the United States and elsewhere, chronicled by Francesco Durante in his essay in this book. Cordiferro was published by Nicoletti Brothers, the Cocce Press, and the Italian Book Company, as well as his and his family's own *La Follia di New York*. Others, like the dramatist and novelist Paolo Pallavicini, published in both San Francisco and New York, and across the Atlantic in Italy (many of the writers in this exhibition had at least some of their works published in Italy as well as in the United States).

Next, while there were some (like Luigi Galleani) who only wrote political tracts, many of the writers wrote richly dramatic and imaginative, as well as political, works, whether for didactic reasons or as a release from their political activities: besides Cordiferro and Pallavicini, Arturo Giovannitti stands out as a dramatic writer of depth and accomplished poet, as well as political writer, and Gigi Damiani, a political philosopher, was a forceful

Italian playwright (cat. 84–87), albeit of political dramas published in the United States, though there is no evidence that he even visited this country. Even a straight political figure like Italy's Errico Malatesta used in an American publication the traditional Italian literary technique of having an average worker ask questions of another while at a café together, building into a crescendo of an understanding eventually of the evils of capitalism and the plight of the worker (cat. 81).

Nor did serious political writing mean that these authors were not engaged in the real world. Jean-Paul Sartre, had he known them, would have applauded the quality of *engagement politique*, the ability of these writers to break away from their desks to lead factory workers in strikes, as well as to lead an even broader range of anti-fascists in demonstrations against Mussolini, and they did so not as one-offs, to enhance their literary credentials, but rather as an integral part of who they were, as their political activities endured in a concerted, consistent way over time. These writers include, besides Giovannitti, Ezio Taddei and Efrem Bartoletti, among others. They worked as miners and organizers of miners in Italy, in Pennsylvania and the Mesabi range of Minnesota, as well as leaders during particularly trying events, like the 1912 Bread and Roses strike in Lawrence, Massachusetts, led by Giovannitti and Tresca (cat. 112, 115, 148). Some, like Carlo Tresca, went on regular *giri di propaganda*, *i.e.*, propaganda tours, stirring up workers on the West Coast (where Tresca was sometimes barred by company officials who feared his ability to stir up otherwise complacent workers) as well as the East Coast, not just in cities like New York, but in regional locales like Utica and Buffalo (see cat. 117, 118).

Fourthly, the level of competence of the publishers who could nurture and encourage high-quality writing was itself fairly high, even if the books they produced were rarely striking examples of the book arts. Native Italian speakers, of course working in their own language, were employed by book publishers who were already experienced and relatively sophisticated either in business (or soon became so) (*e.g.*, Tocci, De Martino) or as journeymen in the book arts (*e.g.*, Attilio Coccè and Alberto Nicoletti, trained as typographers and linotypists in Italy), even if few of the works in this exhibition are models of contemporary trends in book design or printing, Taddei's works being the exception. At least a few — especially Tocci,

De Martino, Ettore Nicoletti and Adamo and Claudio Coccè — were literary editors (as well as businessmen) who had some idea of nurturing and spreading literary talent from both sides of the Atlantic.

Finally, *there were bookstores*, Italian bookstores, lots of them, not only in the major cities, that served as the locus for not only the books themselves, but for the people who bought and read them. Some, like the Italian Book Company or Rossi's, stocked works of all kinds, and sheet music as well (cat. 134, 142c); others were so-called "red bookstores" (cat. 56) or the more high-minded sounding Libreria Sociologica in Paterson (cat. 81), which stocked radical materials well represented in this exhibition. Nor were these isolated examples: one grammar writer, Angelo De Gaudenzi (cat. 9), also maintained a business as "editore e librai" (publishers and booksellers), which offered in an advertisement in the *1905 Italian American Directory* (cat. 49) "at your request to send a 'prospectus' for the establishment of a bookstore to be supplied with books *at reasonable prices*." Whatever their political perspective, the existence of bookstores — and the commercial encouragement of more bookstores to meet an evident demand —reflect a communal interest in books and a developing book culture.

The essays that follow this introduction suggest the richness of this enterprise. The first two are by Italian scholars, classically trained in Italian literature before they encountered American history, and who can thus look at the Italian literary output in the U.S. with a detachment and objectivity few of us here have. Martino Marazzi's *And the Word Was Made Inkcarnate: From Oral to Written to Published Literature in Italian America* is an insightful analysis of how Italians in American moved from spoken to written, and thence to published language in an amazingly short historical period, the move that parallels Robert Viscusi's brilliant apothegm about the wrenching experience of Italians coming to America: "A whole nation walked out of the middle ages, slept in the ocean, and awakened in New York in the twentieth century."[4] Marazzi shows how that transition elucidates the central linguistic trauma, the "uprooting" from their language parallel to the uprooting from the mother country.

Francesco Durante, the godfather of the study of Italian literature in the United States, creates a vivid portrait of one of the most important of these writers, Riccardo Cordiferro, a writer whom Durante considers an "archetypal" Italian American, in that he best personifies "those characteristics that were considered in his contemporary America to be typically Italian: incurable sentimentality; exaggerated populist passion in politics; grandiose and ornate (if not downright histrionic and borrowed from the grand opera stage) in word and gesture; and an unrepentant seducer's spirit combined with a paradoxical, quasi-religious worship of the domestic virtues."[5]

Robert Viscusi, whose attunement to issues of language and identity is that of one classically trained in Latin and Greek, as well as English and American literature, provides a series of poignant reflections as well as scholarly observations. The work he examines is one of the more lavishly produced books, an elephant folio, half of which is composed of essays reflecting the progress of Italians in America, and the other half of which is a directory of prominent Italian American businessmen of the time, *Gli italiani negli Stati Uniti d'America* [Italians in the United States of America] (New York: Italian American Directory Co., 1906) (cat. 50). He sees that work in the historical context of the Milan Exposition of 1906, whose planners had called, a year before the Exposition, for production of this work. Viscusi concludes that the Milanesi regarded Italians in America then as perhaps not constituting much more than a revenue-producing colony of Italy, a colony whose prominent members are on display permanently, well captured in this book, almost as if in a zoo (though he does not quite say that), alongside specimens from Italy's failed colonial forays into Africa.

These essays, as well as this exhibition, then, were conceived in praise of these, a different kind of Italian American "pioneer." The shame of it has been that so few of the works exhibited and discussed here have been translated into English and made available to an English-language readership, Italian American or otherwise. With the anticipated publication in 2013 of the translation and publication by the Fordham University Press of Durante's monumental *Italoamericana* (volume 2), however, excerpts from about 65 of these writers will see their first translations into English and begin to fill this significant gap in American (as well as Italian American) studies. My only hope is that this exhibition is also an important step in the same direction.

NOTES

1. See Jean Peters, *Book Collecting: A Modern Guide* (New York: R.R. Bowker Co. 1977); Nicholas Basbanes, *A Gentle Madness: Bibliophiles, Bibliomanes, and the Eternal Passion for Books* (New York: Henry Holt, 1995).

2. See, *e.g.*, Nancy C. Carnevale, *A New Language, a New World: Italian Immigrants in the United States, 1890–1945* (Urbana, Ill.: University of Illinois Press, 2009).

3. See Robert E. Park, *Immigrant Press and its Control.* (New York: Harper & Brothers, 1922); Alexandra DeLuise, "The Italian Immigrant Reads: Evidence of Reading for Learning and Reading for Pleasure, 1890-1920s." *Italian Americana* 30, no. 1 (Winter 2012): pp. 33-43.

4. Robert Viscusi, *Astoria* (Guernica: 1995), p. 22.

5. Francesco Durante, "Riccardo Cordiferro: An Italian American Archetype," in *Strangers in a Strange Land*, p. 18.

MARTINO MARAZZI And the Word Was Made Ink-carnate: From Oral to Written to Published Literature in Italian America

In the beginning was the end. In the final pages of Salvatore Scibona's acclaimed novel by the same title, *La fine*, an old Italian woman who emigrated "for love" from the Roman countryside to Ohio in the 1890s seals the epic with a stream of consciousness which reads like a letter to her beloved. Many things and thoughts pass through her mind, including the following: "Here is what we call a mother tongue. Think of the physical tongue of your mother. Think of your father's kisses on that tongue and how the kisses precede you into the world./ My dear, I have never heard spoken since a word in my mother's tongue. My darling, I forsook it for the promise of you."[1]

I'm proposing here that we look at the books and all the various items on display in the current exhibit as testimonies to a unique phase of dynamic balance between a before and an after. They are, at the same time, the result of an arrival and a point of departure - individually and historically. They are the product of a subtly shifting expressiveness. The tongues and kisses of Scibona's female character looking back at the defining years of her life belong to the complex dimension of mass migration, a *tsunami* sweeping away people's lives, transporting them elsewhere, metamorphosing their culture and inner being with the energy of a centrifugal force. "Mass migration" includes local histories, global economics, wars and persecutions, risks and dreams, poverty and opportunity, uprooting, distance, crushing toil, circadian cycle of hope and despair — and language caught in the midst, clenched to, as it were, a raft, a complex system of cyberlogic daily dismembered and benumbed, striving to somehow reconfigure itself.

Real life, and real spoken words, precede – at least from the point of view of personal histories – the social and cultural landscape rapidly refashioned by the Italian American communities over the other side of the ocean. I believe that if we assume, for the sake of our analysis, a hypothetical typology comprised of three inter-related stages – *Speaking*, *Writing*, *Publishing* – we could better approach a dynamic that has linguistic trauma as one of its epicenters.

Speaking. - Let us start, then, by trying to briefly look at how Italians used their spoken language in the U.S., keeping in mind a sort of caveat: because in fact the actual and obvious weight of the oral dimension can by and large be inferred from written sources, so that if and when we discuss orality, it's as if its improvisational dynamism has been muffled and long gone already. Nevertheless, its vitality gleams through whatever written documents we have available. These are fragile sources, better conveyed by some form of sound recording and/or visual reproduction. I'll try to make do. Some among the shrewdest early observers of the Italian "colonies" worldwide (Amy A. Bernardy (cat. 69), Giuseppe Prezzolini, Renzo Nissim, *et al.*) concur in their keen attention to the fleeting traces of the pliable, unheard-of, innovative use of the venerable Italian language in the new contexts of immigration. The language of Dante combusts with the different linguistic materials of the many distinct Italian dialects, and with the languages of arrival – whether they be English or, in Latin America, Spanish and Portuguese, French (in and all around Paris and the French Midi), and later German. Bernardy even fantasized, as early as 1911, about the day when the future historian would have the full catalogue of the colonial written documents at his or her disposal – a *corpus inscriptionum* (much like the one that scholars of ancient Rome religiously leaf through) made of street signs, posters, flyers, commercial ads, and the like. (Some of these can be found, along with books, among the ephemera on display in this Grolier exhibition.)

Sometimes, even a simple letter can suffice. That's where *lettera*-ture comes from, after all: letters, either mailed back to the motherland, or just plainly and carefully written in longhand. Here are two examples. I was struck, only months ago, when I came across a large, elegant sign painted on the wall of a stone house in a minuscule village to the north of Lake

Maggiore, deep in the Alps. This is a region from which laborers and impoverished landowners started emigrating very early in the 19th century. Many made it to the West Coast of the U.S., which, to make a long story short, explains the birth of the wine industry there. Giuseppe Leoni, a returning immigrant, limited himself to writing down his full name in big capital letters, adding only his arrival point, and the source of his acquired wealth: "Califorgna" – just like that, with a "gn." The painted sign on the entrance wall of his house, built with the money of emigration, marks his proud homecoming: it's a strong proclamation of success, attached to its tangible result, and a self-evident declaration of an identity that is spatially and chronologically defined by the migratory experience. The elemental phonetics highlights the Italian-ness of his American dream: despite the supposedly intense period spent in the remote West, and the equally committed effort at establishing the geography of his *nostos* (homecoming), he adopts with the utmost clarity the grapheme commonly used in Italian for the palatal sound: that "gn" sign is a sort of minimal cultural and linguistic slip; it visualizes in a way acceptable to an Italian-speaking person the foreign-ness of a not familiar name.

The *corpus* of the immigrants' epistolary literature represent another enormous and inexhaustible body of evidence. Every researcher in this field has amassed distinct primary sources. Among my favorites I count the postcards sent in both directions, in part because of the relationship they dramatize between the verbal and the iconic, and furthermore because of the added layers of tenderness, self-vindication, and mischief that can be frequently extracted by a later third party (a contemporary reader) taking into consideration the distance between the sender and the addressee, and the imbalance between their different levels of knowledge. The carefully written mailing card sent to Civiasco, a village of northwest Piedmont, on New Year's Eve, 1901, by Severo ***, a resident of the Lower East Side of Manhattan, is addressed to his friend Florinda Zatti. The verso bears a touching photo of Third Avenue at Cooper Square, with Cooper Union to the left and the Third Avenue El in full motion, speeding north and south. Underneath it, commerce and human traffic. Severo has marked a cross on the upper right of the avenue, next to where he lives on East 11th Street. He refers to the "terza avenida," betraying a familiarity with Spanish: after all, we are informed, a "Carlo" who's close to both correspondents has decided to stay in Barcelona, despite the fact that "io avreba stato molto contento che avesse venutto dove in poco tempo potteva guadagnare molto danaro" (which very roughly translates as *I wood had had very happy that he had cum where in a short time he cood earn much money*). Here, too, the orthography is revealing; there are some mistakes (like in "avreba [*i.e.*, "avrebbe"] stato," instead of "<u>sarei</u> stato"), due maybe to Severo's recourse to an uncommon tense; some forms reproduce "correctly" the dialectal pronunciation and grammar (*anca te* = "anche tu", *i.e. you too*; *poi* = "puoi," *i.e., you can*); and above all, it is fascinating to observe that there is not a single punctuation mark, as if such a brief message was meant mostly in its continuous entirety, almost like the prolonging in ink of a fast and fact-laden street conversation, and thus as if it was not concerned with internal prose rhythms and logical hierarchies. Once it starts with the formulaic salutation, "Cara Florinda," it proceeds in an uninterrupted flow all the way to Severo's signature and address, followed by the only minuscule, but visible, period.

Is Severo Florinda's fiancé? It is tempting to think he might have been; but as far as we know, we can only say that he's ensconced downtown, bewildered by modern urban bustle, and that he is very aware of the economic opportunities around him. He sends wishes; he keeps in touch and promises a real letter in the future. He addresses his female friend with the intimate "you" form. He most probably left Italy for economic reasons, leaving his relationship with Florinda at an uncertain standstill. She needs to be reassured, but he can't (or doesn't feel he can) seriously commit himself. His card has an energetic pull, but manages to waddle in a typically masculine airiness. Here's an atom in the very middle of American capitalism, at the beginning of the twentieth century. His shout back to his familiar hilltown[2] must have been read by Florinda with a mixture of puzzlement and pride, hope and concern. What was this guy actually saying? What was going on in his mind? Are we (and she with us) witnessing the slow formation of a linguistic fault line?

The spoken word is subject to interpretation just like the written word. Examples like the above are not that dissimilar from the spirit of what scholars of Italian American history consider the master narrative of the

Italian immigration to the U.S., the autobiographical account of Rosa Cassettari[3], where the contagious alertness of this Milanese peasant, turned Chicagoan informer to the benefit of the local school of social work, in many instances lets us glimpse into a performative enactment of her bilingual identity. Rosa's words, no matter how filtered by the professorial editing of her interlocutor Marie Hall Ets, usually resort to Italian bits when at their most spontaneous or emotional. Whenever we hear her speaking Italian, albeit in a flash, we sense that we are entering a particularly charged territory of her memory. And above all, it's the interplay, the negotiation between the two codes, that really counts, the movement back and forth. There is not *one* language on one side, and *another* language on the other side; rather, there is a conscience which operates linguistically on a moving ground.

Writing. – Immigrant writers transport such a dynamic to a different, one could say a much higher, degree. And I'm referring here more in general to a conscious use of artistic expression. That is, writers, artists and intellectuals can be more effective to the degree that they tap into the shared needs and codes of their community. Their creativity can show up on a page, on a canvas, on a stage. The more perceptive observers of the time were quite aware of this:

> But the ill-clad Italians, with their odious pipes puffing out malodorous [sic] smoke, who crowd into the dramatic stable yard and make the atmosphere within the old mule shed unbearable to all save themselves, do not go there for vulgar vaudeville or cheap variety. You would not expect it, and it is hard to believe when you see it, but these ignorant, untutored men, who labor with their hands all day at the worst work in New York, flock to the Star [the Star Theater at 101 Union Street, in South Brooklyn] to see the highest of Italian drama attainable here. They flock there every night and listen enthralled at the words, written centuries ago by the immortal Tasso, the Italian epic poet, who, together with his father, Bernardo Tasso, contributed some of the best of Italian epics. [. . .] The Star Theater is a dirty place to go: it is filthy and sickening to the sight and senses, and one sees men there who surely never wash. Yet with all its dinginess and dirt, its bad odors and mean looking men, it is worth a visit, and if one is of the people of the Italian quarter and doesn't object to the smoke

and grime and understands the Italian language, it might be worth enough visits to cover at least a canto of "Jerusalem Delivered."[4]

This full re-enactment of *Jerusalem Delivered*, performed at the Star Theater with marionettes, is a bold statement. What was happening was the conscious appropriation and re-use of styles and languages passed down through the centuries along the Italian peninsula and elsewhere. To different degrees, all the major voices of the Italian American communities crafted their stories and poetry transporting the home-grown tradition to the new shores. Such a modus operandi was risky but inevitable and necessary, in order to win approbation and consent; repetition had to go hand in hand with openings.

Reassure and dare is the emblem of an immigrant art which is at the same time popular, multi-layered, and ephemeral. Pulp fiction lives side by side with the diabolically intense skits of the vaudeville multilingual theater of Eduardo Migliaccio, a/k/a Farfariello. The romantic potboilers by Paolo Pallavicini — exemplified in this exhibition by his *Tutto il dolore, tutto l'amore* (San Francisco, 1926) (cat. 61) — embellishing the life of a mostly imagined Italian middle-class in California, were at some point in such demand as to appear in the columns of the colonial newspapers in San Francisco, and at the same time to be printed by major publishers back in Italy.

Arturo Giovannitti, the first great bilingual Italian American poet, poignantly called *The Cage* (eloquent title) "a poem of rotting tradition and living men."[5] He had composed it on a Sunday, in 1912, unjustly detained in Salem Jail; and its first publisher had been *The Atlantic Monthly* — just like a decade later Pascal D'Angelo, author of *Son of Italy*, was to be read both in *The Nation* and in the New York-based nationalist monthly, with strong Fascist leanings, *Il Carroccio*.

Italian immigrant artists can count on a public attuned to their culture. This is not surprising, since they are well and truly part of it, being for the most part immigrants themselves, largely self-taught, and more often than not used to doling out a meagre living with an assortment of jobs. Gigi Damiani, a/k/a Simplicio, a leader of the hyper-active anarchist subterranean network, can flaunt his familiarity with the real common ground of most Italians at the time, the language of the opera, when he inserts in an otherwise virtuosic but rather inane parody of fascist opportunism three joyous and sonorous lines like the following: "Addio banchetti, addio ragazze belle,/ e facili guadagni,/ "clamori e canti di battaglie addio!" ("Farewell banquets, farewell fair girls,/ and easy money,/ 'farewell shouts and songs of battles!'").[6] That is, he is quoting from Arrigo Boito's free adaptation of Shakespeare's *Othello*[7] for Verdi's opera, one of his late masterpieces. It is telling that Shakespeare is served to an immigrant public (striving to unshackle it from its torpid social and political conformism) through the mediation of Verdi and Boito. Can you be more aptly bicultural than this?

Such a playful and sophisticated intertextuality affects at different levels the creativity of the immigrants' art, and constitutes an indispensable prerequisite if we want to approach without naïveté the varied and adventurous world of the immigrants' publishing world, in both its commercial but also cultural components.

Publishing. – Arrival point. When you publish, you decide to go public. And in so doing and being, you forge a public. What was previously an intellectual operation which required recognition as a hypothesis now tests itself in front of a real audience. Your public is no more a double of the mind, but a real paying entity and, on occasion, it votes with its feet. A substantial degree of mutual linguistic understanding is paramount; and so is a close relationship with the territory. If your public has a high degree of returns, both physical and imaginary (if daydreaming and being informed about the motherland remain a staple of everyday life, as they did), then you should also consider stretching as much as possible your activities, in a variety of ways, on both sides of the Atlantic.

More plainly, the appearance of an Italian American publishing world means that an Italian American public is born, *i.e.*, acquires the consciousness of being such. Italian Americans existed before Frugone e Balletto, before the Italian Book Company, before New York's *Il Progresso Italo-Americano*, San Francisco's *La Voce del Popolo*, and stores like E. Rossi on Mulberry and Mott. But such ventures testify to a new rise in status and self-confidence. *The same linguistic and expressive phenomena which we have tried to exemplify above now make it into print.*

Here, then, are the books and items on display. There's a difference between being a native speaker (no matter how traumatized or energized by the encounter with a different culture, depending on a myriad variables) or being a writer (using and/or abusing tradition) — and, on the other hand, making your appearance on the social stage, becoming a read item, metamorphosing into an author. Books do that. You may still be halfway between a god and a jester, but your voice doesn't just produce a narcissistic echo any longer: the publisher bets on its response and its recognizability. The name above the title is now, potentially, a beacon for a community.

The histories of the Italian American publishers (and there were, literally, thousands of them up to the 1970s, scattered all around the U.S.) are replete with big and little facts, with anecdotes, with acts of courage, as well as with acrimonious bickering — Luigi Carnovale's 1909 *Il giornalismo degli emigrati italiani nel Nord America* (cat. 63) provides lots of evidence of the latter — with grand or petty failures (and, less often, successes), with opportunistic schemes and political feuds. Taken collectively, they can represent, in some way, a metaphor of the entire Italian immigrant culture.

Italian publishing in the U.S. started in the mid-19th century, in the fiery climate of the Italian Risorgimento, and soon expanded and adapted to the gigantic wave of immigrants from the peninsula (arriving in steerage class with other hundreds of thousands of southern and eastern Europeans). While always, by necessity, open to both worlds, from the 1920s they also increasingly showed signs of interaction with the surrounding linguistic landscape.

Simply put, the English language takes over more and more newspaper columns as we get closer to the outbreak of World War II: not only "English sections" begin appearing as a rule on the last page, but Italian American authors venture into bilingualism (Giovannitti, Tresca), book publishers like the Società Libraria Italiana (Italian Book Company) print volumes in both languages, and typical "American" products, such as the comic strip, quickly eschew the short, goofy Italian translations. Newspapers like the *Corriere d'America look* American (see their elegant use of pictures, and the overall layout of its pages) way before their Italian counterparts in the peninsula. And after World War II, a New York magazine like *Divagando* anticipates Mondadori's *Epoca* in imitating, at least superficially, the graphics of *Life*.

On an individual level, more and more the authors of the Italian American community show their keen attention to a close rapport with their audience. "Publishing," *i.e.*, mingling with the public, is for them, literally speaking, an essential dimension of their popular activity. That is why, especially until World War II, these two dimensions (authorship and publishing) represent, in the Italian American world, almost two communicating vessels. They mirror and they strengthen one another, following the biological trajectory of a generation which had come of age in the years of the Great Migration, between the end of the 19th century and World War I.

So, Tresca and Giovannitti rally the "ethnic" crowds of the unionized workers; Migliaccio/Farfariello cheers the undifferentiated spectators of the neighborhood theaters, and, later, local radio station listeners; and newspapers of all orientations show an unfailing devotion to the most diverse products of "colonial" literature (fiction, poetry, op-eds, even drama). And as it had rapidly formed with strong homogeneous characteristics, so that culture will gradually but inevitably disperse from the 1950s on, to be replaced by new ways of being "public," and eventually turning its back on the Italian language.

NOTES

1. Salvatore Scibona, *The End.* New York: Riverhead, 2009: 308.

2. Not far from the birthplaces of the parents of such distinct Italian American personalities as novelist Mari Tomasi and politician and military officer Charles Poletti.

3. Marie H. Ets, *Rosa. The Life of an Italian Immigrant.* Madison: The University of Wisconsin Press, 1970.

4. "Local Italian Theater Crowded Every Night." *The Brooklyn Daily Eagle*, December 3, 1899:7.

5. See Arturo Giovannitti, *The Cage* (Riverside, Conn.: Hillacre, 1914), at colophon.

6. Simplicio, *Coraggio e avanti!*, in *Sgraffi* (Newark: Biblioteca de L'Adunata dei Refrattari, 1946:93). See cat. 87.

7. Verdi's *Otello*: Act 2, Scene 3.

MARTINO MARAZZI is assistant professor of Italian literature at the Università degli Studi, Milan, Italy and has been a Fellow of the Italian Academy for Advanced Studies at Columbia University. He has written widely on literary and cultural relations between Italy and the United States, editing various works by Italian American writers. His most recent books are *Voices of Italian America. A History of Early Italian American Literature with a Critical Anthology* (in paperback (New York: Fordham University Press, 2012); first edition (Madison, NJ: Fairleigh Dickinson University Press, 2004), and *A occhi aperti. Letteratura dell'emigrazione e mito americano* (Milan: FrancoAngeli, 2011). He is the author of two books of fiction: *La fine del Purgatorio* and *Filogenesi* (Milan: Sedizioni, 2008 and 2010).

FRANCESCO
DURANTE Riccardo Cordiferro:
An Italian American Archetype

Riccardo Cordiferro is, in a sense, the most typical of first-generation Italian American writers, in that he best personifies those characteristics that were considered in his contemporary America to be typically Italian: incurable sentimentality; exaggerated populist passion in politics; grandiose and ornate (if not downright histrionic and borrowed from the grand opera stage) in word and gesture; and an unrepentant seducer's spirit combined with a paradoxical, quasi-religious worship of the domestic virtues. In other words, he represented the Italian male, appealing and at the same time rather untrustworthy on account of his ever-changing, capricious and unpredictable character.

A little-known portrait photo buried in the pages of the prestigious 20th-century American magazine, *The Bookman*,[1] corresponds precisely to these preconceived notions. Cordiferro is discussed under the mouthwatering title, "An Anachronism in Bohemia." The anonymous author asks himself, "Where is the old, Bohemian spirit of Henry Murger, the time-honored belief that the poet must be more careless, more improvident, more unaccountable and more unexpected than other men?" And he answers himself that the spirit lives on in Cordiferro and in the poems of his last book, *Singhiozzi e sogghigni* (Hiccups and sneers), a work, published in New York by the press of the "Araldo Italiano," that covers the long period from 1893 up to that work's publication in 1910. The anonymous writer reminds the reader that the weekly *La Follia di New York*, full of the "spontaneous passion of the lower part of the Italian peninsula," was established in 1893.[2] Cordiferro, the writer recounts, was the poet, and his brother, Marziale Sisca, dealt with the practical aspects of publishing the journal. In the early days, the two brothers ate when they could, and the ability to publish the periodical was in the hands of Providence. And yet, a bit at a time, a "little band of orthodox Bohemians" rallied around Cordiferro's inspirational poetry. Cordiferro "sometimes wrote his poems for the next issue of the paper from the interior of a jail where he had been unkindly imprisoned for criminal libel."

As the years passed, however, Marziale created a place for himself in society: he became middle class and prosperous, he married, he moved his family into a nice house complete with servants, and he drastically reduced his appearances in the more popular coffee houses of the old Little Italy. His brother, Alessandro (Alessandro Sisca being the generally-known real name of Riccardo Cordiferro), did nothing of the sort. On the contrary, throughout the period he "keeps the old traditions relatively intact." Certainly, "he is better dressed than of old and a little more regular, and the paper now has ten or twelve pages and many advertisements, and the temptation for a poet to see the eloquence of American ideas is very strong." And yet, "Cordiferro still nurses the Muse" and "proudly maintains that, in spite of his clothes and the money he can borrow from his brother, he is still a poet at heart," something that, consistent with the sympathetic *Bookman* article, emerges clearly from the pages of his new book that is "so full of tumultuous feeling and lyric emotion."

Returning to the title, "An Anachronism in Bohemia," we see that Cordiferro's bohemian spirit did not appear anachronistic only in America and in the cities where, almost a half-century earlier, writers of the same temperament used to linger into the wee hours at tables at the Pfaff beer hall. The bohemian spirit was also anachronistic in Italy. Indeed, it could be said that the very same famous Puccini opera, *La Bohème*, was, in 1896, almost a tombstone. Still, the association of Cordiferro with Puccini's Rodolfo can be considered just about total. The Parisian garret inhabited by artists; the Café Momus; the articles written for magazines; and, obviously, the loves of anxious young girls weakened by consumption (Mimì and Musetta), all transport us to a world extraordinarily similar to the world of which the bard, Riccardo, sings.

As far as Italian literature goes, the Sicilian poet, Giuseppe Aurelio Costanzo (1843-1913), thoroughly evoked this world in a collection that preceded Puccini but bore the truly Puccini-like title, *Gli eroi della soffitta* (The heroes of the garret). The book was first published in 1880 and an additional five editions, at least, were published by 1904. No doubt Cordiferro must have been exposed to this very popular volume as a model in his formative years in Naples, where he studied with such prestigious teachers as Francesco De Sanctis, Luigi Settembrini and Silvio Spaventa, and where Costanzo also had his start.

And so it was that, in an act of spontaneous acceptance, Cordiferro felt himself a full-fledged member in the company of the "Many [who] refuse to bend their backs to the rod / Or their necks to the halter " and who, "Like lions and eagles / Strong and wild hate the crib and flock / And yearn for the chase and flight, / But without a morsel in the mouth or a spur in the flank."[3]

Cordiferro's identification with this company must have been all the more profound in that, in the meantime, it had assumed "political" significance. And Cordiferro – the very young Cordiferro of the 1890s – just like the Cordiferro impassioned in old age by his adoption of anti-fascist ideals, with his contributions to magazines such as *Il Martello* (The Hammer) of Carlo Tresca or *Il Nuovo Mondo* (The New World) of Augusto Bellanca and Luigi Antonini, reveals in America his "subversive" tendencies, clearly not channeled by any rigorous party discipline. On the contrary, those tendencies resulted from a natural sympathy for the humble and oppressed, for the "lowest" to whom he had to feel a deep sense of brotherhood. In the vast field of emigration from Italy at the end of the 1800s, this intellectual company could hardly remain insensitive to the anarchist and socialist speeches frequently made by able Italian compatriots who were part of an exhilarating oratorical tradition. This "political" element is present in Cordiferro's work, moreover, in an ingenious way: not as the product of complex rational analysis, but in a sense that could be described as "poetic."

In 1911, the same year *The Bookman* reviewed his book (a rare privilege for a first-generation Italian American), Cordiferro also was reviewed in *Novatore*, the "free review published every 15 days for all the energetic young who have something new and ingenious to say," edited by the anarchist Libero Tancredi (real name: Massimo Rocca) in New York at 500 East 16th Street. *Novatore* dedicated a short review[4] to a leaflet recently edited by *La Follia,* a poem in the form of a monologue in hendecasyllabic blank verse titled *Il pezzente* (The tramp). And it is as if Tancredi – who, moreover, would soon return to Italy and then, in 1919, become a fascist, which he remained at least until the assassination of Giacomo Matteotti in 1924 — took advantage of the occasion to give Cordiferro a little "lesson" in political discipline.

The theme of *Il pezzente*, a story of "a starving man thrown into prison for his hunger," was not new; "rather, it was," said Tancredi, "one of the themes that was in vogue among the sentimental subversives, when the revolution was not so much considered the triumph of a capable and strong working class against the soft and useless bourgeoisie," as much as "an obscure and angry vendetta of the boundless and miserable masses against society's fortunate ones."[5] In Cordiferro's monologue, the poor "tramp," compelled to beg for charity on the frozen streets of a New York blazing with Christmas holiday plenty, recovers at some point his dignity. This, notes Tancredi, "demonstrates that denying charity is the most noble action that one could take, if for no other reason because this could instill in the beggar, after his blind revolt against the man who refuses to be charitable, the certainty that both in individual and in larger social relationships, one gets to keep only what one has the force and the merit to take."[6]

This is certainly an argumentative reading, among other reasons because Cordiferro's monologue, created for the stage and meeting (according to multiple sources) popular acclaim in the Italian community's small theaters, ends with the work's key scene, a scene that is the exact opposite of an affirmative position based on class consciousness. In a *coup de théâtre* clearly inspired by the puppet theater of the Grand Guignol, the tramp, imprisoned after having attempted armed robbery, strangles himself with his own hands. But Tancredi glosses over this detail. He stops at the class consciousness-raising of the tramp, and he notes: "And it is precisely in the conclusion flowing spontaneously from this little work that one finds its subversive value."[7]

A certain anachronism is almost the natural condition of the immigrant, on whom falls the task of perpetuating on the shore where he makes landfall the image of his own land of origin exactly as it was at the moment of his departure. Nevertheless, one cannot help but note that Tancredi pretended not to know that *Il pezzente* was the late-maturing fruit of a fundamentally pre-political creative idea based on a text from at least sixteen years earlier: its first printing appears to date back to 1895. Riccardo Cordiferro was just twenty years old at the time, having been born at San Pietro in Guarano, a small town in the province of Cosenza, in Calabria, on October 27, 1875.

In Naples, where his father Francesco, also a poet, moved to work on the court house staff, Riccardo made his debut early, publishing a few poems in short-lived magazines such as *Napoli letteraria* (Literary Naples). In 1886 he entered the San Raffaele a Materdei seminary. His vocation could not have been very strong if, as legend would have it, he was expelled for having expressed anti-clerical views and he began to enjoy the company of well-known leaders of the radical left, including Giovanni Bovio and Arturo Labriola. In 1892 he left for America, settling in Pittsburgh, possibly to avoid military service in Italy. He later went to New York, where his father and brother, Marziale, joined him.

Alessandro Sisca started the magazine *La Follia* in 1893, when he was not quite eighteen years old. At that moment his career began as the "bard" of the Italian colony of the Lower East Side. Cordiferro, his favorite among many pseudonyms that he used at the beginning became, as a practical matter, his established name. The name may find its origins from reading Walter Scott, but this is not clear. With this and other names he published *La Follia;* and his works also appeared in other publications, from *La Sedia Elettrica* (The Electric Chair) to *The Haarlemite* to, significantly, *La Questione Sociale* (The Social Question) of Paterson New Jersey, one of the most authoritative and combative anarchist leaflets in the United States, founded in 1895.

All of Cordiferro's vast output – drama, poetry, journalism – had a very strong "social" bent, the work of an artist who was socially engaged, though without a precise party orientation. In this sense Cordiferro did not distance himself much from the general tendency of Italian "colonial" literature which, at least until the rise of fascism, was pretty much all of the same color, slightly red. Still, one can recognize in Cordiferro a true leader of a literary movement, a founding father who, until 1894, worked with other mythical figures such as Antonio Maiori and Pasquale Rapone, the two most celebrated heads of theatrical companies and dramatic artists in Little Italy. Cordiferro's writings for these two leading artists included *L'onore perduto* (Honor lost) (1901), a social drama in four acts fortunate enough to be performed until the 1930s and to command a sequel in 1906 entitled *L'onore vendicato* (Honor avenged).

Without entering into the details of the plot of the two plays, generally they advance a very powerful argument against the wickedness of the wealthy, of the exploiters, and in particular of the prominent sharks — bosses and bankers — who grow fat at the expense of their poor fellow countrymen. Cordiferro's rhetorical paraphernalia is, as previously mentioned, borrowed from the Italian social tradition, from poets such as Costanzo, Mario Rapisardi, or Olindo Guerrini (and possibly one might add to the list Italy's first national poet and first recipient of the Nobel Prize for literature (1906), Giosué Carducci).

Anti-clericalism, an ingredient hardly alien in Italian literature of the Risorgimento and post-Risorgimento, weighs heavily in Cordiferro's work. A garish example of this anti-clerical bent is found in the text of Cordiferro's conference presentation, *The Priest through History* (Barre, Circolo di Studi Sociali, 1915), read publicly in a number of different fora from Buffalo to Brooklyn to Toronto, in confirmation of an intense evangelical effort that he undertook side by side with the anarchists. The insistent and bombastic tone of the work weighs even more heavily and prompted the more refined literary types (including the "American," Giuseppe Prezzolini, whose political views, moreover, were opposed to those of Cordiferro) to respond with disdain. Notwithstanding these limitations, Cordiferro's impact was real and unique, particularly in his ability to focus on the reality of the immigrants, to align himself with their hopes, their desires, their incurable nostalgia as well as the tenacity and leonine courage with which they figured out how to invent a new life for themselves across the ocean.

One could conclude, based on what has been said about Cordiferro, that he was, in essence, a revolutionary writer, the son of an era that assassinated kings, emperors, and presidents. And yet, it would be an incomplete portrait. As Cordiferro described his work, in something of a humble confession in the preface to a collection of his poetry, *Poesie scelte* (Selected poetry) (1928), "the only secret I have learned is the ability to portray a profound sense of what I see around me simply and clearly."[8] He might have added that he obtained that deep sense through a profound sharing of those experiences, including many difficult moments that marked his life from the time when, in 1897-98, he suffered the deaths first of his wife, Annina Belli, and then of his children, Emilia and Franchino. In the end, the

theme underlying all of Cordiferro's work is real life lived and then transformed into an ideal according to the tastes of the times; life with its tragic
and its sweet moments, with its tears and laughter.

Also in 1911 Cordiferro wrote his most famous verses, the only lines
that guaranteed him universal fame: the lines of the Neapolitan song, *Core
'ngrato* (Ungrateful heart) (cat. 22c), one of the finest examples of the
genre. The song is a lament of the abandoned lover of the beautiful Catarina (Catarì) who has become incapable of recognizing in the singer the
man who dedicated his entire life to her. "Don't you forget / that I gave you
my heart, Catarina / Don't you forget!" The song, *Core 'ngrato*, is also an
anachronism. The music was composed by maestro Salvatore Cardillo who,
like Cordiferro, emigrated from Naples to New York. Cardillo cloaked the
verses in a score that was simultaneously operatic, solemn, dramatic and
filled with pathos, closer to the late romantic style of Francesco Paolo Tosti
than to the more modern style of Giacomo Puccini. The true appeal of *Core
'ngrato*, making it one of the most fateful Neapolitan songs of any period,
lies precisely in this quality of being "ancient," in requiring a tenor voice
capable of hitting a bold B flat in the high-pitched finale: a voice compa-
rable to that of his friend, Enrico Caruso who, not coincidentally, was the
first great performer of this song (followed by, among others, Tito Schipa,
Carlo Buti, Placido Domingo and Luciano Pavarotti).

Love, therefore, is the theme. A love that, by the way (remarkable if one
recalls that the lyrics were written by a ferocious, self-proclaimed enemy of
the clergy), prompts the heartsick lover to seek comfort from his confessor who is a "holy person" but who also, in his own way a practical man,
advises the lover, "My son, let her be." This brief religious interlude aside,
love and revolution are the classic pairing.

Among Cordiferro's contemporaries we find this combination in the
personality of Carlo Tresca. Cordiferro was Tresca's equal in these matters,
even if Cordiferro's lovers were all (unlike the lovers of the famous anarchist labor leader) of humble origins. Lucia Fazio was an actress and the
daughter of actors. Her marriage to Cordiferro in 1899 was his second one,
and her letters to her Riccardo are instructive. The letters between Lucia
and Riccardo can be found at the Immigration History Research Center of
the University of Minnesota. A number of Lucia's letters brim with jealousy

for a man known to favor amorous adventures. One letter, dashed off from Hoboken on December 11, 1898 following one of their many arguments, informs Cordiferro that their four-year relationship is over. Lucia confronts Riccardo with his too-numerous escapades. "No, you are incapable of loving holily, ideally. I pity you because you did not make yourself into what you are; the women you have encountered have made you so. Oh, how I have cried, and how much I have cried. . . . I have cried not only when I have known you but also when I have read your verses. And how many times have I prayed to the God you have mocked. I, who have told you not to kiss me, you have hated. Go ahead, hate me, disdain me, think of me as a kept woman, whatever you like to think. This is the last time I write you. . . . Be happy, and I hope you find a woman who will make you happy."[9]

As we know, the woman he finds will be the same Lucia. She will take on the role of the consort who is patient, understanding, silent. So much so that Riccardo, imbued with libertarian doctrine that certainly included free love, did not hide his multiple appetites, to the point of recalling his "lovers on the trains, in the electric cars, in the parks, in the coffee houses, in the restaurants, in the hotels, in all the discretely quiet corners of our frequent amorous encounters," as he wrote in the previously cited preface to *Poesie scelte.* The charm in all this lies in how genuinely bohemian and melodramatic it is: this is the real cultural soup, the cultural background of Riccardo and of poor Lucia who, in the previously quoted letter, lets off steam in such a way as to prove, for those who have been rejected, surprisingly prophetic: "My God! How ungrateful the human heart is!"

In a word, it's as if there were no distinction between life and art, as if each character could declare (as does Tosca): "Vissi d'arte, vissi d'amore" (I lived for art, I lived for love). Nor does the chord of pathos and sentiment exhaust Cordiferro's poetic resources. A writer capable of grasping all literary forms and finding nourishment in all sources, he is perhaps even more effective in satire, a form he practiced throughout his career, particularly in *La Follia*. His collection, *Brindisi ed augurii* (Toasts and salutations) (New York, Società Libraria Italiana, 1917) (cat. 46), contains, for example, a toast made by a completely illiterate, prominent immigrant, on the occasion of a picnic organized under the auspices of a leading Italian American society. Preceding by a decade or so a little masterpiece of first-generation literature, Pasquale Seneca's story, *Il Presidente Scoppetta, ovvero La Società della Madonna della Pace* (President Scoppetta, or The Society of Our Lady of Peace) (cat. 66), on a topic thoroughly examined by many other writers (not the least of which was Eduardo Migliaccio's character, 'O cafone c'a sciammeria (bumpkin in a tuxedo), Cordiferro, in his "toast" set in triplets, displays a lively ability to mimic the improbable language of a certain category of immigrant who enjoyed economic success but came from the humblest origins. We are treated to the ever-evolving Italian American pidgin, a picturesque form of speech of extraordinary expressive power, in which a speech (Eng.) becomes not a discorso (It.) but, instead, a spiccio (ph. SPEE-che-oh); a business (Eng.) is not an affare (It.) but a bisinisso (bee-zee-NEES-oh); and a solemn promise is one to repay one's associates bai-baie (by-BY-eh), meaning by and by. On many other occasions, notably including the "comic satire" *Il prisco cavaliere* (The knight of olde) (cat. 22b),[10] Cordiferro launched contemptuous attacks on this portrait of a self-styled personage. In the personage's toast, however, there appears a trace of sympathy. Cordiferro appears to say, yes, this person is truly an ignorant bumpkin, but he is someone who broke his back and merits his good fortune. Let's listen to the successful bumpkin for a moment:

> *Voi sapete però che una perzona*
> *strutta non so, ma quanto abbasta saccio*
> *per decidere in caso una quistiona.*
> *Del resti, io non m'imbiccio e non m'imbaccio,*
> *giacché rebbo penzaro al bisinisso:*
> *ca si quillo falliscio, io po' che faccio?*

(You know I ain't no educated guy, still I know enough ta figure out what's what. All that other stuff, I couldn't care less; all I gotta care about is the business, because if that goes down, what am I gonna do?)

Cordiferro's very good ear allows him to deal confidently with the eloquent babble of the great personage. In his own, unique way, the personage borrows from the language of his new home. Drawing on the rich and variegated background of his Italian dialect of origin, the personage breathes southern Italian tonality into those once all-American words. The Italian dialect, even more than the adopted American terms, is twisted as the prominent immigrant pronounces words in such a way as to place him definitively in a specific inland area in the region of Campania. He says "perzona" instead of "persona;" "so" instead of "sono;" "saccio" instead of "so;" "m'imbiccio" instead of "m'impiccio;" "rebbo" instead of "debbo," and so on, not to mention some comic ambiguities, for example when he says "strutta," corresponding to the Italian word "istruita" (educated or cultured) but which could also mean, in Neapolitan dialect, "distrutta" (destroyed). The Neapolitan dialect is one of those areas in which Cordiferro most distinguished himself and in which he achieved greatly appreciated results. His contribution to Neapolitan song has already been mentioned. There is also, however, a Cordiferro from Calabria in harmony with the family tradition that he received from his father, Francesco Sisca, the author of a Calabrian poem entitled *Lu ciucciu* (The donkey) (cat. 21). The son was no lesser than the father, and one of his many books was *Ode alla Calabria* (Ode to Calabria) (cat. 72) (known to this writer in its 1933 edition published in Buenos Aires; it was not unusual for a first-generation literary work to move quickly from one America to another).

Notwithstanding the fact that the more apparent side of Cordiferro's cultural development related to his years in Naples, he remained faithful as well to his roots in Calabria, one of the regions of Italy that most contributed and continues to contribute to Italian immigration; his connection remained strong and a source of pride. Cordiferro felt such pride notwithstanding the not-always-flattering reputation of the people of Calabria, who ". . . pòrtanu | Na mala nduminata, | Ppecchi la capu tenanu | Cchiù tosta e na granata (. . . have a bad reputation because their heads are harder than a grenade)." *Ode alla Calabria.* Cordiferro, with the help of another colonial, Francesco Greco, wrote a poem in the Calabrese dialect on the martyrdom of Sacco and Vanzetti. In delivering this eulogy Cordiferro did not feel the need to limit himself to the dialect of his own personal background. Indeed, there remained in his memory the image of an enchanted agro-pastoral world high in the mountains with torrents and streams of the freshest water and clear skies; a wilderness that, on the skids of memory, can obscure the proverbial wilderness of America. (Indeed, if the waters of

Calabria are the freshest, then the waters of America seem to him "bbruoru e baccalà," codfish soup.) Cordiferro saw that, to some degree, Calabria also had an ungrateful heart. Calabria saw to it that its people had to leave to seek their fortunes elsewhere. This was not cause enough, however, to allow the children of Calabria to declare that they did not love their native land:

> *Tu érramu luntanu me mandasti,*
> *Nchiuvandume a ssu scuògliu,*
> *Ma io bene te vuogliu*
> *Nsinca campu.*[11]

(You sent me far away like a tramp, nailing me to this reef, but I'll love you for as long as I live.)

Riccardo Cordiferro died in New York on August 24, 1940.

(Translated by Richard L. Mattiaccio)

1. No. 5, vol. XXXII, January 1911, pp. 450-451).

2. See, e.g., cat. 27.

3. Giuseppe Aurelio Cortanzo. *Gli eroi della soffitta*. Roma: Libreria Alessandro Manzo, 1880.

4. *Fra le stampe*, series II, year II, no. 1, January 1, 1911.

5. Ibid.

6. Ibid.

7. Ibid.

8. Foreword to: Riccardo Cordiferro, *Poesie scelte*, Campobasso: Edizioni Pungolo Verde, 1967.

9. Alessandro Sisca Papers, IHRC 2408, Box 1, Folder 5.

10. There is a play of words here, in that the word "Prisco" means "of olde" but it is also the Cavaliere's surname.

11. *Poesie scelte.*

Francesco Durante is the author of *Italoamericana. Storia e letteratura degli italiani negli Stati Uniti, 1776–1943* in two volumes, the second volume of which will be published next year in translation in the United States by Fordham University Press. His most recent books are *Scuorno* (2008) and *I napoletani* (2011). He has translated various American authors, among them John Fante and Bret Easton Ellis.

ROBERT VISCUSI The Universal Exposition

Thirty-three years ago, I was just beginning to do research in Italian American literature. Visiting the library at the Center for Migration Studies in Staten Island, I came upon an enormous book, a guide to Italian American life, published in 1906. It was called *Gli italiani negli Stati Uniti d'America* (cat. 50), and it was produced on a scale that dwarfed all the other books by and about Italian immigrants I was finding that day. The first half of the book was full of prose that I ignored, because my Italian was almost non-existent in those days. But the entire second half of the folio was filled with photos, and these fixed my attention.

It was like touring the imaginations of my forebears. My grandfather, my godfather, and many friends of theirs were small-to-middling proprietors in and around New York City. These men lived to produce things. Even today, I can never think of them without those things all around them. My grandfather had a small machine shop and gave piecework jobs to all the housewives in the neighborhood. My godfather had a small "art-novelty" factory that baked liquid latex in plaster moulds to produce mannequins and other display items that he would drive around the city and deliver to his many clients in the advertising and window-dressing trades. Such entrepreneurs were common in the Italian American world of the 1940s and 50s. Back in 1906, many of their most successful antecedents had bought their own pages in *Gli italiani negli Stati Uniti d'America,* where they could see themselves in large portrait photographs, dressed as prosperous burghers, right next to photos of the plants, the shops, the machines, the furniture, the villas, the whatever-it-was that had made them important. Ever since the day I first turned the heavy pages of this book, it has remained for me a reminder that, for many of these new Americans, as Matthew Frye Jacobson has put it, "immigration was a capitalist strategy."[1]

Some Italian American novelists, Helen Barolini and Mario Puzo more than most, have understood this fact of life and have made the family romance of capitalism the armature of their fictions. But very few have given the flavor, even the aroma, of small production the way these photographs did — at least for me that day, who had a memory bank on this topic ready to stir at the slightest suggestion.

Thus, when I recognized this elephant folio looming among the smaller, and often ephemeral, publications in James Periconi's stunning collection, I thought, "Yes, I'd like to write about this!" And I have done so. But something had happened to me in the past thirty-three years that had changed the book for me and, would consequently alter the essay I was about to write. I had learned to speak, read, and write in Italian. In the process, I had spent a good deal of time in Italy and among Italian speakers in the United States as well. I had learned to think like an Italian. So this huge book, when I returned to it, had become larger yet. The Italian agenda that produced it, to which I will turn in a moment, was suddenly vivid to me. And the capitalist imaginaries of my grandfather, my godfather, and their predecessors in the Italian colony of New York looked very different when seen against that background.

It turns out that this work was produced for the Universal Exposition in Milan in 1906, for a pavilion called "The Italians Abroad." The Milanese view of the subject startled me when I first began to look at it, but the more I thought about it, the more interesting it became. And that is the theme of this essay.

The books in the Periconi collection all have the organic character of an onion or a peach pit. Substantial, firm, complete, but containing at the center a vacant space. Between the words *Italian* and *American,* some emptiness subsists. What is this void? Does it represent the language barrier, formidable in 1906, the year I want to talk about? Does it represent the cold Atlantic, more fearsome then than now? Does it speak for the social no-man's-land between the Italian immigrants and the American natives in the United States?

All of the above, to be sure. Indeed, the space between two such words as *Italian* and *American* in the naming of a sub-national minority is the theme of a very large literature. Psychology, sociology, political science, international economics, immigration history, ecclesiastical geography, intergroup dynamics, women's studies, and criminal conspiracy are only a few of the discursive arenas that have contributed to the study of compound identities in sub-national minority studies. And each one of these fields requires its own theoretical dynamics of desire, disconnection, and displacement. *Gli italiani negli Stati Uniti d'America* occupies a place in this entire geography of dissatisfaction. It was published in the year of the Exposition in Milan. Its editors chose as a publisher one who knew how to get Italian Americans to subscribe to a book about themselves and their enterprises. The Italian American Directory Company had just issued, in 1905, a more conventional listing of the names and addresses of a great number of Italian Americans who were prospering in major cities in the U.S. (cat. 49). *Gli italiani negli Stati Uniti d'America* was supported by similar subscriptions, but it had a more ambitious cultural goal: indeed, we may say that it was a dossier of the petit-bourgeois reality that filled the vacant space in the expression *Italian American*. That may seem a fanciful description. It is not. Spectacle, like any complex construction, requires parts that remain invisible.

The spectacular event to which the book specifically belonged was that same Universal Exposition of Milan in 1906. This book was produced to serve the occasion. This Exposition, the first international fair in Italian history, was staged to mark the completion of the Simplon tunnel that connected Brig in Switzerland with Domodossola in Italy. On average, 3,000 workers per day, mostly poor Italians, had worked on this tunnel for seven and a half years. At 20 miles, the completed passage was, and for seventy-six years would remain, the longest tunnel in the world. A marvel of engineering, as well: trains traveled through it on electric power. Transport, suitably enough, was a major theme at this Milan Expo: visitors could fly in balloons and ride on an elevated railroad; there were airplanes, and the entrance to the Exposition in Parco Sempione (Italian for Simplon) was built to replicate the Domodossola entrance to the great tunnel. The Milan Exposition, in retrospect, appears a preparation for the Futurist Manifesto of 1909, with its praise of speed, flight, electricity, and machines. Surrounding the celebration of the announced theme in 1906 was the Universal Exposition's development of what had by now come to be the given theme of any such exposition in those days: the naturalization of imperial ambitions.[2]

Beginning with London's Crystal Palace in 1851, universal expositions had become the favored means of drawing large portions of a population into a single place, and of there accustoming visitors to the notion that the growth of sovereignty and of captive markets belonged to an ordinary, inevitable, ideologically taken-for-granted form of "progress." Such expositions moved forward on a double track: first, they continually celebrated "progress" (each such exposition featured new industrial innovations that were making industrial and territorial expansion plausible); and, second, they represented the peoples of the world as chapters in a vast catalogue of the dominant and the dominated.

Gli italiani negli Stati Uniti d'America reflects the second part of this agenda. In doing so it presents the Italians of the United States in a double optic, first showing them as seen in the eyes of the Italian bankers, bureaucrats, and politicians who had the most practical use for information about their enterprise, and then displaying these colonials as they themselves wished to appear to those same metropolitan worthies. The effect is both dramatic and intimate.

The late French sociologist Pierre Bourdieu divides the social world into the dominant and the dominated. Then he divides the dominant half into its own dominant and dominated parts.[3] This upper half and its inner chambers are what we see here. We look through the eyes of Italy's global captains in the first half of this book, and then, familiar with that point of view, we look at the local captains of the United States Italian colony. The relations between these two parts are complex. But, after I had read the first part of the book, now that I was able to do so, I realized that the second part would never look the same to me again: its heroes faded against the background of their more dominant metropolitan cousins. The more these Italian Americans resembled the economically dominant Milanesi, the less acceptable, indeed, the less visible, they became. We at least can examine these photos. It is not clear how many people ever did so at the fair in Milan.

The bankers and economists in Italy were interested in Italian America as a market for Italian exports, and they were attentive to its labor power and to its economic advance. From the preface:

The authorizing committee of the Milan Exposition for the exhibit "The Italians Abroad," by the circular of 20 June 1905 sent to Presidents of Chambers of Commerce established in our most important centers of emigration, announced a collective graphic Exposition, in a publication on the model of the volume *The Italians in the Argentine Republic* (Buenos Aires, 1898), one that would give a picture of the conditions and possibilities of the individual colonies, showing how much Italian labor can produce in them.[4]

"Individual colonies," never "individual colonials." The point of view is relentlessly ministerial, metropolitan, and cosmopolitan. The visitor comes away interested in the worldwide network of Italian technical ambitions, trade relationships, artistic influences, its capacities for labor and artisanal production.

The volume, following the model and the idea of the Authorizing Committee, should consist of two parts: the first, general, composed of monographs which treat the various questions that might pertain to Italian emigration and the development of commerce and of exchanges of every sort between the Mother-Fatherland and the individual regions; the second, composed of monographs that would present the most eminent persons and the most important companies and industrial, commercial, and agricultural firms of our communities.

"The most eminent persons and the most important companies and industrial, commercial, and agricultural firms of our communities." This is no doubt how the worthies in those photographs would sometimes see themselves, at one with their firms and their eminences. It also hints that these *prominenti*, since they had in effect paid for the volume, would form its one secure readership.

The key to understanding this work is that it represents and reinforces the imperial/colonial view of the "Italians of the United States of America." Those American Italians inhabit a vacancy in the prospect. They are interesting to businessmen, but only as trading partners — not for any other reason, and not especially to anyone else. "The Italians of the United States" did not excite much attention, though people admired the pavilion "The Italians Abroad" where it shared space with other global Italians. A reading of the volume suggests why people did not find its subjects enormously exciting.

The essays in the first part include a fairly complete, and remarkably sober, survey of the ways that Italians were prospering in the United States. Under the rubric of "Immigration," Luigi Aldrovandi gives a mixed picture of the flow of population, always balancing the pluses and minuses not really of immigration, but rather of emigration: very concerned about what this movement means to Italy, whether it can be judged a net gain or loss. The prominent journalist Adolfo Rossi (see cat. 68) provides a general survey of where Italian laborers ("La mano d'opera Italiana") were working in the United States: in large cities; on railroads, farms, and orchards; in coal mines — expressing the opinion that it would be better were the Italians settling in a wider range of situations. Guido Rossati provides an amply detailed list of notable agricultural settlements and initiatives undertaken by Italians from New Jersey to California. There are surveys of maritime trade between the U.S. and Italy, of the commerce in Italian value-added exports such as silks, fruits, foods, mineral and chemical products, manufactures, works of art, and automobiles, as well as a brief survey of American exports to Italy.

The most vivid passages in this part of the volume are the Homeric catalogs of what Italians were doing in the United States. They built businesses in macaroni, rag-picking, plaster figures, furniture, artificial flowers, flags, uniforms, gloves, hats, carts and wagons, sweets (ice creams and candies); printing, lithography, and binding; cigars and tobaccos; and musical instruments. The roll-call of artisans is possibly more suggestive to us than it would have been to citizens of a metropolis in early-twentieth-century Italy, where this Shakespearean cast was a normal assortment: shoemakers, weavers, stonecutters, bricklayers, bread bakers, pasta makers, waiters, cooks, pastry cooks, carpenters, cabinetmakers, decorators, figurine makers, mosaicists, typographers, printers, florists, colorists, plasterers, house painters, hat makers, glove makers, instrument makers, mechanics, pressers of shirts. All this might have excited the interest of prospective contractors, who were thinking of doing business in New York or Boston, and needed to know what artisanal resources were available. The chances are, again, that very few people ever reviewed this material.

There are comprehensive discussions of Italo-Americans in politics, of churches and parochial schools, of settlement houses in Manhattan and

Brooklyn. Antonio Stella provides a very detailed report on the hygienic conditions under which Italians were living in North America. His essay is grimly subtitled, "The Deterioration of the Race." There are studies of the teaching of Italian in American colleges and universities and in the Italian schools of New York, studies of the instruction in New York City's public schools. There is a very brief survey of the colonial press, and a similarly cursory survey of artists and professionals, and, surely of interest to prospective investors and emigrants, an ample conspectus of Italian American real estate holdings. This leads the way to the most specifically colonialist part of the book. First, Bernardino Ciambelli, the "Homer of the migration" (cat. 10, 135), offers an essay entitled "Columbus Day," about the national effort, begun and consummated in Pueblo, Colorado, to have October 12 declared a national holiday. Ciambelli specifically links this campaign to the Columbian Exposition of 1893 in Chicago. Next comes an ethnographic essay on the usages, customs, and feasts of the Italians in the United States. An essay on sport in the Italian colonies. Two essays by the noted scholar Amy Bernardy on the Italians of Boston, and surveys on the "colonies" of Rhode Island and of Buffalo.

This massive folio is itself an exhibit. The first part of it might belong to a library of reports, fit company for the *Bollettino dell'Emigrazione*, published every year from 1901 through 1927 by the Commissariato Generale dell'Emigrazione of the Ministero degli Affari Esteri. Only in the later essays – Ciambelli on Columbus Day, Amy Bernardy on the North End of Boston – does the tone reflect something of the intense social passions of life in the Italian colonies of the United States. Compared, however, with the steady outpouring of radical literature in the colonies that constitutes a significant part of this Grolier Club exhibition, this is still polite writing, very respectful of the established order of things.

Good manners, even to excess, provide the overwhelming tone of the second half of the book. The *prominenti* who advertise themselves here clearly want to be regarded as the equals of the people who are going to be looking at their photographs in Milan. The book's introduction frankly explains that the expenses of publication were borne by selling space for these ambitious exercises in personal display. These many pages are something like a *Who's Who* of the colonies: one meets the people who owned the furniture stores and bakeries; the people who supplied American drawing rooms with ornamental plaster and furnished them with occasional tables in parti-colored marble, standing on legs carved in the shapes of gryphons. One grows tired of the doctors and big-bellied eminences in every variety who have themselves photographed wearing ornamental moustaches as big as walrus tusks. They advertise their dwellings, edifices that seem to look out at passersby from corner plots in small cities and practically cry out, "Internist!" "Undertaker!"

While such portraits of mansions and artists' studios were important to their proprietors, their competitors, and their clients, and were even putatively useful to the Milanese merchants who may have used the book to seek out business contacts in the United States, these photographs did not make much of an impression in Milan, not even inside the pavilion of "The Italians Abroad." In a recent essay, Patrizia Audenino conducts a thorough analysis of that pavilion, and reports that some people complained that it "was not a success," adding that the only part of it the public really liked was the Eritrean exhibit, where there were free peanuts they could grasp. There was also a presentation of a wide selection of Eritrean goods aimed at lucrative trade with Italy. The pavilion's jury gave the Eritrean exhibit its grand prize.[5] Indeed, as she suggests elsewhere, the only exhibit based upon such books as this (there were volumes submitted by other colonies as well) was the quiet display of the books themselves, sitting demurely in showcases or lying on tables for visitors to peruse, it being tacitly understood that it made sense to leave the contents as taken for granted, but unseen. It apparently did not even interest the Milanesi to dramatize in some way, let's say, the dozens of crafts that were practiced in Italian America. Nowadays, we would love to see those pastry cooks and cabinetmakers and mosaicists at work. In Milan in 1906, no doubt, one could see such things at the corner of any street.

Even in photographic reminiscences of the Universal Exposition, one encounters many photo essays based upon the Eritrean exhibit in "The Italians Abroad." The Eritreans made for a popular attraction, practically a sideshow of racist exoticism, thick with high grass and enlivened by plenty of witch doctors, half-naked dancers, big cats, masks and spears and drums. While it was easy to see that the *Comitato Ordinatore* had sober economic and social concerns in mind when it sent out its request to Chambers of Commerce in Italian colonies asking for reports on public hygiene and the state of education in the colonies, it is also easy to see that the people who promoted and actually frequented the fair were neither convinced by, nor even aware of, any spectacle that might have accompanied those reports: earnest portrait-photos of the leading attorneys and surgeons in small Pennsylvania cities did not excite attention or comment, nor did they in all probability appear outside the covers of their tomb-like albums. These undramatic colonials with their Savoyard moustaches in effect occupied a structurally vital vacancy at the heart of the system of international trade, a system that was and would continue to be a main support of Italy's rising economic status among nations. But it is clear that the worldly Milanesi who frequented the fair were not impressed by the diplomas and suburban machine shops of successful Italians in Yonkers and Newark. These well-to-do emigrants – who could not escape being colonials, who could not help appearing to belong to the dominated half of the dominant class – clearly put all their efforts into looking like their superiors, who, alas, were not much interested in that spectacle.

Italians in Italy preferred a more dramatic exhibition of their imperial victories and prospects. They preferred the equivocal glories of what were called "state colonies" (Eritrea, Benadir) to the less-splendid assets of what were called "free colonies" (as Audenino points out, these were the innumerable places in the world where the Italian exodus actually settled and, more often than not, made good).[6] The dominant class of Italians in 1906 did not, perhaps, foresee what an international victory it would be for Italy when the children of Italian emigrants became high school principals and successful architects in the United States. Despite Italy's already disastrous history in Africa, most Italians would go on for a long while thinking that their nation's real imperial future was destined to fulfill itself among the exotics in the phenotypically subaltern settlements south of the Sahara. It is perhaps the case that the dominant parts of dominant classes have little taste for the dominated parts of those same dominant classes – their lesser cousins, as it were – but instead prefer the truly dominated: the illiterate, the distant, the strangely dressed, the racially excluded, the stylistically exciting. The Milan Expo took place in the decade known for the vogue of African masks and drums in Paris and Milan.

Spectacle is a convenient way of organizing a panoramic view of a complex reality. But it has this weakness, that it may appeal more to the viewers' narcissism than to their realism. With the superior wisdom of another century to reflect upon events, we might conclude that upper-class Italians gradually and reluctantly would come to see that their real international respectability would owe more to their successes selling macaroni in the Bronx and high-end leather goods in Manhattan than it would ever gain from their adventures subjecting darker peoples and then photographing them alongside giraffes and zebras. It is clear to us now that the prosperity of Italians had a firmer basis when it rested upon trade and cooperation with Italians Abroad in free colonies than it ever could in state colonies, where it rested upon forceful oppression of peoples whom the Italians might find picturesque but could scarcely begin to understand. The great economist Luigi Einaudi, later the second president of the Italian Republic, as early as 1900 rejected ideas of "expanding Italy through military conquest rather than through the peaceful expansion of trade and commerce," and he accused militarist colonialists of "insane visions of colonial adventures in sterile places that would bring forth nothing but blood and shame."[7]

Oddly, though, when Italy's would-be African empire disappeared after the Second World War, the steady and reliable Italians Abroad still did not come into the spotlight. Instead, Italy's worldwide Mafia rose to prominence as a theme for film and other forms of popular fantasy.[8] The appeal of the exotic and the shameful, it may be, is so central to the dynamics of international spectacle, that the dominant classes of Italians and of Americans as well, have persisted in disavowing the reality of boring Italian Americans who wear three-piece suits and live in prosperous respectability. In their places, the Italian American demiurges of the international spectacle have come to occupy a permanent pavilion in the imaginary Universal Exposition. There, they populate a violent conspiracy, stylish, dramatic, and illicit forever. Who wants accountants when you can have *consiglieri*?

Are the earnest Italian Americans forgotten? Are the memories of their colonial achievements lost in a cold void where no sympathy can ever find them? Not for me. And I had hoped to write an essay that could share that sympathy with others. But I have not managed it. I have kept seeing Milan around the edges of the photographs. I could not take my eyes off that gleam of trams and turbines and Leonardo's engines of war. I could hear the profits from abroad, money Italians had earned in the copper mines of Colorado and in the twenty-mile electrified tunnel of Simplon, flowing like underground rivers into the foundations of this city's monumental banks. And when I look at *Gli italiani negli Stati Uniti d'America*, I see those moustachioed grandfathers and godfathers under the pitiless gaze of Milan's Futurists and, indeed, of all its fashion police. The old Italian Americans are wearing double-breasted suits that fade in the glamour of this city, its mirrors, its glittering mastery of style. I want to speak of their achievements, their dreams, but I cannot get them back into New York City and Cleveland, where they were somebodies, cannot separate them from Milan, from the minor, very minor, but apparently permanent places it has assigned them in the Universal Exposition.

NOTES

1. I heard him say this at a seminar at Brooklyn College on the work of Oscar Handlin. Jacobson has told me he was paraphrasing John Bodnar, *The Transplanted: A History of Immigrants in Urban America* (Indianapolis: Indiana University Press, 1987).

2. See Paul Greenhalgh, *Ephemeral Vistas: The* Expositions Universelles, *Great Exhibitions and World's Fairs, 1851–1939* (Manchester: Manchester University Press, 1988), pp. 52–112.

3. Pierre Bourdieu, *Distinction: A Social Critique of the Judgment of Taste,* trans. Richard Nice (Cambridge: Harvard UP, 1984), uses this geometry of relative power positions to explain the social forces that produce and predict the judgments of taste.

4. Luigi Aldrovandi, "Prefazione," *Gli italiani negli Stati Uniti d'America* (New York: Italian American Directory Co., 1906), p. iii [translation mine].

5. Patrizia Audenino, "La mostra degli italiani all'estero: prove di nazionalismo," in P. Audenino et al., eds., *Milano e l'Esposizione internationale del 1906: La rappresentazione della modernità* (Milano: FrancoAngeli, 2008), p.119.

6. Patrizia Audenino, "Il lavoro degli italiani all'estero nell'Esposizione internazionale di Torino del 1911," in *Archivio storico dell'emigrazione italiana* (Asei), numero monografico, *Il Cinquantenario dell'unità d'Italia (1911) e l'emigrazione,* edited by Giovanni Pizzorusso, vol. 7 (2011), pp. 11–17.

7. Cited by Audenino, "Il lavoro degli Italian all'estero."

8. Guy Debord, *Comments on the Society of the Spectacle,* trans. Malcolm Imrie (London: Verso, 1998), p. 67, introduces the idea of the necessity of the Mafia to the international spectacle.

Robert Viscusi is executive officer of the Wolfe Institute for the Humanities and professor of English at Brooklyn College. He is the editor-in-chief of the forthcoming translation of Francesco Durante's collection of writings of all of the authors in this exhibition, *Italoamericana: History and Literature of the Italians in the United States: 1880–1943* (Fordham University Press, 2013). A poet, he is also the author of the forthcoming *Ellis Island*, to be published by Bordighera Press in 2012. The author wishes to thank Patrizia Audenino, Ombretta Diaferia, and Linda Lentini for their assistance in preparing this essay.

Catalogue

Learning the language

1 ⟡ Lorenzo Da Ponte. *Poesie varie di Lorenza* [sic] *da Ponte*. New York: Pubblicate dall'autore, 1830. Second edition.

This work, "published by the author," was dedicated to Domenico Rossetti di Scander, a wealthy patrician from Trieste mentioned with affection in *Memorie di Lorenzo Da Ponte* (New York, 1829-30), in appreciation for his putting up the always-impecunious Da Ponte (b. The Veneto, 1749; d. New York, 1838) as a guest during the latter's visit to Trieste. With his libretti for Mozart's *Don Giovanni*, *Le nozze di Figaro* and *Così fan tutte* written in another lifetime, in his receding past, in the U.S. Da Ponte often self-published his own Italian poetry and translations of English poetry into Italian, for his private Italian students. Here, before there were specialized Italian printers, an American one, J. H. Turney, was the "Stampatore" (printer). Examples of Da Ponte's translation in the *Poesie varie* are Byron's *Prophecy of Dante*, a free translation of LeSage's *Gil Blas*, and a poem of his own. This "second edition"follows the first appearance of the Byron and LeSage translations, which were published in 1821, in New York, as well as at the end of the third volume (1830) of the second edition of *Memorie*. The manner in which the present copy is bound (in original paper boards) is probably the way that most of his students purchased and maintained their copies.

Besides his writing and publishing poetry (and his *Memorie*) in America, Da Ponte also wrote and published simple dramas here for his private students and those at Columbia College, where he became its first professor of Italian in 1825. Da Ponte imported Italian books (classics, readers, grammars and dictionaries) and, in addition to using them with his own students, distributed them throughout the country to support the then-new fashion of teaching Italian in American colleges. His private students included well-to-do New Yorkers and their families alike, including William Cullen Bryant, Clement Clark Moore, Gulian Verplanck and the Livingstons. Da Ponte and his brother Carlo maintained a bookstore (perhaps out of their home), and in 1827 published the *Catalogo dei libri italiani depositati alla Biblioteca Sociale di New York* (Catalog of Italian books deposited at the New York Society Library), at which library Da Ponte had started an Italian Library Club, with many prominent New Yorkers, such as his private students, among the subscribers.

Da Ponte's aim, as he explained in his *Storia della lingua e letteratura Italiana in New-York* (History of Italian language and literature in New York) (New York: Gray e Bunce, Stampatori, 1827), was to overcome New York's then-present cultural deficit (as compared to Boston and Philadelphia). While he says in his *Memorie* that only he taught Italian in New York, this work reveals that when he returned in 1819 to New York after a period of living in Pennsylvania, Da Ponte found that several of his compatriots had established themselves as Italian teachers. He thought well of some of them, but held many others in contempt as imposters. Da Ponte persuaded his student, and later congressman, Verplanck to get the Library of Congress to purchase Italian books published in Italy.

2 ⊹ Carlo Alfieri. *De Porquet's Italian Phrases, or, Il fraseggiatore toscano: A copious choice of Italian sentences to facilitate a complete knowledge of the formation of the verbs and syntax of that elegant tongue.* Boston: S. Burdett & Co., 1832. Third edition.

Reflecting the widespread interest in learning Italian in this era in the U.S., this Italian grammar was, like Longfellow's work (cat. 3), published in 1832 in the U.S., by the self-proclaimed "foreign booksellers," S. Burdett & Co. of Boston. This "third edition, revised and corrected" is noted on the title page to be "revised and improved by the American editor." This edition is stated to be "by Carlo Alfieri, Professor of the Italian language, London," although Louis Philippe R. Fenwick de Porquet himself appears still active in 1832, as his publication of other language works (in Italian, French and Spanish) as late as the 1840s suggests. The advertisement for the current edition, following the title page, notes that "the present Elementary book" is "now very popular in London." A similar Italian grammar was published by J. Avezzana in New York in 1841, also authored by Alfieri from the work originally by de Porquet.

3 ⊹ Da H[enry] W[adsworth] Longfellow. *Saggi de novellieri Italiani d'ogni secolo, tratti dà più celebri scrittori, con brevi notizie intorno alla vita di ciascheduno* [Samples of Italian short story writers of each century, drawn from the most celebrated writers, with brief notes on the life of each one of them]. Boston: Presso Grey e Bowen, 1832.

Although remembered now for his poetry, Longfellow was first and foremost a scholar and teacher of several foreign languages, Italian included. This work, Longfellow's first published study in Italian, is a reader containing stories of many Renaissance authors, including Boccaccio and Machiavelli, and was printed during Longfellow's professorship at his alma mater, Bowdoin College, in Maine. Following his time at Bowdoin, in 1836 he succeeded George Ticknor, professor of modern languages, at Harvard.

4 ⊹ Pietro Bachi. *A Grammar of the Italian Language.* Boston: Charles C. Little and James Brown, 1838. Simultaneously published in London by Richard James Kennett.

Born Ignazio Batolo, Bachi (b. Palermo, 1787; d. Boston, 1853) received his law degree at the University of Padua, but fled the country in opposition to Bourbon rule in 1815. He became instructor of Italian at Harvard in 1826 (a year after Da Ponte's appointment at Columbia), under the advocacy of George Ticknor, the first Smith Professor of Modern Languages, a major supporter of hiring native speakers for instructing modern languages; this occurred only two years after Bachi's arrival in America. As a result of Ticknor's effort, Bachi was the first Italian-educated faculty member appointed at Harvard. A popular teacher, Bachi had as students Henry David Thoreau (for four years), Oliver Wendell Holmes, Edward Everett Hale, and James Russell Lowell.

5 ⁛ Alfonso Arbib-Costa. *Lezioni graduate di lingua inglese.* New York: Francesco Tocci, 1906.

6 ⁛ Alfonso Arbib-Costa. *Italian Lessons.* New York: Italian Book Company, 1914. Seventh edition.

7 ⁛ Alfonso Arbib-Costa. *Advanced Italian Lessons.* New York: Italian Book Company, 1924. Third edition.

Arbib-Costa (b. Livorno, 1882; active, New York, 1900-1930), professor of romance languages at the College of the City of New York, wrote texts designed to help students of English and Italian. First published in 1906 by Francesco Tocci at his Emporium Press in New York, *Lezioni graduate* (Graded lessons) was written in Italian to teach English to Italians and was reprinted for decades afterwards by Tocci's later venture with Antonio De Martino and others, the Società Libraria Italiana, the most important of all the Italian language publishers in America. Società Libraria Italiana and the Italian Book Company are one and the same (cat. 9, 16, 36, 42, 45-46, 134-141, 143).

Of course none needed to learn English (and standard Italian) more than the immigrants themselves, whose social culture in Italy had remained largely one of oral transmission: immigrants took to America's "self-improvement" culture (cat. 5), as reflected in significant library usage by Italian immigrants and noted in a 1913 New York Public Library usage study by John Foster Carr (cat. 144a, b). This study led to the publication of many grammars and readers (1906, 1911, 1913, 1930) for immigrants eager to learn both languages.

8 ⁛ Alberto Pecorini. *Grammatica-enciclopedia italiana-inglese* [Italian-English grammar-encyclopedia]. New York: Nicoletti Bros., 1912.

First published by the Nicoletti Brothers in 1911 "for the Italians in the United States," and reprinted by that same important early publishing house several times during the decade, this work by Pecorini (b. Italy, 1881; d. Argentina, 1957) later also went through many editions, reflecting its evident success, beginning with a second edition in 1919 and continuing as late as 1952, when it was reissued by both the author's own Libreria Nuova Italia (New Italy Booksellers) and also in New York by Forzano & Fleri (under the title of *Nuovissima grammatica enciclopedia italiana-inglese*).

In New York, at the beginning of the 20th century, Pecorini (like many of the other writers whose works are on exhibition here) managed an Italian newspaper in America, in his case, *Il Cittadino* (The Citizen) for some years. In preparing his *Grammatica,* as he noted in the preface of this work, he "had in mind specially the middle class of Italian workers in the United States," those who "while not having followed, in Italy, studies beyond elementary school, nevertheless had a knowledge of the Italian language that makes them able to appreciate a good and practical grammar." His goal was to offer a method of learning English that was different from that used in existing works produced either in Italy or the United States, works geared more to advanced students in a classroom setting.

In 1909, Pecorini published *Gli americani nella vita moderna osservati da un italiano* (The Americans in modern life, observed by an Italian) (cat. 74). Pecorini was no reclusive grammarian: Giuseppe Prezzolini of the Casa Italiana at Columbia called this journalist one "of those misfits: adventurers, people of talent, whether exploited, or blackmailers, eccentric and excited, at times subversive, then nationalists, sometimes anarchists, sometimes semi-scholars, other times bankrupt; always ready to fight with the pen and perhaps with punches in defense of their ideals and of their persons, and attack the ideals and persons of others, in a tone rising many octaves above the level of their financial means and of the circulation of their periodicals."[1] He also published, in English, for The Massachusetts Society of Colonial Dames, *The Story of America* (Boston: Marshall Jones Co., 1920).

9 ❧ A[ngelo] De Gaudenzi. *Nuovissima grammatica accelerata: Italiana-inglese ed enciclopedia popolare con pronunzia. Divisa in 11 parti* [The newest accelerated grammar: Italian-English and popular encyclopedia with pronunciation. Divided into 11 parts]. New York: Italian Book Company, [*ca.* 1944].

This work was widely popular and frequently reprinted; the copy here, lacking a publication date, contained 11 parts, and was printed no earlier than 1944 (its "brief history of the U.S." recounts the events of 1944 that ended World War II). The first edition was originally issued in 1896. An advertisement boasts of the "Edizione 1905" of this work in the *1905 Italian American Directory* (cat. 49) as having "grown into XI Parts, adding a brief history of the U.S.," and running to 400 pages. (Curiously, a "last edition" in between these two issues, dated 1914, contained 13 parts, according to the title page, recounting events in its "brief history" only to 1898.)

De Gaudenzi, the corporate secretary and then president of the Società Libraria Italiana in its early years, includes in this work, besides conventional grammar and lists of vocabulary, nomenclature and pictures of tools for various trades (such as tailor, blacksmith, carpenter, watchmaker), useful phrases and sample form letters in both languages. These include delightful love letters, marriage proposals, and appropriate responses: "[I] have never dared to explain my great love for you." To a jealous lover, an appropriate reply, counsels this work, might be "Your words are entirely out of place, and I do not believe that the friendship of a[nother] gentleman, known to my father, could have displeased you. I have not yet promised to seclude myself entirely from society and friends. . . ."

Imaginative literature of the great migration

10 ⟨ Bernardino Ciambelli. *La trovatella di Mulberry Street, overro La stella dei Cinque Punti* [The foundling of Mulberry Street, or: The star of Five Points]. New York: Società Libraria Italiana, 1919.

Ciambelli (b. Lucca, 1862; d. New York, 1931) was the most celebrated and prodigious novelist – as many as eight novels of his were in print and for sale at the bookstore of *Il Progresso Italo-Americano* (advertisement, July 5, 1896) – as well as journalist in early 20th-century Italian America, contributing to several newspapers and journals simultaneously throughout New York, including *Il Progresso, La Voce del Popolo* and *La Follia di New York* (cat. 27). Called Little Italy's Eugène Sue,[2] he published several serial novels of Italian American life, usually weaving intricate plots of corruption, criminal women, and outrageous activity in a mixture of Zola and Poe. This novel is no different, intertwining the lives of "the foundling," Luigina, and the daughter of a millionaire, Annie Richardson.

Though one of Ciambelli's dreams – to have his works translated into and published in English – was never realized, that did not slow his industriousness in other writing projects. Known for Balzac-like all-night bouts of writing, and his serial publications, *letteratura d'appendice,* distributed as appendices tucked into successive issues of a newspaper, he also engaged in political organizing among Colorado mineworkers. Alfredo Bosi, who is generally restrained in describing writers, calls Ciambelli in *Cinquant' anni di vita italiana in America* (cat. 32) "one of the most popular and prolific colonial writers and journalists, capable of setting out in one night, from the first scene to the last, a big play in five acts, of writing a whole novel of the most sensational kind or of filling with the freshest material about all of the Italian colonies in 8-pages: Bernardino Ciambelli!" (p. 408). See also, cat. 49, at pp. 153-155 ("Columbus Day") and cat. 135.

11 ⟨ Menotti Pellegrino. *I tre cavalieri di Trinacria* [The three knights of Sicily]. New York: Menotti Pellegrino, 1929.

This cloak-and-dagger "historical novel" set in mid-19th century Italy, prefaced with a poem that praises fascism and wishes Mussolini a long life, follows Pellegrino's first novel, *I misteri di New York* by 26 years. Francesco Durante and

Martino Marazzi mention Pellegrino in their scholarly work, and the Library of Congress's *Catalog of Copyright Entries* issued for the year 1929 lists this novel. The dramatic composition and motion picture categories in the *Catalog* for the year 1938 also list *I tre cavalieri* with the subject heading *"Madre Sicilia,"* its location there suggesting Pellegrino adapted his work to either a screenplay or for a stage play.

Little more is known of Pellegrino or his first work, published by the obscure firm of Tipografia Italiana Unione De Luca & Benedetti. *I misteri di New York*, a novel that speaks of crime, corruption and political entanglements within and outside the Italian community, is an "almost indecipherable hodgepodge."[3] Despite that, it opens with a paean to New York to which anyone now can relate: "NEW YORK! . . . the cradle of fortune sought by the disinherited of all peoples! . . . [the place that represents] America for the majority of the innumerable worshippers of the powerful almighty Dollar."[4] Other than this discussion by Marazzi, no biographical information about Pellegrino can be found in modern scholarship, such as that of Durante, or in any of the contemporary sources, such as Flamma, Schiavo or Bosi.

Ezio Taddei

Ezio Taddei (b. Livorno, 1895; d. Rome, 1956) was involved in Italian politics at an early age: at thirteen he was arrested for involvement in a demonstration connected with a nurses' strike in a Roman hospital. When released from prison, he found the doors of his home closed to him, and began life as a vagabond. He was sentenced in February 1922, along with 32 other anarchists, by the Court of Assizzes in Genoa for conspiracy to destroy several private and public buildings. Overall Taddei spent 18 years in Italian jails, first for his anti-bourgeois activities and later for his anti-fascist activities; these experiences animated and fueled much of his writing. War and imprisonment fostered his desire for social justice, reinforced by his reading, especially 19th-century Russian realist novels. The Russian radical Mikhail Bakunin, who arrived in Italy in 1864 and believed in immediate armed revolution, attracted intellectuals like Taddei; he and anarchist Errico Malatesta recur as models for the fictional alter egos under which Taddei wrote.

As is evident from the translations into English of several of his volumes, Taddei (unlike most of the other writers in this exhibition) enjoyed a significant, however brief, success in American intellectual circles. A frequent critic of the racist and anti-immigrant fervor in the U.S., in New York he was welcomed by Carlo Tresca and, following Tresca's assassination in February 1943, made an impassioned speech on the street outside the offices of the radical newspaper *Il Martello* (cat. 118) about the need to find the assassin.

12 ⊹ Ezio Taddei. *Il pino e la rufola* [The pine tree and the mole]. New York: Edizioni in Esilio, 1944.

The Cocce Press, which printed this and all the works of Taddei featured here, was founded in 1922 by Adamo and Attilio Cocce, who subsequently launched the second printing house of *Il Progresso Italo-Americano*. With a dedication to the Italian worker, and a message on the rear cover in Italian that reads, "This volume costs 5 dollars which goes completely to the benefit of the anti-fascist movement in Italy," this political novel is set in the dilapidated post-war suburbs of Taddei's birthplace of Livorno, Italy. This work was translated into English by Samuel Putnam and published by Dial Press in New York one year after this Italian version was issued. Putnam also translated Taddei's *Le porte dell'Inferno* (Roma: A. Mengarelli, 1945), published by Dial as *The Sowing of the Seed* in 1946.

13 ⊹ Ezio Taddei. *Alberi e casolari* [Trees and barns]. New York: Edizioni in Esilio, 1943.

One of Taddei's early novels, dedicated to Nicola Brunori, the acclaimed physician tried and convicted in 1913 for extortion who served three-and-one-half years in prison. This copy is inscribed by the author to one Paolina Krewer.

14 ⊹ Ezio Taddei. *Parole collettive* [Collective words]. New York: S.E.A. [Società Editrice Americana], 1941.

This work, with a preface by the writer Alfredo Segre, comprises seven stories, written in the late 1930s during the last few of Taddei's 18 years of imprisonment in the Fortezza di Civitavecchia in Italy. The artist for these sketches spread throughout the work, and probably also the unsigned collage depicted on the cover, was Costantino Nivola (b. Orani, Italy, 1911; d. Southampton, NY, 1988), a Sardinian graphic and fine artist and sculptor. Fearing for the safety of his Jewish wife, Nivola fled Italy with her for America in 1939, where he became art director of *Interiors* and *Progressive Architecture*, the first non-American admitted (in 1972) to the American Academy of Arts and Letters, and an intimate of de Kooning and Jackson Pollock. The American edition, *Hard as Stone*, was translated by Frances Keene and published in New York by New Writers in 1942.

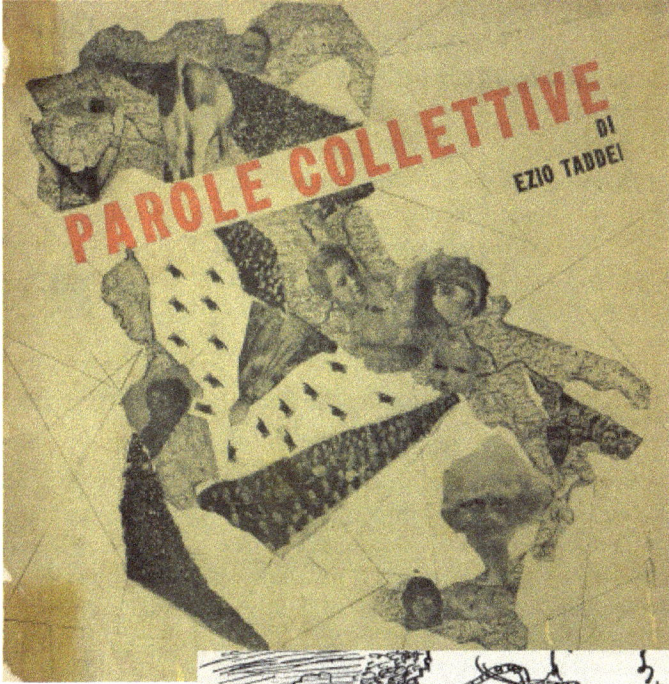

15 ✠ Camillo Baucia. *I miei ragli. Raccolta di sonetti* [My brayings. A collection of sonnets]. New York: Nicoletti Bros., 1909.

This collection of 50 sonnets is one of two known works by the Baltimore-based musician and professor of literature, Camillo Baucia. Active in the local Dante Alighieri Society in Baltimore, Baucia was called the "champion marathon pianist in Europe."[5] The *Time* article reported that after a grueling 52 hours of playing in a two-man piano-playing marathon contest, the aging pianist was urged to desist on doctor's orders, and did so, while playing "Maryland, My Maryland," yielding the championship to his opponent.

16 ✠ Giuseppe Cadicamo. *Tennysoniane: "Nothing will die," "All things will die." Versione libera*. New York: Francesco Tocci, 1909.

Cadicamo (b. Cosenza, 1842; emigrated to U.S. in 1894) published this free translation version of two well-known poems by Tennyson on the centenary of his birth. In his dedication, Cadicamo lauds the great Victorian poet as an "impassioned and constant friend of Italy and of Garibaldi." A colorful figure in New York's Italian colony, Cadicamo is depicted by Bernardino Ciambelli in two novels, including *La trovatella di Mulberry Street* (cat. 10), where he figures as composer of a chorus set to music by countess Gilda Ruta.

Francesco Tocci, who published (as in this case) or simply printed, even after 1910 (as with cat. 19) through his Emporium Press in the first two decades of the 20th century (cat. 142a), was one of the founders in or about 1910 and first president of the most prolific of all the American Italian-language publishers, the Società Libraria Italiana. This company, to which Tocci transferred copyrights he had held when publishing as "Francesco Tocci, Editore," often, even in its early years, operated under its name in English, the Italian Book Company. Tocci's self-proclaimed driving ambition, set out (before the Società's first work was published) in the 1906 *Gli italiani negli Stati Uniti d'America* (cat. 50 at 452-455), had long been to make Italian books available and popular among Americans as well as Italians.

17 ✠ Calicchiu Pucciu [Calogero Puccio]. *Lu sonnu di Monsignuri X: Poimettu in lingua siciliana* [The sonnets of Monsignor X: Short poem in Sicilian]. Brooklyn: Tipografia Italiana del Rinascimento, 1912.

Pucciu (b. Italy, 1876; d. New York, 1927), or Puccio, was a sculptor and carver, with a studio in Brooklyn, as well as an accomplished dialect poet who began to publish verses in the literary and political magazine, *La Follia di New York* in 1906 (see notes preceding cat. 21). This work is dedicated to Riccardo Cordiferro. After several trips to Italy on a sculpting project, he was back in New York by 1922. Treated in a hospital on Wards Island, he fell into a depression and attempted suicide by jumping into the East River. Rescued, he died two days later of pneumonia.

18 ⊹ Carlo Salvo. *Flamma alitur* [The fire still burns]. New York: Nicoletti Bros., 1916.

Preface by Luigi Roversi. Salvo (b. Italy, 1889; active in New York through 1948), a freelance journalist, came to the U.S. in 1905. Based in New York, he collaborated in Italian language dailies and magazines in both Italy and the U.S., writing both prose and, like this work, poetry that was often filled with patriotic sentiments in restrained style. This copy is inscribed by Salvo to *Il Carroccio*, and thus was probably a gift to Agostino de Biasi. He was the editor of two periodicals: *La Rassegna*, published monthly, from 1920-1922 and *Vita Italo-Americana*, published weekly, from 1920-1929. In addition to managing two publications, Salvo contributed to the newspaper *La Voce d'Italia* (edited by Igino Manecchia).

19 ⊹ Nicola Fusco. *Le variazioni*. New York: Il Carroccio Publishing Co., 1916. Second impression / Second thousand.

Printed by Tocci's Emporium Press. Despite its always nationalistic, and later pro-fascist, political ideology, *Il Carroccio* published fiction and poetry of all types, both in serial publication and through its book publishing arm, as in this work. The lyrical poems of *Le variazioni* include songs of praise of nature, but also sad songs of memory and of exile, sometimes dedicated to the glory of the homeland, to "faraway Italy which today suffers a holocaust to the demon of war but will reemerge tomorrow redeemed and immortal." Fusco was based in Pittsburgh, which contained a substantial Italian community. In the *1905 Italian American Directory* (cat. 49), issued about a decade before the appearance of *Le variazioni*, there are six pages of ads and individual entries about that city, but Fusco is not to be found among them.

20 ⊹ Pietro G. Varvaro. *S[an] Giovannino*. New York: [n.p.], 1943.

Born in Palermo, Varvaro (active 1910-1950s) lived in New York in relative obscurity, visited often by Italian friends from what remained of the Sicilian nobility, such as the Prince of Niscemi. He was also friends with Italian singers, musicians and conductors, such as the Metropolitan Opera's Giulio Gatti-Casazza. Varvaro was far better known in Italy, where he was more often published, and revered as a "*poeta modernissimo*." This three-page poem is dedicated to Piero Tozzi, the Italian artist who discovered Michelangelo's lost marble work, "San Giovannino," and was a gift to me from the author's daughter, Aurora Varvaro Gareiss, a renowned environmentalist in New York City.

Riccardo Cordiferro

Cordiferro (b. Cosenza, 1875; d. New York, 1940), born Alessandro Sisca, became involved at an early age with the literary and theatrical environment of Naples, to which his family had moved from Calabria. He published his first verses at age 18, and composed the lyrics for many Neapolitan songs, performed, among others, by Enrico Caruso. Cordiferro's well-known "Core 'ngrato" (1911) (cat. 22c) has been sung and recorded by Andrea Bocelli, Luciano Pavarotti and others. See Francesco Durante's essay, "Riccardo Cordiferro: An Italian American Archetype," pp. 18-29.

Emigrating with his family to America in 1892, soon thereafter Cordiferro founded the weekly literary magazine *La Follia di New York*, together with his father Francesco (1839-1928), who was also a poet (cat. 21), and with his brother Marziale (cat. 27). The work for *La Follia,* combined with his intense literary productivity, absorbed Cordiferro completely, and gave him a vehicle by which to publish several of his works, such as *La vendetta* (cat. 22a). Approbation for the magazine's notable success on the East Coast led him to make frequent trips throughout the country and beyond to give theatrical presentations and poetry readings, and to engage in debates, very often with political overtones.

Though not committed to any one strain of leftist thought, Cordiferro maintained close contact with anarchist and socialist circles, which resulted in more than one arrest and constrained him to resign from directing *La Follia.* In 1895, his drama, *Il pezzente* (The tramp), ran for hundreds of performances and became a standard in the repertory of amateur players in revolutionary political circles. See Durante, "Riccardo Cordiferro," pp. 21-22.

Beyond the political, Cordiferro was perhaps more drawn to satire, the comical, and the sentimental, including songs and Neapolitan impersonations. He wrote poetry all his life, and dedicated himself to comic theater. Cordiferro was principally responsible for the flourishing of colonial poetry: by his decisions of who to publish in *La Follia*, he became the arbiter between old world and new world literary styles, effectively, a guarantor of the new literary culture of the Italian American colony. He was among the collaborators of Carlo Tresca's radical newspaper, *Il Martello* (The Hammer) (cat. 118) even into the 1930s.

21 ⚓ Francesco Sisca. *Lu ciucciu. Poema in dialetto calabrese* [The donkey]. New York: Tipografia Sisca & Sons, 1913.

The only known book-length publication of Sisca *père*, this poem was a "bilingual" collaboration — Calabrian dialect by the father, and Italian translation (as well as preface and notes) by his son, who took the pen name Riccardo Cordiferro. Though the family was Calabrian by birth, the curiosity of this work is that the Siscas had built their reputation in Italy as masters of the Neapolitan

F. SISCA

IU CIUCIN

Prezzo del volume: $1.00

dialect (*e.g.*, *Core 'ngrato*) (cat. 22c); contrast this with the popularity of Cordiferro years later as a poet writing in the Calabrian dialect. This copy belonged to Calabrian-American poet Pasquale Spataro, who featured examples of poetry by both Francesco Sisca and Riccardo Cordiferro in his anthology, *Poeti calabresi in America* (Bergamo, 1957).

22a ⊁ Riccardo Cordiferro. *La vendetta. Lirica in versi liberi* [Vengeance: Lyrics in free verse]. New York: La Follia di New York, [*ca.* 1933].

This 15-page lyrical text is inscribed "*Alla scrittrice Anna Lannutti con sincera ammirazione / Riccardo Cordiferro / New York, 22 Gennaio 1933*" (To the writer Anna Lannutti with sincere admiration, Riccardo Cordiferro, New York, January 22, 1933).

22b ⊁ Riccardo Cordiferro. *Il prisco cavaliere* [The knight of olde]. Brooklyn: F. Sparacino, [*ca.* 1924].

This copy of another bound poem, a comic satire – the title is a play on words, as "prisco" means "ancient" or "of olde," but it is also the horseman's name – is also inscribed to Anna Lannutti: "*Ad Anna Lannutti, gentile e fervida cultrice della Muse, per ringraziarla della parole di loda e di plausa/ scritte dopo la lettura del mio sonetto 'Fine l'anno' / Riccardo Cordiferro / New York, 20 Gennaio 1933*" (To Anna Lannutti, kind and ardent cultivator of the Muses, to thank her for her words of praise and approval written after the reading of my sonnet, 'End of Year').

22c ⊁ [Sheet music]. Salvatore Cardillo (music), Riccardo Cordiferro (lyrics). *Core 'ngrato*. Milano: G. Ricordi, 1911.

One of the most enduring 20th century Neapolitan songs, still popular today, *Core 'ngrato* was a signature work sung by Caruso and Luciano Pavarotti, and remains a favorite of Andrea Bocelli.

23 ⊁ Federico Mennella. *Rapsodia napoletana*. New York: Cocce Press, 1944.

Rapsodia is an epic story of the history of Naples from its founding as a Greek colony, composed of 105 sonnets written in the Neapolitan dialect. It includes a preface by Agostino de Biasi, publisher of *Il Carroccio* during most of its run. Besides this accomplished work, Mennella (b. Naples, 1894; d. New York, 1954), a businessman and trade official living in New York, wrote the dialect page in Cordiferro's *La Follia* for years, and published at least two other poetic works in New York, *Le canzoni de l'ora* (1945) and *Napule d'aiere* (1944). Mennella's grandson and namesake is a member of the Grolier Club.

DRAMA

Ludovico Caminita

Ludovico (born Michele) Caminita (b. Palermo, 1878; d. New York, 1943) was active in the first decades of the 20th century in anarchist circles in Barre, Vermont, and elsewhere. After his conversion from socialism to anarchism as the result of a debate he held with Spanish anarchist Pedro Esteve, he became editor of *La Questione Sociale,* of Paterson, the most important anarchist newspaper at the time and the one that Luigi Galleani worked for in his first years in the U.S. Caminita directed another periodical, *L'Era Nuova*, which was suppressed by the authorities in 1917, and followed that by founding the clandestine newspaper, *La Jacquerie.* He also submitted poetry and essays to the Siscas' non-militant *La Follia di New York* as well as to the militant *Cronaca Sovversiva* in Barre. Caminita was arrested on February 14, 1920, during the middle of the 1920s "Red Scare," along with twenty-eight others in a raid that thereby wiped out the entire staff of *L'Era Nuova.* Living for some time in Hawthorne, New Jersey and later in Scranton, he avoided deportation according to at least one account (disputed by some) by giving up names of fellow leftists, earning him the enmity of the godfather of all Italian journalist-anarchist-labor leaders in America, Carlo Tresca (cat. 116).

24 ╊ Ludovico Caminita. *Sonata elegiaca: Dramma*. Brooklyn: Tartamella, 1921. Second thousand.

Inscribed by Caminita on August 22, 1935 to Dr. Cloyd H. Marvin, rector and president of George Washington University. This drama, first performed on May 16, 1921 at the Olympic Theatre in New York, starred the most celebrated actress in Italian American theatre, Mimì Aguglia, and was directed by Clemente Giglio. *Sonata elegiaca* was an instant hit, perhaps explaining why it was issued by two different publishers in the same year (the other being A. Fontanella in Paterson, New Jersey). The "Second thousand" on a copy published in the same year as the play's first production is thus probably not puffery. This still-early edition manages to include many laudatory reviews of the play by Cordiferro, Roversi and Italo Stanco, among others, in Italian newspapers and magazines, such as *La Follia di New York* and *Il Progresso,* in an appendix.

Sonata elegiaca follows the life of a rich American writer, Errico Parson, who supports the cause of the workers during a strike out of love for a typical proletariat militant, Lillian Owen. The love triangle extends further: Parson's jealous wife, with the help of her admirer, manufacturer Giovanni Oliver, conspires to accuse and imprison the radical Owen. Their efforts bring success, as Lillian is convicted of perpetrating a dynamiting attempt, and dies in prison.

25 ╊ Ario Flamma. *Fiamme: Dramma in un atto. Memorie di un suicida* [Flames: Drama in one act. Recollections of a suicide]. New York: Ario Flamma, 1911.

This volume consists of two works: a popular play originally written, performed, and published in Rome in 1906 (before getting a second life with this publication), followed by *Memorie*, a short story. Flamma (b. Cattomosetta, Sicily,

1882; d. New York, 1961) emigrated to America in the first decade of the 20th century. During the First World War, he was a volunteer in the U.S. army. He lived in Chicago as secretary of the Italian Chamber of Commerce, and then moved to New York, where between 1922 and 1924 he was the director of the magazine *Il Vaglio*. "I have been in America for ten years, stubbornly following the bitter and harsh path of art. I am still surprised that I have not yet forgotten my Italian, given that the three million Italians in America speak every dialect but Italian."

Flamma claimed preeminence for having pioneered attempts to draw middle-class themes onto the popular stage of New York's Little Italy (though he also boasted of successes on Broadway). He was one of the few Italian writers of the era who managed to get his work translated into English, and first self-published a volume of translations of youthful plays, *Dramas*, in New York in 1909. Some years later, he succeeded in getting "Fiamme" translated and published in English as *Flames & Other Plays* (New York, 1928).

26 ⅙ Silvio Picchianti. *La "Montanina." Melodramma in 3 atti. Musica di Salvatore Iodice*. [*ca.* 1930s]. Spiralbound typescript.

A gift to me from Gloria Iodice, whose husband composed an operatic score to this libretto. Though he sometimes composed music, Picchianti, a Florentine who had published in Italy before immigrating to the United States in the early 20th century, also wrote libretti or melodramas on commission from composers such as Salvatore Iodice. And although the libretto for *La "Montanina"* was written in the 1930s, Iodice set the work to music twenty years later for a competition in Rome. Unfortunately, the work was withdrawn from competition before the submission could be made; thus, it was never performed.

Picchianti (b. Florence, 1908; d. New York, 1987) dedicated himself to musical theatre in America, preferring plots about exiled families, middle-class interiors, and stories of love and adultery. But he did not omit the patriotic and social muse, nor musical comedy and poetry. He wrote in both standard Italian and Florentine dialect. *La "Montanina,"* named for the city's curfew bell at that time, takes place in mid-15th century Florence on the feast of Calendimaggio (the first of May), a kind of Carnevale or Mardi Gras, and involves a jealous husband and a despondent but murderous lover.

Iodice (b. Naples, 1900; d. New York, 1966) came to New York at an early age, studying piano with the aging Hungarian pianist, Rafael Joseffy. In 1919, he went to Paris to study composition with Camille Saint-Saëns, returning to New York in 1922. He made several lengthy trips back to Naples, where he gained some fame as a composer; the great Italian tenor, Tito Schipa, sang one of his songs at its debut performance.

27✛ Marziale Sisca. *La Follia di New York* [The Folly of New York]. Vol XXXXIII, No. 1. New York: Italian National Magazine, 1935.

This satirical weekly magazine was founded in 1893 by Francesco Sisca and his two sons (see discussion before cat. 22a), Marziale, who ran the magazine early on and well into the 1960s, and Alessandro, better known as Riccardo Cordiferro, who became one of the leading men of letters in the Italian American community. Boasting the variety of *La Follia's* offerings, an ad appears on the rear

VOL XXXXIII — No. 1
Sunday, January 6, 1935
Office: 154 Nassau St.

CAT. 27

of Cordiferro's lyrical verse, *La vendetta* (cat. 22a), in Italian, translated here as: "Every issue contains: an article of the most important matters of the moment; numerous pages of variety; original short stories, sketches, and dialect poetries; chronicles of art; a page for men; a page in English; an installment of an unpublished story, etc." A very young Frank Capra and Rodolfo Valentino appeared in its pages, as well as many of the writers represented in this exhibition, including Pucciu (cat. 17), Caminita (cat. 24, 40), Caruso (cat. 30), Roversi (cat. 33a), Seneca (cat. 66), Cenerazzo (cat. 77) and of course, Ciambelli (cat. 10, 135a).

La Follia was concerned not only with political and social themes (such as the indictment of fake doctors who exercised their profession in the colony — Dr. Collins, perhaps (cat. 47)? — or the bankers who enriched themselves by swindling immigrants), but also with cultural issues. The pages of *La Follia* also contained works of many well-known Italian writers not part of the American scene, from Salvatore Di Giacomo to Mario Rapisardi. The contributions of Italian opera stars, popular in America, ranged from Enrico Caruso, who drew his amusing caricatures for the paper (gathered into a volume by Marziale Sisca in 1908, see cat. 30), to Tito Schipa and Beniamino Gigli.

28 ᛭ E. M. Grella. *Vita. Satirico Settimanale* [Life. Satiric Weekly]. Vol. 1, No. 7 (December 1929) and Vol. 2, No. 2 (January 1930). New York: E. M. Grella, 1929-30.

Two issues of the heavily-illustrated satirical weekly magazine, the covers each displaying a political caricature in addition to the magazine's staple, a dancing smiling faun, all by Italian cartoonist Giovanni Viafora. Little information exists about E. M. Grella (not even his first name), though he does appear in several articles and journals of the early 20th century, and a 1918 issue of *The Fourth Estate* lists him as owning three newspapers: *Il Giornale Italiano* (The Italian Journal), *L'Araldo Italiano* (The Italian Herald), and *Il Telegrafo*. Of his four publications, this seems to be the only humor magazine.

29 ᛭ Agostino de Biasi. *Il Carroccio* [The Chariot] *(The Italian Review)*, Vol. IX, no. 6. New York: Il Carroccio Publishing Co., 1919.

Agostino de Biasi (b. Sant'Angelo dei Lombardi [Avellino], 1875; d. New York, 1964) was the editor of the newspaper *L'Eco dell'Ofanto* (named after the Ofanto, a river that flows through Avellino) before immigrating to the United States in November 1900 to become managing editor of the newspaper *Il Progresso Italo-Americano* (1900-1904; 1906-1911). De Biasi founded the conservative newspaper *L'Opinione* in Philadelphia during his hiatus from *Il Progresso*, and also ran the newspaper *Il Telegrafo*, bringing monarchist principles to all the newspapers he wrote for or directed.

In 1915, on the eve of Italy's entrance into World War I, de Biasi founded this monthly magazine, which he directed, with a regular correspondent in Rome, Enrico Corradini. The first issue announced "Italian emigrants — intellectuals and workers, those who are real Italians both in relation to foreigners and within themselves — must undertake the task of defending the name of Italy by voice and with the pen, just as their brothers are charged with the defense of the frontier with their weapons." This serial publication also exhorted Italian Americans to return to Italy and fight against the central powers, though de Biasi never himself returned to Italy to do so. Slowly *Il Carroccio* turned more fascist under his direction: he used the

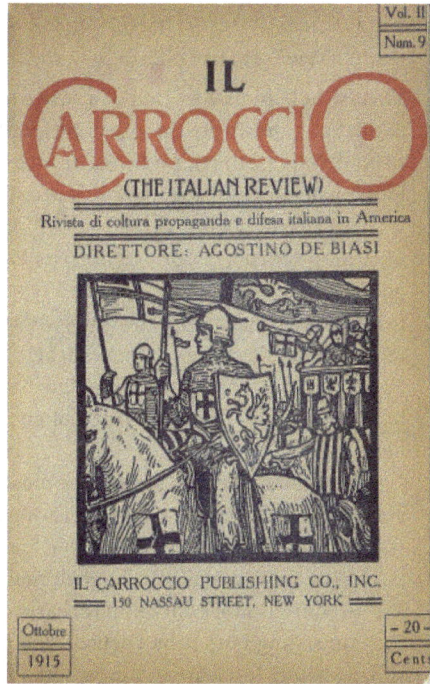

CAT. 29

April 30, 1921 issue to establish the New York Fascio (NYF), a fascist program comprised mainly of war veterans and former syndicalists. But some time later, believing himself to have a "pure Fascist conscience," de Biasi resigned from the NYF. When *Il Carroccio* began to publish confidential information, the Partito Nazionale Fascista (National Fascist Party, PNF) expelled de Biasi, and a fascist boycott against *Il Carroccio* ruined the magazine. De Biasi appealed to Mussolini for re-entrance into the PNF in 1930, which was granted in 1933. *Il Carroccio*, however, long eclipsed by *Il Grido della Stirpe* in popularity among American fascist sympathizers (see note before cat. 128 and cat. 131), never regained its popularity, and was officially discontinued in 1935.

Its politics notwithstanding, *Il Carroccio* played a positive role in promoting non-political, Italian-language, American literary output, especially from two talented women writers, Dora Colonna and Caterina Maria Avella. It thus fairly enough called itself, on the cover of every issue, a "*rivista di coltura*" (magazine of culture), as well as one of "*propaganda e difesa Italiana in America*" (propaganda and defense of Italy in America).

30 ⧉ Enrico Caruso. *Caricatures in four parts / Caricature in quattro parti*. New York: La Follia di New York, 1908.

This is the rare first edition of a series of editions of this popular collection of caricatures drawn by the great Neapolitan tenor, Enrico Caruso (b. Naples, 1873; d. Naples, 1921). *La Follia di New York* published Caruso's caricatures in individual issues for years before gathering them in book form.

Caricatures begins with a brief bilingual text of Caruso's life, and includes illustrations of many world figures, including political leaders as well as those in opera, music and theatre. Part II, "Types of Our Colony," includes sketches of many writers and publishers whose works are featured in this exhibition, including those of Mayor des Planches (cat. 78), Luigi Roversi (cat. 33a), Francesco Tocci (cat. 5-6, 16, 19), and Marziale Sisca (cat. 27). Later editions of this collected work lack "Types of Our Colony," reflecting the decline and passing of "our colony."

Those later editions, such as the most commonly available one (dated 1965), also lack the biographical entry at the outset, the ads at the end, and most of the Italian-language material. However, they do contain Caruso's letters, accompanied by translations into English that are not found in the original edition. These editions also contain more caricatures than earlier printings, reflecting the continuing output by Caruso, who published drawings for *La Follia* until shortly before his death in 1921 at age 48.

Histories, biographies, directories

31 ⧉ Luigi Cavallaro. *Pionieri ed eroi della storia americana* [Pioneers and heroes of American history]. New York: Frugone, Balletto & Pellegatti, 1907.

Perhaps reflecting how early in the period of the Great Migration he was writing, Cavallaro's work is not about Italians, but rather sets forth the "life and the works of illustrious men in the history of America." This is the only item in this collection from the important early New York publisher of Italian works, Frugone, Balletto & Pellegatti. In the late 19th century, when the firm was just Frugone & Balletto, the publishers made an important and early "find" of Bernardino Ciambelli, publishing seven novels of the greatest Italian language fiction writer to come from the "colonia italiana" (cat. 10, 135a). The 1906 edition of *The Trow Copartnership and Corporation Directory of the City of New York* lists "Frugone, Balletto & Pellegatti Publishers," yet the 1901 directory only lists Frugone & Balletto, so the addition of Pellegatti occurred shortly before publication of this work.

Pionieri ed eroi contains appendices about the Declaration of Independence, the "real war cry of an oppressed people yearning for liberty," and the United States Constitution, "said by Gladstone to be the most stupendous work that the mind of man has ever produced." Cavallaro, of whom little is known, dedicated his work with reverent affection to Dr. Melville Knox Bailey, founder and president of the Italo-American Educational League, "ardent apostle of the instruction and well being of the Italians in America."

32 ⊹ Alfredo Bosi. *Cinquant' anni di vita italiana in America* [Fifty years of Italian life in America]. New York: Bagnasco Press, 1921.

This copy inscribed in 1922 to Luigi Barzini, the great Italian journalist and founder of the U.S.-based *Corriere d'America* (The American Courier). *Cinquant' anni* is the first history of Italians in America, the composition of which arose from a meeting between Bosi and King Vittorio Emanuele of Italy in 1901, at which the king expressed curiosity about the now-established Italian colony in America. Like many of the American imprints in this exhibition, this copy was acquired from a book dealer in Italy, one who presumably obtained it from the estate of or a descendant of Barzini, who had returned to Italy after his sojourn in America.

Bosi's work encompasses a broad sociological and historical review of the Italian experience in America. Reflecting on both good and bad aspects of the culture, the text includes chapters on illiteracy, *L'analfabetismo: La gran piaga d'Italia* (Illiteracy: The great curse of Italy), as well as on lynching, *Il linciaggio: La gran piaga d'America* (Lynching: The great curse of America). On the latter, he counted 3,224 lynchings over a period from 1888 to 1918, including the famous 1891 New Orleans lynching of 11 Italians, which became an international *cause célèbre*. Bosi also wrote of American legislation to stop the inflow of Italians as "undesirable immigrants," while at the same time he wrote of Italian Americans enjoying their successes in the dramatic and pictorial arts, in commerce and industry, and in Italian journalism in America.

33a ⊹ Luigi Roversi. *Luigi Palma di Cesnola e il Metropolitan Museum of Art di New York*. New York: Metropolitan Museum of Art, 1898.

This copy, with an inscription to "the most noble Madam Contessa Valdrighi" dated 1899, is a hagiography of the Torinese count, Palma di Cesnola, who arrived in America penniless (but of noble birth). Though impoverished, he learned English quickly, and began teaching English and French. He married Mary Isabel Reid, a student of his from a good New York family, and later passed an officer's exam to rise to lieutenant colonel. In that position he joined a regiment to protect President Lincoln. Luigi Roversi (b. Bologna, 1859; d. New York, 1927) was the secretary and assistant to di Cesnola as the first director of the Metropolitan Museum of Art after the war and Cesnola's service as U.S. ambassador to Cyprus. Di Cesnola's collection of Cypriot artifacts still continues to occupy a separate room at the Met.

Roversi led a diverse career: lecturer for the Board of Education of New York on themes of civic education, literature and art; literary and drama critic; and teacher at the People's University, promoted in New York by the Socialist Party. Trained as a lawyer in Italy, he was a correspondent of *La Gazetta* of Torino and other Italian newspapers, and wrote literary pieces in *appendici*, laid in between newspaper sheets for *La Patria* (The Fatherland) of Bologna. After immigrating to America, he became a contributing editor of *Il Progresso Italo-Americano* and *L'Araldo Italiano*, and the politico-literary editor of *La Follia di New York*, and associated with several Italian newspapers as the New York correspondent. Besides this work, Roversi also published *Ricordi canavesani. Luigi Palma di Cesnola a Rivarolo Canavese e a Cesnola*. (Memoirs from the Canavese: Luigi Palma di Cesnola at Rivarolo Canavese and at Cesnola) in 1901, about Cesnola's voyage to his hometown area in Italy.

33b ⧆ Vincenzo Polidori to William Shipman, Esq., autograph letter signed, New York, on *Il Progresso* stationery (2 & 4 Centre St., Staatz [*sic*] Zeitung Building, December 3, 1885.

Polidori was *Il Progresso* co-"editore-proprietari" (for five years) with Carlo Barsotti, probably in the period when Roversi was a contributing editor for *Il Progresso*. This letter to William Shipman of Stony Brook, New York, attorney for the landlord of the *Il Progresso* building, is Polidori's transmittal of a rent payment on behalf of an unknown party.

Vincenzo Vacirca

Vincenzo Vacirca (b. Sicily, 1886; d. Italy, 1956) was a member of the Socialist Party of Italian Workers by age 16, and organized the first union of peasants in Ragusa in Sicily at that tender age, for which he was subsequently arrested and imprisoned. In 1911 he was elected a member of the Chamber of Deputies in Bologna and visited Russia, where he interviewed Lenin, Trotsky and other Communist leaders for his articles published in *L'Avanti!* Condemned to five years in prison by the judges of Siracusa for his anti-fascist writings, Vacirca returned to the U.S. in 1925, only to meet the fascists' continued pursuit.

A writer both of novels and fiery political speeches, he was serially compelled to flee (or in some cases, expelled) from Brazil, Argentina, and Austria. In New York, between 1913 and 1919, he managed the newspapers *La Lotta di Classe*

(Class Struggle); in Chicago, *La Parola del Popolo* (The People's Word); in Boston, the daily *La Notizia* (The News), and the socialist weekly *L'Internazionale* (The International). Radicals Arturo Giovannitti and Carlo Tresca were good friends and comrades of Vacirca in political struggle.

It wasn't only his writing that was fiery: Vacirca spoke at political rallies, and one in Newark turned into a brawl, with gunshots and a knifing. He was the first publisher of *Il Nuovo Mondo* (The New World), the first anti-fascist daily newspaper outside of Italy, located in that East 10th Street building which Vanni Montana later characterized as "the citadel of Italian American anti-fascism," and to which Cordiferro contributed. In 1926, he was deprived of Italian citizenship, and his goods and property were confiscated. Later, he participated in forming the Partito Socialista dei Lavoratori Italiani, and from a rigorously anti-Communist position, directed the party nationally from 1949 to 1952.

34 ⁙ Vincenzo Vacirca. *La Russia in fiamme (22 mesi di rivoluzione)* [Russia in flames (22 months of revolution)]. New York: Casa Editrice "I Giovani," 1919.

The subject of *La Russia in fiamme* is one Vacirca knew well from his interviews (while a senator in Italy) with Lenin and Trotsky: the Russian Revolution, from its inception in 1917. The first few pages feature quotations in French (Romain Rolland) and English (Longfellow), as well as from Maxim Gorky, who is quoted in Italian, calling for the complete overthrow of the Bolshevik regime whose censorship of Gorky's newspaper strained their relations.

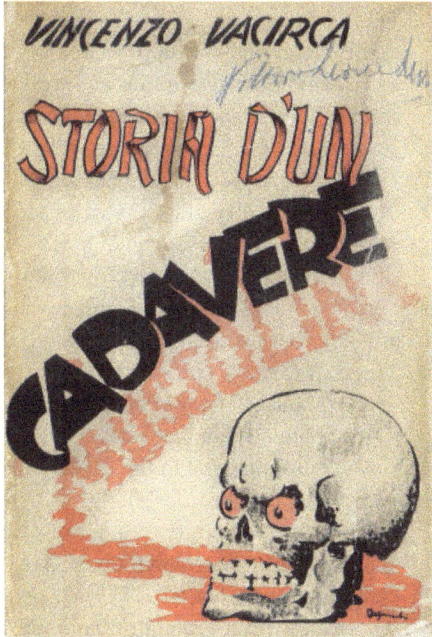

CAT. 35

35 ⁙ Vincenzo Vacirca. *Mussolini. Storia d'un cadavere* [Mussolini. History of a cadaver]. New York: La Strada Publishing Co., 1942.

Vacirca's anti-fascist biography of Mussolini covers the period from his growing up in poverty to his rise to "Il Duce" in 1925 and emperor in 1936. The bright pictorial cover (artist unknown) is illustrated with a graphic drawing of a red-eyed skull; the blood trailing from the skull's base spells "Mussolini" for the cover title.

36 ⊁ Salvatore Viola. *Il libro dei santi* [The book of the saints]. New York: Variety Bazaar & Italian Book, 1942.

The front cover provides some bibliographic information in Italian, translated here as: "Printed exclusively for the newspaper *L'Italia* 1500 Stockton Street, San Francisco, Cal." A rare hybrid (published in New York, but printed for a San Francisco newspaper), Viola's work reflects the Catholic faith that most of America's Italians followed faithfully, the significant anti-clerical minority notwithstanding. This work names and describes the saint, or saints in some cases, for every day of the year, as well as a list of patron saints for each profession. A native of Pescara, the birthplace of poet Gabriele D'Annunzio, Viola (active, 1930s–1940s) was director of the Permanent Italian Book Exhibition in New York (a bookstore founded in 1928 to establish connections between Italian publishers and the American book-buying public), with its 50,000 volumes in Italian, studied music at the New England Conservatory of Music, and worked at international book stores in Boston and New York. He directed the Italian section of *The Atlantic Monthly*, and wrote for the newspaper *Il Corriere Siciliano*, and the magazines *Giovinezza* (Youth) and *La Settimana* (The Week).

37 ⊁ Baldo Aquilano. *L'Ordine Figli d'Italia in America* [Order Sons of Italy in America]. New York: Società Tipografica Italiana, 1925.

This work traces the development of the OSIA, the most durable of Italian American fraternal organizations, as well as the Italian immigration that gave rise to its formation. The OSIA took an active role in the support of Mussolini when he rose to power in November 1922. Its Supreme Venerable, Giovanni di Silvestro, attempted to pledge the loyalty of the OSIA to Mussolini and purge the organization of "radicals." Fiorello La Guardia, Arturo Giovannitti and others opposed this action, thus sparking a serious and long-lasting crisis within OSIA, ending with formation of a separate fraternity in February 1923. Later that year, Arturo Giovannitti and labor leader Luigi Antonini were purged from the OSIA's ranks.

A free-lance journalist, Aquilano (b. Chieti, 1885; d. New York?) directed out of Milan the daily, and still one of today's most popular Italian-language newspapers, *Il Corriere della Sera*, from 1911 to 1913 and thereafter *Il Messaggero*, a weekly published out of Paterson and Passaic, New Jersey. He also contributed to several weekly and monthly magazines. In 1907, Aquilano joined the OSIA and was instrumental in the development of that organization's laws and rituals. A believer in broader commerce between the U.S. and Italy, he founded the Italian Tourist Institute. Besides this work, he wrote about his native Abruzzo (and mining in Allegheny), the Italians of Long Island (with preface by Theodore Roosevelt), Woodrow Wilson, socialism and syndicalism and the origins of American literature, among other topics.

38 ⫶⊕ Ario Flamma. *Fiorello La Guardia.* New York: Worthy Printing, 1934.

Published only a year after La Guardia was elected mayor of New York City, this work by Flamma is, for the first half, a meditation on the vagaries of wealth, prosperity and our national illusion during the Depression. Only starting at p. 46 of this 76-page essay does he begin in earnest to discuss La Guardia's life. Flamma concludes this work with evident pride that after electing mayors in 29 other cities, Italians finally elected a mayor to the country's most important city.

39 ⫶⊕ Ario Flamma. *Italiani di America: Enciclopedia biografica.* New York: Casa Editrice Cocce Brothers, 1936.

After its publication in 1936, this work was reissued as "Volume II" in 1941 (by S. F. Vanni) and as "Volume III" in 1949 (again by Cocce), with some additions and deletions. Its great value for the researcher is that it is unlike similar works written by the even more prolific Giovanni Schiavo, whose English-language *Italian American Who's Who*, issued annually between 1935 and 1967, was filled mostly with biographies of doctors, lawyers and businessmen. Rather, Flamma's directory is replete with short biographies of journalists and other writers (indeed, "pubblicista," free-lance journalist, is perhaps the profession that appears most frequently in the work), as well as of many artists and musicians of the time, such as Salvatore Iodice (cat. 26).

40 ⫶⊕ Ludovico Caminita, Sr. *Obici: Biografia.* New York: Tipografia Editrice Scarlino, 1943.

Caminita describes the source of inspiration for this biography: walking up Broadway one evening with an editor of *Il Corriere d'America*. The sight of the electric sign at 47th Street and Broadway advertising the Planters Peanut and Chocolate Company, founded by Italian immigrant Amedeo Obici, prompted Caminita to think about how Obici's "genius, his feverish work and pioneering spirit overcame every obstacle and asserted himself superbly in the industrial life of this great nation." An exception to Caminita's typical anarchist-inspired production (cat. 24), this work was presumably a kind of potboiler written to pay the bills.

41 ⫶⊕ Riccardo Cordiferro. *Gabriele D'Annunzio nella vita e nell'arte* [Gabriele D'Annunzio in life and in art]. New York: Cocce Brothers, 1938.

A lengthy essay on perhaps the then most celebrated political, journalistic and literary figure of Italy, who was also known for the torrid love affair he carried on with actress Eleonora Duse. D'Annunzio had a significant impact in the United States among the Italians. In particular, his brand of journalism inspired either admiration or heavy criticism among Italian writers participating in the ongoing debates (see Carnovale, cat. 63) on the quality of Italian American journalism. D'Annunzio's nationalistic fervor for Italy is considered to have unfortunately helped nurture the climate in which fascism took hold. This work is a long-after-the-fact transcription by Cordiferro of a lecture he gave several times in Connecticut, New York and New Jersey, mostly from 1918–1924. His last lecture was in March 1938, in the hall of the La Guardia Political Club in New York, just a few days after D'Annunzio's death.

42 ⊁ Paolo Pallavicini. *La guerra italo-austriaca (1915–1919)*. New York: Società Libraria Italiana, 1919.

Pallavicini (b. Torino or Milan, 1886; d. San Francisco, 1938) began his American writing career in New York, publishing this work with the Società Libraria Italiana, before moving west. He spent a good part of his last few decades on the West Coast, writing and producing radiodramas, such as his 1933 *Nella terra del sogno* (published by the San Francisco newspaper, *L'Italia*), and more sentimental fiction such as *Tutto il dolore, tutto l'amore* (cat. 61).

Martino Marazzi dryly calls *La guerra italo-austriaca* a "hyperconformist outburst of exasperated nationalism."[6] An earlier work published by the company, in 1911, contains the same unthinking patriotic support of Italy's war with Turkey (cat. 136).

43 ⊁ Anonymous. *In memoria della Rev[erendissi]ma Francesca Saverio Cabrini: Fondatrice e Superiora Generale delle missionarie del S. Cuore del Gesù, volata al cielo in Chicago il 22 Dicembre 1917* [In memory of the Most Reverend Frances Xavier Cabrini: Founder and General Mother Superior of the Missionaries of the S[acred] Heart of Jesus, rushed to heaven from Chicago, December 22, 1917]. New York: A. Bernasconi, 1918.

A lengthy tome dedicated to the memory of Mother Cabrini (née Francesca Saverio Cabrini), the first United States citizen canonized by the Catholic Church. Known and respected throughout Italian America, Cabrini initially relocated to America on papal orders, and not only founded the Sacred Heart Missionary, but also orphanages and hospitals throughout the United States and elsewhere. This work predicts Cabrini's canonization, which came to fruition many years later, in 1946, and includes translations in English, Spanish, French and Portuguese of encomiums to Cabrini given at various funeral and memorial services around the world. The letters "A.M.G.SS.C.J." are printed at the top of the cover and title pages, "A maggiore gloria del santissimo Cuore di Gesù" (To the greater glory of the most holy Heart of Jesus). A slightly shorter version of the same work was also published in 1918 in Rome by the Scuola Tipografia Salesiana.

44 ❧ Franco Lalli. *La prima santa d'America* [The first saint in America]. Brooklyn: Fortuna Publishing Co., 1944.

La prima santa d'America reflects the intense pride in Mother Cabrini that continued to exist nearly thirty years after her death. Although she was not canonized a saint until 1946, the title of this work predicts it with certainty, which is not surprising given the lengthy gestation period that usually precedes canonization. Cabrini was known as "the Saint of the Emigrants" and "the Italian Saint," and was the first U.S. citizen to be so honored with the title. The Italian American pride was all the greater in that the first American saint was an Italian, rather than the Irish, whose less than hearty welcome to their later-arriving, non-English speaking fellow Catholic immigrants no doubt contributed to the anti-clericalism of the *sovversivi* (subversives) (cat. 109-111). Lalli and the writer of the preface to this work, Pietro Novasio, teamed up again two years later in *La strada della gioia* (cat. 48).

45 and 46 ❧ Giovanni Molinari. *Raccolta di discorsi per ogni occasione* [Collected speeches for every occasion] [and] Riccardo Cordiferro and Giuseppe Valvo. *Brindisi ed augurii* [Toasts and greetings]. New York: Società Libraria Italiana, 1917.

Each of these two identical editions – printed simultaneously in Rome and in New York – appears from their title pages and covers to be two works bound in one, but each in fact is one text divided into six separate parts. Parts 1-3 are comprised of Molinari's model speeches and commemorative discourses, in prose, "for all occasions." Parts 4 and 5 are all poems written by Valvo and Cordiferro, respectively, that are toasts and good wishes for weddings, banquets and other celebratory occasions. Part 6, titled *Altri Brindisi* (Other Toasts), is a modest contribution of six pages of poems by a fourth author, Modestino Sessa, though, unlike the first three, he is not credited on the title page.

   The red cloth version was printed in Italy and the brown cloth printed in the United States. Small differences may be found: the American issue is of a slightly smaller format, lacks the half-title for Molinari's work that is found in the Italian printing, has fewer pages, and a smaller typeface. Also, this copy of the Italian printing contains a misplaced gathering: the signature of the gathering comprised of pages 113-144 is misprinted as "3" instead of "5," thus pages 113-144 are duplicated. It begs the question, how many other issues were affected by the same printing error? In its early days, this publisher often had its works printed in Italy; a large distance between publisher and printer . was bound to lead to more errors of this kind. Though bearing the same date,

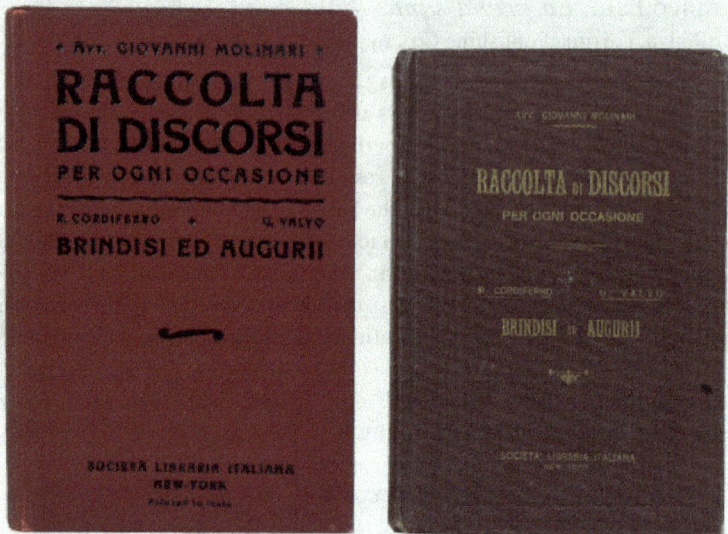

the American edition may well have resulted from dissatisfaction of the publishers with the mistakes of the binding by the printer in Italy.

47 ⚹ Professor E. C. Collins, M.D. *Guida alla salute: Il come prevenire le malattie, come curarle, come riguadagnare la salute, estesa descrizione delle cause, sintomi, e trattamento di tutte le malattie del corpo umano con un capitolo sul matrimonio e la vita sessuale* [Guide to health: How to anticipate illnesses, how to treat them, how to regain health, extensive description of the causes, symptoms, and treatment of all illnesses of the human body with a chapter on marriage and sexual life]. New York: E. C. Collins / New York Medical Institute, 1904. Second fifty thousand copies.

Though little information is available on Collins, an issue of *The Medical Standard* dated 1896 announces his medical residency in Hicksville, NY. Later, he appears to have been fined $150 for advertising his medical practice without first seeking legal authorization. That a work on health "written exclusively for the Italians in America" by this non-Italian could dare to have a chapter "on matrimony and sexual life," including discussion of both "sexual indifference" and nymphomania, is itself noteworthy.

Practicing at the New York Medical Institute on West 34th Street, Professor Collins boasts on the inside front cover the "number of sick people cured in every state" of the U.S. by his medical methods, enumerated state by state – could he have been one of the fake doctors working in the immigrant community indicted in the pages of *La Follia* (cat. 27)? Collins is quick to note that of these 20,196 patients, most of whom were permanently "cured," "only a quarter were actually examined by me personally," the rest by his original method by correspondence. The "object of this book is to teach to my fellow citizen Italians how to stay in good health, and how to recover it in case of sickness."

48 ❧ Pietro Novasio, Franco Lalli and Elisa Odabella. *La strada della gioia* [The road to joy]. New York: Liberal Press, 1946.

This work, with a cover illustration by W. Vercellino, is a series of philosophical essays, apparently all written by Pietro Novasio, about the "art of life," with barely a page gone by before the writer invokes Schopenhauer, Emerson, Vico, Aristotle, Manzoni, Lao-Tse and Dostoyevsky in rapid fire. Franco Lalli explains in the preface that Novasio, a former deputy in the Italian Parliament, was a self-proclaimed political exile living in New York, where he broadcast a regular radio program from his office at the New York Public Library's 42nd Street Research Library. Bolded advice to the reader includes nostrums such as "Weak men wait for opportunities; great ones know how to create them." Odabella's specific contribution to the work is not specified, but may be the last chapter, translated here as "The Rules of a Good Life," printed in a smaller-sized typeface.

49 ❧ Italian American Directory Co. *1905 Italian American Directory: Guida generale per il commercio Italo Americano / General guide for the Italian American trade*. New York: Italian American Directory Co., 1905.

Attempting to fill the same need that American city directories had long performed, this Italian American directory is notable for its national (and international) scope. It leaves no possible advertising space unused, with a lively multi-colored stamped cloth cover and even text inked to the fore-edge (for "Maffei & Co.," who were "Consegnatori, Agenti & Rappresentanti [di] Prodotti Alimentari e Vini" (Consignors, Agents and Representatives of Food Products and Wines) at 304 West Street in Manhattan. The names and addresses of Italians in the directory were organized by borough (within New York City), and then by trade. Italians in 44 of the then-48 states as well as Washington, D.C. were listed by name, and organized by county and trade. A demographic map of the U.S. shows the distribution of Italians across the country, and their population in each state. New York easily held the largest Italian population, with 612,128 Italians (including my grandfather, Joseph Periconi, listed under "barbers," at 1703 Madison Avenue in East Harlem in Manhattan). The states are ranked

down, with second most populous, Pennsylvania, with a population of 241,425 Italians, and Oklahoma with the fewest, with 76.

Among the all-Italian language advertisers from New York was that of the author of the *Nuovissima grammatica accelerata*, Angelo De Gaudenzi (cat. 9), here "editore e librai" (publishers and booksellers), which offered "at your request to send a 'prospectus' for the establishment of a bookstore to be supplied with books *at reasonable prices*."

50 ⊹ Italian American Directory Co. *Gli italiani negli Stati Uniti d'America* [Italians in the United States of America]. New York: Italian American Directory Co., 1906.

Published as a result of the organizing committee of the 1906 Milan Exposition directing Italian Chambers of Commerce around the world to prepare a volume in a series about "gli Italiani all'estero" (Italians abroad), this Italian-language work was an ambitious one, a collaboration with, and actually published by, the same publisher in the year following the more conventional *1905 Italian American Directory* (cat. 49). Part I of this rare elephant folio work contains essays by what can be considered an all-star cast of Italian writers, from then inspector of immigration Adolfo Rossi (cat. 68) on Italian manpower in the U.S., Alfonso Arbib-Costa (cat. 5-7) on Italians in public schools, Alfredo Bosi (cat. 32) on the failure of the Italian colony in New York to establish a true Italian school, Bernardino Ciambelli (cat. 10, 135a) on Columbus Day, and Amy Bernardy (cat. 69) on the Italians of Boston. Part II comprises 290 of the 473-page total, and is a directory of advertisements and summaries of Italian American businesses. Included here is a description of Francesco Tocci's Emporium Press (cat. 5, 16, 19), in which Tocci describes his goal to help make Italian books available and popular among Americans as well as Italians. See Viscusi, "Universal Exposition," above, pp. 30-41.

A moveable feast: Galleani and Borghi

Luigi Galleani

Galleani was one of the anarchist movement's most eloquent writers and spellbinding orators, heir to the great Errico Malatesta in Italy and elsewhere, a political agitator and charismatic anarchist leader, and a prolific political publisher. Mentor to Sacco and Vanzetti, the peripatetic Galleani was born in Italy, and lived in various venues in the U.S. from 1901 until he was deported back to Italy in 1919. He first settled in Paterson, New Jersey in 1901 to be the editor of the then-most important anarchist journal, *La Questione Sociale*. Then, after starting *Cronaca Sovversiva* in 1903, he moved to Lynn, Mass. (cat. 51) until the postmaster in Lynn refused to mail the newspaper *Cronaca Sovversiva* and his books, at which time he repaired to Barre, Vermont (see, *e.g.*, cat. 92). He was prosecuted for violating anti-leftist laws, especially the 1918 Anarchist Exclusion Act.

This act, which permitted the government to shut down publication of the *Cronaca Sovversiva* in that year (and deport Galleani and other editors of the newspaper subsequently), had been passed by Congress largely in response to the bombings that Galleani incited his followers to undertake (see cat. 52) through his publications as well as his personal direction: he even published a manual on how to make bombs ("La salute è in voi!" (Health is in You!)).[7]

Galleani's deportation in 1919 arose as much from his newspaper and pamphlet publications that were themselves regarded by the authorities as incitements to violence, as it did from his actual and attempted bombings. He and his followers of the individualist school of anarchism were wary of not only electoral politics but also of syndicalism, *i.e.*, the use of trade unions to bring industry and government under the control by direct action, such as strikes and sabotage, the preferred methods of Carlo Tresca, among others. Because of these doctrinal differences, as well as Tresca's immense personal charm and popularity, Galleani's followers were even more determined to destroy the reputation and thus the effectiveness of Tresca, despite the anti-fascist views they shared in the 1920s and 1930s.

Like his unlikely ally Armando Borghi, Galleani was internationally well known, so that even his deportation from the U.S. hardly put a stop to his influence. *L'Adunata dei Refrattari* (The Gathering of the Recalcitrants) became the successor newspaper to the *Cronaca Sovversiva*, begun and run by his followers in the U.S. after Galleani's deportation in 1919. Its publishing arm released many full-length works (typically, collections of shorter pieces) like those exhibited here, as well as pamphlets, sometimes without Galleani's authorization, due to his being unreachable in exile on the island of Lipari. *L'Adunata* also published Galleani in Europe, *e.g.*, in Rome as late as 1947, often using the same printer's mark (a mermaid-like torchbearer) he used in the earliest of his works. The international character of the movement had long been clear: in one work, readers of an Italian-language edition of *Organizzazione e anarchia*, published in Paris (by L. Chauvet) sometime after 1925, are urged in a message in the inside rear cover to buy a copy of Galleani's *La fine dell'anarchismo?*, published in the United States (Newark) in 1925 (cat. 53).

51 ⊁ Mentana [Luigi Galleani]. *Madri d'Italia (per Augusto Masetti)*. Lynn, Mass.: Cronaca Sovversiva, 1913.

A pamphlet of 24 pages, this work addresses Italian mothers about the injustices of a nation whose sons return from war, mutilated and undone. In particular it calls for the release of Augusto Masetti, a soldier who, during the Libyan war, is alleged to have assassinated a colonel and rallied the troops with the adage, "Down with the war! Long live anarchy!" It was from his headquarters in Lynn and Barre in the second decade of the 20th century that Galleani led his overtly anti-imperialistic, revolutionary movement, leading to his deportation in 1919.

52 ⊁ Mentana [Luigi Galleani]. *Faccia a faccia col nemico: Cronache giudiziarie dell'anarchismo militante* [Face to face with the enemy: Judicial chronicles of militant anarchism]. East Boston: Edizione del Gruppo Autonomo, 1914.

This text is a lengthy work containing fifteen articles and essays from (and printed by the book publishing arm of) Galleani's newspaper, *Cronaca Sovversiva*, describing various bombings by militant anarchists and their trials that inevitably followed, though prior to the more famous 1917–1918 bombings discussed in Angelo Faggi's book (cat. 96). The best-known members of the militant Gruppo Autonomo, Nicola Sacco and Bartolomeo Vanzetti, worshipped Galleani as "our master." The possession of radical literature like this work, and the need to hide it from the authorities, is the likely cause of the arrest, a few years later, of Sacco and Vanzetti, on May 5, 1920, during the course of a roundup of Galleanisti, who were suspected of taking part in recent bombings. In the process, they were linked to the South Braintree robbery in the wake of a failed attempt to retrieve the car, under repair, they needed, probably in order to collect and hide radical literature like *Faccia a faccia*.

53 ✚ Luigi Galleani. *La fine dell'anarchismo?* [The end of anarchism?]. Newark: Vecchi lettori di Cronaca Sovversiva, 1925.

This is in part the transcript of an interview between socialist and anarchist writer and attorney for the anarchists, Francesco Saverio Merlino, and Cesare Sobrero of the Italian daily, *La Stampa*, and in part, following the interview, Galleani's analysis of the discussion, and his response to Merlino's claim to the reporter that anarchism was dead. One of the adventures of Merlino during this period was the duel between the "cold, Nordic" Merlino and the "suave and dashing" Mussolini, then director of the *Popolo d'Italia*, recounted wonderfully by Eugenio Camillo Branchi in the December 1927 issue of *Il Carroccio*. A lengthy printed "inscription" by Galleani "to comrades in America, in remembrance of the battles fought together for so many years" precedes the title page in this copy (and presumably the entire run). Many years later (in 1982), this work was translated into English by Galleani adherent, and long-time editor of *L'Adunata dei Refrattari*, Raffaele Schiavina, assisted by Robert D'Attilio.

54 ✚ Luigi Galleani. *Medaglioni. Figure e figuri* [Sketches. Characters and suspicious types]. Newark: Biblioteca de L'Adunata dei Refrattari, [1930].

Originally published in *La Questione* or *Cronaca Sovversiva* between 1901 and 1920, this is a collection of Galleani's articles on various important movement characters, Italian and otherwise, published by the book-publishing arm of the newspaper begun by Raffaele Schiavina and other Galleanisti after Galleani was deported in 1919. The preface states that this volume was published during Galleani's exile on the island of Lipari, and thus without his express consent. Galleani lived in confinement and isolation on Lipari from 1926 until shortly before his death in 1930 or 1931.

55 ✚ Luigi Galleani. *Una battaglia* [A struggle]. Roma: Biblioteca de l'Adunata dei Refrattari, 1947.

The first 65 pages of this work reprint and expand upon an earlier Galleani work, *Contro la guerra – contro la pace – per la rivoluzione sociale*. In addition to the original essay, the work includes over fifty articles written from the beginning to the end of World War I. Published in Italy by the American *L'Adunata*, *Una battaglia* was collected and designed to enable Italians in the homeland to gain a sense of what their co-nationals living in America were experiencing.

Armando Borghi

Armando Borghi's unflattering biography of Mussolini was too dangerous to be released in Italy: after Mussolini's rise to power in 1922, publishing a work criticizing Mussolini soon became impossible. Simply for speaking in the Italian Parliament in June 1924 against fraud (and violence) employed by Mussolini in the recent election, United Socialist Party chief Giacomo Matteotti was within days thereafter murdered by the fascists. In 1925, measures that gave the government powers to gag the press were passed. Emergency laws in 1926 suppressed every political party and every newspaper other than those of the fascists. It was in that context that anarcho-syndicalist Borghi arrived in the U.S. in or about November 1926, where he was joined by his lover, Virgilia D'Andrea (cat. 82). Shortly thereafter, in 1927 he published *Mussolini in camicia* in Italian in the only safe place to do so at the time, New York. This work became internationally popular, was translated into French and published in Paris (1932), in Amsterdam in Dutch (1933), and then translated into English from the French edition, not the Italian original, and published in London (1935). *Mussolini in camicia* was again published to America, but in English, in 1938 using the same British translation, and was not published in Italy until 1947, not long after the war's end and Mussolini's execution.

In Italy, Borghi ranked second in Italy only to the legendary Errico Malatesta as its most important anarchist, so that when he arrived in the U.S., Borghi expected to be the foremost Italian anarchist there (Galleani having been deported some years before). However, Carlo Tresca, who as a fellow "organization" anarchist might otherwise have been his natural ally, was in the way, and Borghi surprisingly thus aligned himself with the anti-organizational anarchist Galleanisti and their *L'Adunata dei Refrattari*, a move that he eventually came to regret. Like the Galleanisti, Borghi attacked Tresca not only on ideological grounds but also on personal ones.

56 ⊁ Armando Borghi. *Mussolini in camicia* [Mussolini in a night-shirt]. New York: Edizioni Libertarie, 1927.

When it first appeared in New York, in its original Italian, it was edited and promoted by three anarchist clubs, Gruppo Anarchico di South Brooklyn, Circolo Volontà, and Circolo Operaio di Cultura Sociale. Such clubs existed to advance culture, knowledge and a working-class consciousness among Italian immigrants, and formed the intellectual nucleus of the movement, as well as being centers for education, recruitment and propaganda. The *circoli* also provided access to literature through their own "librerie rosse," *i.e.*, red bookstores.

In this work, Borghi traces Mussolini's rise in his native Romagna, whence Borghi also hailed. Describing Mussolini's transformation from young socialist, Borghi explains why Mussolini disowned socialism, how he allied himself with military politics, and answers the question of whether he saved Italy from revolution. "Should he be classed among the heroes or the scoundrels, the charlatans or the idealists . . . ?" It's clear where Borghi came out on those questions, which explains why the work could not be published in Italy during Mussolini's reign.

57 ❧ Armando Borghi. *Mussolini en chemise* [Mussolini in a night-shirt]. Paris: Editions Rieder, 1932. Number "H.C. [hors commerce] 4" of twenty numbered, privately circulated copies printed on alfa foam paper with the original glassine wrapper.

Mussolini en chemise was also issued in a trade edition of a larger print run, printed on cheaper paper.

58 ❧ Armando Borghi. *Mussolini Red and Black*. London: Wishart Books, 1935.

Translated by Dorothy Daudley from the 1932 French edition, rather than the Italian original. It contains an epilogue, "Hitler: Mussolini's Disciple," written in 1934.

59 ❧ Armando Borghi. *Mussolini Red and Black*. New York: Freie Arbeiter Stimme, 1938.

Though not so stated, this translation is identical to the 1935 London edition. It also contains the same 1934 epilogue, "Hitler: Mussolini's Disciple," as the London translation.

60 ⊹ **Armando Borghi.** *Mussolini in camicia.* Bologna: Mammolo Zamboni, 1947.

Front wrapper has the subtitle "*(Storia di ieri e di oggi)*" (History of yesterday and of today) under the title. First publication in Italy. Others have republished it in Italy at least once since 1947, *e.g.*, in a 1961 edition by Scientifiche Italiane (Naples).

Outside of New York and the Northeast

61 ⊹ Paolo Pallavicini. *Tutto il dolore, tutto l'amore: Romanzo d'ambiente italo-americano* [All of the pain, all of the love: A novel in an Italian American ambiance]. San Francisco: L'Italia Press Co., 1926.

CAT. 61

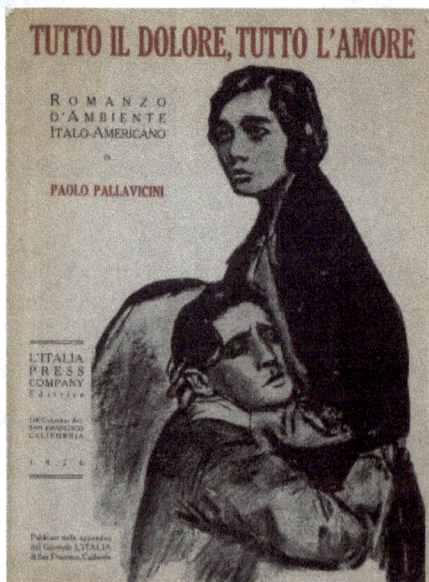

The title page states, "*Pubblicato nelle appendici del Giornale 'L'Italia' di San Francisco,*" (Published as appendices of the San Francisco newspaper, *L'Italia*). Like many of the works of both fiction and non-fiction (*e.g.*, Carnovale, cat. 63) that follow in this section, Pallavicini's romantic novel had been published serially in San Francisco's popular newspaper owned and directed by the *prominenti* ("prominent" and prosperous members of the Italian American community). Like much of Pallavicini's non-political works, this novel presents the intrigues and passions of young second-generation Italians, torn between their roots and the desire for success, and the tormented, drawn-out love affairs that reflected the conflict between affection for their family and striving to be American that separated them from parental love and guidance. This work was also printed in Milan by Sonzogno in 1937.

62 ⊱ Cesare Crespi. *San Francisco e la sua catastrofe* [San Francisco and its catastrophe]. San Francisco: Tipografia Internazionale, 1906.

After the Italians of New York, those of San Francisco (and Chicago) probably had the most well-developed network of periodical press, theatre, literature, associations and other forms of collective efforts, including unions. Crespi's dramatic "you were there" description of the 1906 San Francisco earthquake, and of the killing fires that followed, would surely be considered one of the great accounts of that horrific event, had it been written in or translated into English. "The night of the day following [the earthquake], after a forced march of 52 miles, on the hills that flanked the public gardens of the Golden Gate. . . suddenly, [I saw]. . . . the valley below, a valley on fire, an inferno. The eye could not see the extent of it. . . . there were sudden eruptions. . . ." This work also contains 27 photographs of the devastation, entitled "*Tra le rovine*" (Among the ruins).

Like Pallavicini and Caminita, Crespi was a political as well as a literary figure. An ardent and unremitting leader of California's anarchists and socialists, Crespi (b. Milan, 1857; d. San Francisco, 1948) was involved in a number of political newspapers and journals. Author of *Per la patria* (For the country), the book of revelations of Carlo Camillo Di Rudio, an Italian patriot and naturalized American who participated in the failed attempt on Napoleon III and fought in the battle of Little Bighorn, Crespi also wrote sketches and stories (*e.g.*, *Fantasia di Natale* (Christmas fantasy) in *La Voce del Popolo* (Voice of the People), December 25, 1915) and in 1900 gave life to the anarchist review *La Protesta Umana* (Human Protest) with Enrico Travaglio and then Giuseppe Ciancabilla. Among the other newspapers he founded or oversaw was *Era Democratica* (Democratic Age). In 1916, he attacked the "reactionary insanity" of Tom Mooney's prosecution and trial for a bombing during San Francisco Preparedness Day. His pieces were printed in various newspapers throughout Italian America. In particular, in the last phase of his life, he collaborated on a series for the socialist *La Parola del Popolo*.

63 ⊱ Luigi Carnovale. *Il giornalismo degli emigrati italiani nel Nord America* [Journalism of the emigrant Italians in North America]. Chicago: Casa Editrice del giornale "L'Italia," 1909.

Though himself a founder of a newspaper, *Il Pensiero* (Thought) in 1904 in St. Louis, Carnovale denounces Italian American journalism in this work. In one of the newspaper articles collected here, Carnovale writes, p. 10, "this poor intellectual and moral organism - Italian American journalism - nothing but an ugly parasitical beast, a 'filthy, fraudulent image invading the world with its stink.' Everyone feels qualified to aim their darts (luckily, less poisonous than dirty) of backbiting, of the worst kind of slander, of the most ferocious persecution and

the most vulgar scorn against it." Born in Calabria, Carnovale came to the U.S. in 1902. He used the newspapers for which he wrote to voice his anti-clerical opinions, as well as to express the frustrations of all Italian Americans seeking civil justice for their less fortunate expatriates.

64 ❧ Arturo Giovannitti. *Quando canta il gallo.* [When the rooster crows.]. Chicago: E. Clemente & Sons, 1957. First edition, December 1957; no. 63 of unstated limitation.

Inscribed by Giovannitti in January 1958, one year before his death, to his good friend, Onorio Ruotolo and his wife, Lucia. Ruotolo was a sculptor and teacher at the Leonardo Da Vinci Art School in New York for working men, whose most famous graduate was sculptor and designer Isamu Noguchi. Giovannitti, one of the few truly bilingual Italian American writers, was an equally powerful force in the literary and theatrical arena as he was in the political arena (see cat. 113–115). This work is a sort of tribute rendered for him by his old companions at *La Parola del Popolo.*

65 ❧ Domenico Saudino. *Sotto il segno del littorio I: La genesi del fascismo* [Under the sign of the lictors I: The origin of fascism]. Chicago: Libreria Sociale, 1933.

The stunning front and back covers of *Sotto il segno* were illustrated by Fort Velona (b. Calabria, 1893; d. New York, 1965), a socialist and labor organizer who became best known for his anti-fascist cartoons, which were reproduced widely in the Italian American press. Among other experiences, Velona was clubbed unconscious by fascists at one of their rallies when he shouted "Death to Mussolini!" upon hearing the name of "Il Duce" raised (see cat. 124). The first cartoon as a text illustration (opposite p. xvi) is by Ratalanga, the *nom d'artiste* of Gabriele Galantara, one of the co-founders of and chief cartoonist for *L'Asino* (cat. 109–110). The publisher, "Social Bookstore" was an arm of the Federazione Socialista Italiana.

Saudino (b. Piemonte, 1889; d. Chicago, 1964), son of a tailor, came to the United States in 1912, where he became a writer, an anti-fascist, a publicist of socialist and anti-clerical causes, and long-time contributor to the newsletters *La Parola del Popolo* in Chicago and *Il Corriere del Popolo* in San Francisco. This work, which discusses fascism in Italy only, was the first volume of a projected two-volume work; the second volume, *Le attività del fascismo negli Stati Uniti* (The activities of fascism in the United States) was never published (its manuscript is in the Immigration History Research Center in Minneapolis). The first volume was translated into Greek, apparently causing a diplomatic protest by the Italian government. During the 1930s and 1940s, Saudino was published widely in Italian newspapers in the United States, Italy, Argentina, and Mexico, and during the 1950s, he served as editor of *La Parola del Popolo*.

CAT. 65

66 ⊹ Pasquale Seneca. *Il Presidente Scoppetta, ovvero La Società della Madonna della Pace (dalla sua fondazione al suo scioglimento)* [President Scoppetta, or The Society of Our Lady of Peace (from its founding to its dissolution)]. Philadelphia: [n.p.], 1927.

This parody by Seneca (b. Benevento, 1890; d. Philadelphia, 1952), a professor of languages at the University of Pennsylvania, reflects the bitter laugh of early Italian American comedy. It is filled with a corrupted version of dialect, along with comic drawings, and an "outrageous narrative, full of double-entendres," a "wry extended joke" on the divisions that stifled the Little Italies.[8] This work was dedicated to the king of early Italian American comedy, Eduardo Migliaccio, also known as Farfariello. A year after publication as a book, it appeared in twelve illustrated chapters in *La Follia di New York* (cat. 27).

The narrative is a story about a garrulous shop owner turned politician, Francesco Scoppetta, who founds an organization named "The Society of Our Lady of Peace," of which he is sure to be president. He is painfully surprised when he learns of his well-qualified running mate (whom Scoppetta calls his "anniversary" instead of his "adversary"), Angelantonio Squaglianzogna. Seneca uses Scoppetta's effusive character and misplaced jargon to mock his fellow Italian Americans, but all the while embracing his culture – the title page declares, "*Scritto per diverter tutti e non offender nessuno,*" that is, "Written to amuse all and offend no one."

CAT. 66

Looking homeward

67 ❧ Dario Papa and Ferd[inando] Fontana. *New-York*. Milano: Giuseppe Galli, 1884.

Though neither this nor any of Fontana's (or co-author Papa's) other works were published in the United States, *New-York* is included because like many of the works on exhibition here, it illustrates a frankness, thoroughness, intensity and texture in Italian about their experiences in America that is largely lacking in English-language works by Italians, who were in general loathe to disclose their dirty laundry to Americans. It graphically depicts the spectacle of the degradation and misery of Italian immigrants. Documenting the epic of the great Italian migration, it strongly presents the way the phenomenon of America was perceived in Italy: a mixture of surprise, frustration, and disdain.

Unlike the works of many of the travel writers, whose disdain and contempt for *Italiani fuori* (Italians outside of Italy) stand out, this work shows an understanding that while some of the immigrants' problems stemmed from the mockery, prejudices and hostility they faced from Americans, Italy itself had left the mass of peasants brutalized in the first instance.

A journalist, opera and operetta librettist, poet and travel writer, Fontana undertook the trip providing the material for *New-York* in the United States from New York, where he worked as a journalist for less than a year, to San Francisco in 1881–1882. Papa remained in the U.S. for more than a year, was appointed editor of *Il Progresso Italo-Americano*, and returned to Italy in 1883 to found the newspaper *L'Italia del Popolo*.

68 ❧ Adolfo Rossi. *Un italiano in America*. Milano: Casa Editrice la Cisalpina, 1899.

Rossi (b. Veneto, 1857; d. Buenos Aires, 1921) was first published December 13, 1880 in the first issue of *Il Progresso Italo-Americano*, where his novella, *Lo Zingaro*, was printed in the appendix. In America, after he worked at odd jobs, Carlo Barsotti employed him to manage *Il Progresso*; he later returned to Italy, where he published this work. Rossi vividly portrays the world of the first Italian colony of New York close at hand: the reader enters into the squalid hovels of the usurers; into the ill-famed bars of Five Points, and into the presence of Irish prostitutes and taciturn bosses who exploited laborers.

Even after returning to Italy, Rossi continued to travel and publish extensively, including in *Nel paese dei dollari: Tre anni a New York* (1893) (In the country of dollars: Three years in New York), which first appeared as a collection of articles issued in the *Tribuna* of Rome. Named inspector of emigration, he carried out missions in Brazil, where he wrote of the effects of laws against the exploitation of Italian agricultural workers. He also worked in the United States, where he produced a series of letters, *Per la tutela degli italiani negli Stati Uniti* (For the protection of the Italians in the United States), in 1904. He was promoted to commissioner general of emigration and in addition was vice commissioner and consul in Paraguay and minister plenipotentiary in Argentina, where he remained until his death in 1921.

69 ‡ Amy A. Bernardy. *America vissuta* [American experiences]. Torino: Fratelli Bocca, 1911.

Bernardy was a pioneering journalist in Italy in the early 20th century, and published this work on social life in Italian America. Born in 1880 in Florence, daughter of a Savoyard Italian mother and the American consul to Florence, she wrote for the popular *Il Corriere della Sera* (The Evening Courier) and for the Italian magazine *La Donna* (Woman). She loved to travel, and in seeing how poorly Italians fared after they emigrated, immigration of Italians became her theme. She denounced Italy's failure to provide for its emigrants in other countries, especially given the deplorable conditions in which Italians worked in American factories. Her other major work on the same subject is *Italia randagia attraverso gli Stati Uniti* (Italy wandering across the United States) (Torino, 1913).

70 ‡ Paolo Pallavicini. *Per le vie del mondo* [Along the highways of the world]. Milano: Sonzogno, 1933.

This work also appeared as a serial published under the title *Il romanzo d'un emigrate* (The novel of an emigrant). The main characters are its just and strong hero, Bruno Speri, who also appears in *L'amante delle tre croci* (The lover of the three crosses), and a rich California heiress, Adriana Rosenthal. The work sympathetically depicts "our other army that travels periodically along the highways of the world in search of work, because the great common mother [Italy] is too small and too poor to provide for all." Pallavicini also published in New York and San Francisco (cat. 42, 61).

71 ‡ Matteo Teresi. *Con la patria nel cuore. La mia propaganda fra gli emigranti* [With the fatherland in my heart. My propaganda among the immigrants]. Palermo: D'Antoni, 1925.

In this collection of articles of his more varied arguments (one of them is entitled "In defense of prostitution"), Teresi (b. Palermo 1875; active in U.S. from 1907), after obtaining his doctorate in jurisprudence in Italy, came to America in 1907. He wrote for *L'Araldo* in Cleveland and settled into work in Rochester,

N.Y. with a private banker. He published several works in the U.S., including the one featured here. Teresi tried passionately to defeat the restrictions applied to Italian immigration in the Johnson bill of 1925. He upheld the reasons for Americanization as the purchase "of new, diverse, and characteristic values: the engrafting of the Italic offshoot onto the great trunk of American life." He argues that "the best school of Americanism is economic justice, the honest working of free institutions, and friendly respect for the races gathered here so as to enrich with new elements the life of this still young and rapidly developing nation."

72 ᛭ Riccardo Cordiferro. *Ode alla Calabria* [Ode to Calabria]. Buenos Aires: La Voce dei Calabresi, 1933.

This work, published by the book arm of an Italian-language Argentinian newspaper, commemorates and reflects a literary soiree held in Brooklyn in 1930 in which the titled poem was recited (and then published in the January 4, 1931 issue of *La Follia). Ode alla Calabria* also contains, in addition to the poem itself in Italian as written, a translation into the Calabrian dialect by Francesco Greco, and reviews of Cordiferro's title poem that were widely published in Italian newspapers and magazines throughout the United States. Because of Cordiferro's popularity among South as well as North America's Italians, it is not surprising that this poetic work was published in Buenos Aires for the benefit of that city's considerable Italian colony. The existence of such a broad U.S. Italian-language literary audience, and the promotion of common cause with the Italians of Argentina by itself makes this work interesting. Readers of the Argentinian *La Voce dei Calabresi* (The Voice of the Calabrians), which advertised itself as the "popular tri-lingual newspaper of the Calabrian collective," would have known of Cordiferro's plays.

73 ⊱ Corrado Altavilla. *Gente lontana* [Far away people]. Milano: Edizioni Medici Domus, [1938].

A novel of Italian American life by a contributor to the newspapers *Il Progresso* and *Il Corriere della Sera*, Corrado Altavilla (b. Aversa, 1897; in U.S. from 1923). The story focuses on the Sacchi family, a regular lower middle class Italian American family, who realize on their own that the smooth democratic machine of American government is really a façade for the corruption and lies that keep the country running. Centered around a court case where the son, John-Giovanni Sacchi, is tried for the murder of a young prostitute with whom he had a brief encounter, the entire family becomes involved, lowering them further down the class ranks, until they are forced to return to Italy.

74 ⊱ Alberto Pecorini. *Gli americani nella vita moderna osservati da un italiano* [Modern day Americans, observed by an Italian]. Milano: Fratelli Treves, 1909.

This work is a comprehensive text on the United States for young Italians by the author of the later New York publication, *Grammatica-enciclopedia italiana-inglese* (cat. 8). Included in this work is a history of the U.S., discussions on religion, politics, commerce and education, and a section on social class. Pecorini was editor of the newspaper *Il Cittadino* for some time, and encouraged the integration between Italian Americans and the rest of the country. In 1910 he founded the unsuccessful and short-lived Italian American Civic League in an attempt to do so. He was also quick to denounce another Italian American newspaper, *Il Progresso*, because of its main goal, which he saw as to keep all Italians in the United States out of touch with the laws, news, and general activities of the country in which they lived.

75 ⊱ Emilio Cecchi. *America amara* [Bitter America]. Firenze: G. C. Sansoni, 1940.

This copy of a work reflective of a 1930s intellectual European anti-Americanism — rather than an appreciation of the domesticity and endless labor of the average immigrant — is from the library of Leonard Covello, the Harlem-based educator and author of perhaps the most detailed and still useful monographs on the Italian American experience.[9]

Soon after Cecchi completed this compilation of his letters from America, he declared that "the great, true book. . . . of the Italian in America, if it has not been written up to now, . . . [could only be written] in one of those harsh, barbaric, unheard-of dialects that came into existence in our enormous, suffering communities on American soil. In a new language ... or to be more exact: this book, this poem has been written, but in letters of stone; it has been carved into the rock of Manhattan, into the docks in the harbors and railroad tracks . . . on the walls of the mine shafts, in the furrows of endless fields."[10]

76 ⊁ Efrem Bartoletti. *Riflessioni poetiche.* Milano: Gastaldi, 1955.

This copy of Bartoletti's collection of poems is inscribed in the year of publication to an unnamed friend in the mining town of Scranton, Penn., where Bartoletti settled upon his return to the U.S. in the 1950s after spending some years back in Italy. Bartoletti, a miner as well as a poet, published one work in New York many years prior to this one, *Nostalgie proletarie. Raccolta di canti poetici e di inni rivoluzionari* (Proletarian nostalgia. Collection of poetic songs and revolutionary hymns) (Brooklyn: Libreria Editrice dei Lavoratori Industriali del Mondo, 1919).

Bartoletti (b. Costacciaro, 1889; d. Scranton, 1961) was one of the more important Italian members of the I.W.W., who were known as "Wobblies" in America, vigorously participating in the I.W.W. strikes of 1907 and 1916 on the Mesabi Iron Range in Minnesota, about which he reported to the readers of *Il Proletario* with a series of letters from Duluth. His poetry, including revolutionary hymns, either reflected a robust solidarity with his fellow proletarians, or his homesickness for his native Umbria.

77 ⊁ Armando Cenerazzo. *Poesie napoletane. Volume primo.* Napoli: Ciro Russo, 1949.

Cenerazzo (b. Avellino, 1889; d. New York, 1962) was an actor, playwright and writer of poetry, songs, and Neapolitan caricatures who arrived in America at the age of twelve. He collaborated with librettist Francesco Ricciardi, performing duets and Neapolitan songs, as well as with actress Mimì Aguglia. Though this work was published by Ciro Russo, Cenerazzo also worked at the Cocce Press. Cenerazzo published another volume of poems, edited by Alfredo Guida, that was issued later not as volume 2 of this title, but instead as *Rose rosse e rose gialle* (Red roses and yellow roses).

In the last period of his life, Cenerazzo (whose name, as published, appeared sometimes with two n's) would return to Naples every year toward the end of spring, and usually visit his hometown in Irpinia. After the war, his compositions appeared in the pages of *La Follia*. His poems are variously dedicated to his wife Rosarie, and later to Mimì Aguglia, to Enrico Caruso, and to Riccardo Cordiferro. Cenerazzo was head comedian of a company of modest success, active in New York and on the East Coast until the 1910s. His company's varied repertory moved from Punchinello farces to social and historical dramas, and also to contemporary issues, and sentiments typical of the Italian American world of which Cenerazzo (a resident of the Bronx, at least in the last years) was an attentive and sensitive interpreter.

78 ⊱ E[dmondo] Mayor des Planches. *Attraverso gli Stati Uniti - per l'emigrazione italiana* [Across the United States - through Italian emigration]. Torino: Unione Tipografico-Editrice Torinese, 1913.

This copy of the celebrated study by Mayor des Planches (b. Turin, 1851; d. Rome, 1920), written during his years in the U.S., is inscribed by the author to a *baronessa*. During his travels across the U.S., while ambassador to Washington from 1901–1909, this Piedmontese aristocrat collected information on the demographics of Italian Americans living in the United States, and reported his findings in this study. Mayor des Planches extols the virtues of agricultural work, suggesting that Italians would do much better applying their native agricultural talents in the rural South than, seemingly, in the urban centers of the U.S.

Anarchist, socialist, syndicalist, fascist and antifascist political literature

TRANSNATIONAL ANARCHISM

79a ⊱ Armando Borghi. *Errico Malatesta in 60 anni di lotte anarchiche. Storia – critica – ricordi* [Errico Malatesta in 60 years of anarchist struggles. History - criticism - memories]. New York / Paris: Edizioni Sociali, 1933.

That the story of the transnational work of a figure like Malatesta was written in Italian, published in New York, and printed in Paris by an Italian printer, Tipografia Sociali, is testimony to the international nature of the anarchist movement. Borghi, the second ranking anarchist in Italy, after Malatesta, before he left for the U.S. in the mid-1920s, reviews 60 years of Malatesta's life in this

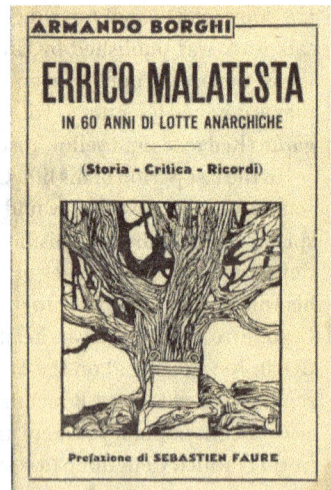

ARMANDO BORGHI

ERRICO MALATESTA
IN 60 ANNI DI LOTTE ANARCHICHE

(Storia - Critica - Ricordi)

Prefazione di SEBASTIEN FAURE

CAT. 79a

work, only a year or so of which was spent in the U.S. In addition to the book's printing in Paris, the introduction by Faure, the French anarchist, is dated Paris, 1933. Originally a socialist, Faure (1858–1942) turned to anarchism in 1888, and developed his theory of synthesis anarchism, the notion that the physical, mental and moral developments of man were all equally important.

CAT. 79b

79b ⊁ Armando Borghi. *Il banchetto dei cancri (dopo Matteotti)* [The banquet of the evil ones (after Matteotti)]. Brooklyn: Libreria Editrice dei Lavoratori Industriali del Mondo, 1925.

This collection of anti-fascist articles Borghi had published, after Matteotti's assassination, in the then New York-based *Il Proletario* is introduced by his preface written from Paris in June 1925. Both the reprinted articles and preface were written by Borghi prior to his removal to America in 1926.

80 ⊁ Vittorio Roudine. *Max Stirner. (Un refrattario)* [Max Stirner. (A recalcitrant)]. East Boston: Edizione del Gruppo Autonomo, 1914.

Roudine wrote this work in his native French, and published it in a bi-weekly periodical in 1911 directed by Henri Fabre in Paris. *Max Stirner* appeared in Italian first in issues of *La Cronaca Sovversiva* between January and April of that year, translated by Luigi Galleani, and was then published in book form in 1914 in East Boston. It concerns the philosophy and work of Max Stirner, a leading "recalcitrant" (a refractory, unwilling individual, disobedient to authority) German individualist and anti-organizationalist anarchist.

81 ⊁ Errico Malatesta. *Al caffè: Conversazioni dal vero* [At the café: Honest conversations]. Paterson: Libreria Sociologica [*ca.* 1910]. Seventh edition.

The Libreria Sociologica (Sociological Bookstore) in Paterson stocked one of the richest and most varied assortments of inexpensive books and pamphlets for anarchists and socialists in the U.S., including social novels and dramas, as well as political tracts such as this one, in the form of a political conversation among five fictional characters. Malatesta believed that while anarchists could not be syndicalists, they could use syndicalist tactics to achieve their goals, and thus could have a role in the development of the Industrial Workers of the World (see cat. 96–106, 114).

Besides Malatesta's work, the Libreria Sociologica published a series by anarchist thinkers that included the work of playwrights and poets, many of whom were in contact with Mexican and Spanish anarchists. This work, as the title suggests, presents a series of conversations between a bourgeois and a student filled with anarchist ideas, and others with varied political opinions. Such conversations in narrative or occasionally dramatic form were a common way of educating and influencing the working men and women whom these writers sought to reach. This kind of presentation contrasted with the more theoretical and philosophical tracts of writers like Renzo Novatore (cat. 90).

82 ⊁ Virgilia D'Andrea. *Due conferenze: Chi siamo e che cosa vogliamo— patria e religione* [Two lectures: Who we are and what we want—homeland and religion]. Newark: Biblioteca de L'Adunata dei Refrattari, 1947.

Virgilia D'Andrea (b. Sulmona, 1890; d. New York, 1933) did not live to see this work published; she died suddenly at the young age of 43. D'Andrea immigrated to the U.S. with her lover, Armando Borghi in 1926 or 1927. She had lost her family at a young age, turned to books for support, and was especially influenced by poetry. In America, she was widely known for her radical poetry, her anarchist activism, and her advocacy of free love. Though a powerful and well-respected female, she did not consider herself an activist for women's rights, but more a promoter of the liberation of all people, especially the lower classes.

In 1922 she published her first book of poetry, titled *Tormento*, about her own personal anguish and social struggles. In *Due conferenze*, she includes two of her public speeches delivered during her lecture tours around the country, published by the *L'Adunata dei Refrattari*, the most internationally influential and longest-running anarchist journal started by Galleani's *Cronaca Sovversivi* colleagues, the Galleanisti, after Galleani's deportation in 1919. Like *Il Martello* – and even, on the opposite side of the political spectrum, *Il Carroccio* – *L'Adunata* particularly sought out articles by women.

83 ⊁ Leopoldo Kampf. *La vigilia: Dramma in tre atti.* [On the eve: Drama in three acts]. East Boston: Edizione del Gruppo Autonomo, 1917.

La vigilia is the first Italian translation "by A.M.G." – who would be known by readers to be Arturo Giovannitti – of Leopold Kampf's popular play, *Am vorabend*. The work was translated from the German original for entertainment as well as for the instruction of Italian working men and women, something that Giovannitti, who grasped the need for something more than political instruction, would understand. Italian American publishers, political and otherwise, published not only material written in Italian, but frequently translated works such as this one. Kampf's play was widely popular, and was also published in Russian, English, and French translations.

Edizione del Gruppo Autonomo was the publishing arm of the anarchist group to which Sacco and Vanzetti belonged, the Gruppo Autonomo (Autonomous Group), which also published Roudine's *Max Stirner* (cat. 80) and Galleani's *Faccia a faccia col nemico* (cat. 52) three years earlier. There were many anarchist groups in Italian America; virtually each one picked its own "nickname" and many created their own imprints.

RADICALS IN THEATRE

Gigi Damiani

Gigi Damiani (b. Rome, 1876; d. Rome, 1953) was an author well published in the U.S., but there is no evidence that he ever set foot in this country. Other than the Detroit-published work (cat. 84), the plays of Damiani were all published in the U.S. by *L'Adunata dei Refrattari*, the Galleanisti publication edited by Max Sartin (Raffaele Schiavina). Damiani, an important anarchist figure in Italy, was a compelling writer who more successfully than any, other than Cordiferro and Giovannitti, used the theatre as a means to promote anarchist ideas. He traveled throughout the world, including Brazil, France, Belgium, Spain and Tunisia. As recently as 1991, a more philosophical and theoretical work, Damiani's *Saggio su di una concezione filosofica dell'anarchismo* (An Essay of a Philosophical Conception of Anarchism) was first published, posthumously, in Pistoia, Italy.

84 ❧ Gigi Damiani. *La bottega: Scene della ricostruzione fascista, dramma in due atti* [The shop: Stages of fascist reconstruction, drama in two acts]. Detroit: Libreria Autonoma, 1927.

A two-act, heavily anti-fascist play published by the Detroit anarchist group's bookstore, the *Libreria Autonoma* (Autonomous Bookstore).

85 ❧ Simplicio [Gigi Damiani]. *"Fecondità." Commedia sociale in due atti* ["Fertility." Social comedy in two acts]. Newark: Biblioteca de L'Adunata dei Refrattari, 1928.

A social comedic drama published by the book publication arm of *L'Adunata dei Refrattari*.

86 ❧ Gigi Damiani. *Viva Rambolot! Bozzetto in un atto* [Viva Rambolot! Sketch in one act]. Newark: Biblioteca de L'Adunata dei Refrattari, [ca. 1930s].

This work depicts the domestic life of a prosecutor who tries to explain and justify his work activities to his daughter in the service of "the Law."

87 ⊁ Simplicio [Gigi Damiani]. *Sgraffi* [Scratches]. Newark: Biblioteca de L'Adunata dei Refrattari, 1946.

This collection of poetry is dedicated to those who have gone through the same struggles that Damiani had suffered.

88 ⊁ [La Parola dei Socialisti]. *La morale di Arlecchino* [The moral of Arlecchino]. Chicago: Tipografia "La Parola" [dei Socialisti], [*ca.* 1910].

While not a play as such, this small pamphlet, first published in Treviso in 1898, tells the dramatic tale of the troubles of an oppressed, slow-thinking comedic servant, a harlequin in the *commedia dell'arte* style of melodrama, a method used by radical writers for the lesson it conveys to simple working men and women, who would understand the hard life of this stock character, the servant Arlecchino, and the impact on him of his mistreatment by his bosses. *La morale di Arlecchino* is volume 24 in the Library of "La Parola dei Socialisti." Apparently the weekly newspaper published many small pamphlets like the one featured here during its five-year life (active from 1908–1913) before it underwent several name changes, to avoid postal authorities' refusal to mail copies to subscribers, and changed its name to *La Parola del Popolo*, under which it operated until 1982.

ANARCHIST-INDIVIDUALISTS

89a ⊁ Gold O'Bay [Tintino Rasi]. *Quaderno No. 1. La grande rivoluzione in marcia*. [Notebook No. 1. The great revolution on the march]. Newark: Gruppi Riuniti dell'Antracite, 1940.

89b ⊁ Gold O'Bay. *Quaderno No. 2. Le basi della società e del diritto* [Notebook No. 2. The bases of society and of the right]. Newark: Gruppi Riuniti dell'Antracite, 1940.

89c ⊁ Gold O'Bay. *Quaderno No. 3. La produzione: Le sue basi, i suoi mezzi, le sue funzione, i suoi scopi* [Notebook No. 3. Production: its basis, its means, its function, its aims]. Newark: Gruppi Riuniti dell'Antracite, 1942.

Gold O'Bay was one of several pseudonyms used by Tintino Rasi (b. Genoa, 1893; d. Philadelphia, 1963). Rasi was an anarchist at an early age in Genoa, where he was under constant surveillance by the police for his political activities. In 1921, along with Renzo Novatore (cat. 90), he edited the anarcho-individualist and futurist journal *Vertice*. During the 1930s, he wrote for *L'Adunata dei Refrattari* in Newark. In 1938, he settled in Philadelphia, and collaborated with Virgilio Gozzoli in New York in anti-fascist activities.

These are the first three journals in a series covering social issues. The first pamphlet introduces itself as the first series of journals or notebooks, *quaderni*, as "*Quaderni sui problemi sociali*" (Notebook of Social Issues), and states that each will address a separate social issue of "our time." Each volume promotes the Galleanisti anarchist newspaper, *L'Adunata dei Refrattari,* on the rear cover.

90 ⊁ Renzo Novatore. *Verso il nulla creatore* [Toward the creative nothing]. West New York, N.J.: Virginio De Martin, 1939.

The cover and, such as it is, title page state "Special Edition Edited by Virginio De Martin / Publisher of *Supermen Literature*, West New York, NJ 1939"; the cover also states at the top "SUPERUOMO: E: ICONOCLASTA" (Superman and iconoclast). Novatore was a prime exponent of a Nietzschean individual anarchism, a philosophy that attacked Christianity and also socialism, democracy and fascism for their spiritual emptiness. This philosophy was somewhat akin to Galleani's non-organizational anarchism without the bombs, but certainly bearing little relation to the anarchism of the organizational kind that led to syndicalism or communism.

Novatore calls for a personal "destructive revolution" in this work, based on the ideas, dreams and desires of the "mighty I," while recognizing that a real revolution had to be more than just a personal one. But he found that all existing political movements doomed the individual to personal mediocrity. This text was published after Novatore's death. There is no evidence that Novatore ever came to America.

91 ⊁ Comitato dei Gruppi Riuniti. *Rivoluzione e controrivoluzione: Manifesto dei militanti e dei Gruppi Anarchici Riuniti del Nordamerica* [Revolution and counter-revolution: Manifesto of the militants and the Reunited Anarchist Groups of North America]. New York: Galilei Club, 1944.

The Galilei Club was another chosen name for an anarchist group, reflecting the independence of its namesake (whose last name the group used, rather than the more familiar first name, Galileo), as well as his battles with the religious authorities. This pamphlet covers many topics, with chapters on the Vatican, Spain, fascism, the Fifth Column, bourgeois government and the social war. The cover features a graphic black and white woodcut on a light blue background of two hands in the clouds. One fights off another clawed hand (presumably the devil's or some force of evil) holding a sharp, bloody dagger.

On the run from the postal or other federal authorities for his publishing and anarchist activities, and looking for a new base of operations after a short time in Paterson, Galleani and his followers found Barre, where Italian stonemasons working in the quarries there, and eager to learn anarchist ideas, had settled. Barre was a comfortable location from which anarchists wrote and published for some of the period of Galleani's residency in the U.S., for *La Cronaca Sovversiva* (until it was closed down under the Sedition Act of 1918).

92 ⊁ [Luigi Galleani]. *Verso il comunismo* [Towards Communism]. Barre, Vt.: Cronaca Sovversiva, 1904.

A very short pamphlet on the types of political views of different people the narrator met while a student at the University of Torino. Possibly as much a warning of the approach of communism as it was an expression of desire for it, this pamphlet was published by Galleani's *Cronaca Sovversiva* (cat. 51, 53, 95).

93 ⊁ G[iuseppe] Ciancabilla, trans. *Tolstoismo e anarchismo: Rapporto presentato al Congresso Operaio Rivoluzionario Internazionale di Parigi dal Gruppo degli Studenti Socialisti Rivoluzionarii Internazionalisti di Parigi* [Tolstoyism and anarchism: Report presented to the Revolutionary Working-Class International Congress of Paris of the Socialist Students Revolutionary International Group of Paris]. Barre, Vt.: Biblioteca Circolo Studi Sociali, [1905?].

A report originally printed in Paris, translated to the Italian by Giuseppe Ciancabilla. Il Gruppo degli Studenti Socialisti Rivoluzionarii Internazionalisti di Parigi was the Parisian socialist group ESRI (Étudiants Socialistes Revolutionnaires Internationalistes) mostly, but not necessarily, composed of anarchists and students.

Ciancabilla (b. Rome, 1872; d. San Francisco, 1904) was one of the most impressive anarchist speakers and writers of the period, but is now one of the least well known. Originally a socialist, after an interview with Errico Malatesta for the journal *L'Avanti!*, Ciancabilla declared himself an anarchist. He traveled around Europe, writing for various newspapers until he was deemed "a dangerous anarchist" and expelled from France. He arrived in the United States just two years before the turn of the century, stopping first in Paterson, and later moving west. Driven out of Spring Valley, Illinois, and then Chicago, by police crackdowns on anarchists in the wake of the assassination of President McKinley in 1902, he finally settled in San Francisco, but died at a young age, 32.

94 ✤ Max Nettlau. *La responsabilità e la solidarietà nella lotta operaia: Rapporto letto alla "Freedom Discussion Group" il 5 Dicembre 1899* [Responsibility and solidarity in the Workers Struggle: Report read to the "Freedom Discussion Group" December 5, 1899]. Barre, Vt.: Casa ed. L'Azione, 1913. First Italian edition.

A short report written by German anarchist Max Nettlau (cat. 121). It was published by the book arm of *L'Azione*, a critical weekly of revolutionary propaganda based in Barre.

95 ✤ Biblioteca del Circolo di Sociali. *All'anarchia: Si arriverà passando per lo stato socialista?* [Toward anarchy: Can we get there passing through state socialism?]. Barre, Vt.: Cronaca Sovversiva, 1905.

Pamphlet No. 4 in a series by the Library of the *Circolo di Sociali*. To Galleani, the likely author of this short work, it was a dangerous error to think that state-based socialism would take the people a step closer to the ideal of anarchy to which Galleani aspired, an error that other countries had clearly made, in his view.

INDUSTRIAL WORKERS OF THE WORLD: SOCIALISM AND SYNDICALISM

The I.W.W. was founded in 1905, but like the rest of the labor unions and American socialist parties at that time, was initially indifferent, if not hostile to the "New Immigrants." Not until the Socialist Party of America established its foreign language federations in 1910–1912, and the I.W.W. led the great strikes of immigrant workers in Lawrence and Paterson in 1912–1913, did the barriers really begin to lift. At the height of the Red Scare it was the "Wobblies" of the I.W.W. who became the chosen scapegoat of the political and legal establishment when the time came to close the doors of a hospitable America for good. In fact, the I.W.W. believed programmatically in internationalism, and the "foreign" membership – especially the Italians – soon became a part of it all. During the trials, in the jails, and in the often fierce debates, the Italians distinguished themselves as one of the most prominent groups. See also cat. 114, 115.

96 ✤ Angelo Faggi. *Uno storico processo di classe: I precedenti e lo svolgimento del processo dell'I. W. W. a Chicago* [A historical class trial: The proceedings and the development of the trial of the I.W.W. in Chicago]. Chicago: Industrial Workers of the World, [ca. 1918].

The title on the cover also states, "Giustizia Capitalista" (Capitalist Justice), not present on title page. This work recounts the mass trial of I.W.W. members from

1917-1918 in the I.W.W.'s hometown of Chicago, in which a total of 820 years of prison sentences were handed down by Judge Kenesaw Mountain Landis, whose later appointment as Major League Baseball Commissioner was controversial. For his role in the trial, Judge Landis became one of the intended recipients of 13 bombs mailed by anarchists in late April 1919 in a plot that was instrumental in the deportation of Galleani, and that followed as well as preceded the passage of politically repressive acts, such as the Sedition Act of 1918, and the ultra-restrictive immigration law of 1924. Faggi (b. Florence, 1885; d. Piacenza, 1967) was deeply committed to the Federazione Socialista Italiana and had been a trade unionist active in Italy, France and Switzerland before coming to the U.S.

Faggi was forced to flee from Italy to Switzerland for leading protests against Italy's war in Tripoli, opposing the majority of Italians in the U.S., who took intense pride in colonialist wars (see cat. 136). After leading demonstrations in Europe against the treatment of Ettor and Giovannitti during the Lawrence Bread and Roses Strike of 1912, Faggi was again compelled to leave his home, and came to the U.S. He replaced Giuseppe Cannata (cat. 101-102) as editor of *Il Proletario*, and brought the newpaper's focus more towards worker organization rather than propaganda. Deported from the U.S. in 1919, Faggi returned to Italy, where he remained vehemently anti-Mussolini, pushing for both a syndicalist revolution and support for the Russian Revolution. Unable to stay out of conflict he again fled Italy, after he and several other leftists planted a fatal bomb at the Diana Theatre in Milan as a protest against bourgeois indifference to the attacks of the fascist *squadristi* (action squad members).

97 |+ Anonymous. *Che cosa è l'I. W. W.?* [What is the I.W.W.?]. Chicago: Industrial Workers of the World, 1923.

Translated from the English original by Mario De Ciampis. De Ciampis was the author of the authoritative short treatise on the history of Italian revolutionary socialism in the U.S. (cat. 106), and writer of, or contributor to, several other works in this exhibition (cat. 98, 103).

98 |+ Mario De Ciampis, ed. *Il Proletario* [The Worker] Saturday, April 28. Chicago: Industrial Workers of the World, 1923.

This is the front page of the May Day 1923 issue of *Il Proletario*, the I.W.W. newspaper edited at various times by Carlo Tresca, Mario De Ciampis, Arturo Giovannitti, Angelo Faggi, Giuseppe Cannata and Edmondo Rossoni. The striking cover illustration, captioned "The heads of the monstrous snakes finally fall, shattered," shows a muscular, bare-breasted woman about to strike, with an axe, a many-headed snake that threatens the children standing behind her, an image that reflects the symbolic importance of May Day among Italian radicals in the New World with the rare use of red (or of any color) ink. Like the masthead des-

sign, it is signed "391," which was the name of the French Dada-ist and Surreal-ist artist Francis Picabia's magazine published at times in Paris and New York until 1924, and whose design colors were also black, red and white.

The potential connection with this French artist is further suggested by a famous article by then-editor Rossoni in *Il Proletario* entitled "Liberty and Blood," in which he wrote, "Liberty is not just a pretty woman. . . . Rather, she is a strong woman with strong breasts and a rough voice, with fire in her eyes . . ." This passage in the Francophile Rossoni's article was based on a 19th-century French poem by Auguste Barbier, which lauded a symbolic Woman Liberty.[II]

The motto of the paper, evident on this page, is "Educazione - organizzazi-one - emancipazione. Conquistando la fabbrica, conquisteremo il mondo [Ed-ucation - organization - emancipation. Subduing the factory, we will conquer the world]. The "Hour for Action" lead story is by Mario De Ciampis. Relatively early on, May Day turned into a more joyous celebration as well, with food, drink and dancing, in addition to poetry readings and dramatic performances, such as

Pietro Gori's *Primo Maggio* (May Day). The verso of this front page contains a poem by Virgilia D'Andrea (cat. 82) entitled "Primo Maggio." De Ciampis was a long-time editor of *Il Proletario*, leading historian of the Federazione Socialista Italiana, and a close associate of Carlo Tresca. Ironically, there was no May Day issue the following year, 1924, because the newspaper was in the middle of moving its base of operations from Chicago to Brooklyn, where it remained. My collection has the full run of 1923–1924 issues.

May Day had its origins as early as 1886, when unions and anarchist groups in Chicago led a series of demonstrations and protests demanding an eight-hour day, resulting in the Haymarket massacre on May 4 of that year, in which several demonstrators and policemen were killed by a bomb thrown at the police. Five anarchists were subsequently executed for their participation, though no evidence linked them to the bombing. France declared May 1 as the international holiday of workers of the world in 1890. Traditional May Day celebrations remained alive among immigrants and the working class even after President Grover Cleveland in 1887 supported the Knights of Labor's recommendation that workers' day be celebrated in September as Labor Day. Early May Day celebrations included strikes, mass protests and demonstrations, often ending in violence and police confrontations.

99 ❧ Justus Ebert. *L'I. W. W. nella teoria e nella pratica* [The I.W.W. in theory and practice]. Chicago: Industrial Workers of the World, [*ca.* 1922].

100 ❧ Vincent St. John. *L'I. W. W.: La sua storia, struttura e metodi* [The I.W.W.: Its history, structure, and methods]. Brooklyn: Lavoratori Industriali del Mondo, [*ca.* 1919].

Like cat. 97, this work and cat. 99 are translations from English-language originals, intended to reach an Italian-language-only audience of workers who could help swell the ranks of the Wobblies.

101 ❧ G[iuseppe] C[annata]. *La tattica sindacalista in America* [Trade-union tactics in America]. Brooklyn: Libreria dei Lavoratori Industriali del Mondo, [1921].

102 ❧ G[iuseppe] C[annata]. *La tecnica industriale e la rivoluzione proletaria* [Industrial technology and the proletarian revolution]. Brooklyn: Libreria dei Lavoratori Industriali del Mondo, 1922.

Giuseppe Cannata succeeded Edmondo Rossoni in the Federazione Socialista Italiana and as editor of *Il Proletario*. The earlier of these two pamphlets contains a section on industrial development in America, the state of sociological develop-

ment, the American Federation of Labor and the "brotherhoods" of railway workers, independent unions, and the I.W.W. Cannata was also, along with Tresca, a
founding member of AFANA, the Anti-Fascist Alliance of North America.

103 ⊁ Giantino [Alibrando Giovannetti]. *Unionismo industriale e sindacalismo* [Industrial and trade unions]. Brooklyn: Casa ed. Lavoratori Industriali,
[1923].

The title page states Giantino as the author, with no publication date; however, this pamphlet begins with an introduction by Mario De Ciampis dated
1923. Like most unionist pamphlets, this pamphlet contains the preamble of
the I.W.W., and also discusses industrial and trade unionism in the U.S. and
Europe. "Giantino" was the pen name of Alibrando Giovannetti (1875-1945).
In Italy, Giovannetti was secretary of the Unione Sindacalismo Industriale's
metalworkers union. A believer in non-violence, he saw peaceful occupation of
factories as a substitute for insurrection. He and Armando Borghi (cat. 56-60,
79) led one such factory occupation in Liguria in 1920.

104 ⊁ Enrico Meledandri. *La crisi del socialismo* [The crisis of socialism].
Chicago: Il Proletario, [1922].

A text by anarcho-syndicalist Enrico Meledandri, with sections titled, translated
here, "The Fate of Socialism," "Inert Maximalism," "Scientific Socialism," and
"Misery and Revolution." Note that the same printer's mark of the I.W.W. appears on the covers of this work, as in the Giantino above (cat. 103). Meledandri
was editor of *Il Proletario* from Chicago in the penultimate year of its publication there.

105 ⊁ Vittorio Buttis. *Memorie di vita di tempeste sociali* [Recollections
of a life in social storms]. Chicago: Comitato "Vittorio Buttis," 1940.

With cover art by Fort Velona, and a preface by radical activist Angelica Balabanoff, the title page of this work states, "*A cura del comitato Vittorio Buttis,
Per onorare il 50.0 Anniversario di servizio fedele alla causa operaia e socialista*" (Edited by the "Vittorio Buttis" Committee to honor the 50th Anniversary
of faithful service to the worker and socialist cause). This memoir of Buttis's
life of and experiences in political activism is illustrated with several black and
white photo portraits of influential Italian Americans, and especially prominent
I.W.W. figures, including "Eugenio Vittorio" Debs, Mother Jones, and Angelica Balabanoff.

By the early 1890s, Buttis (b. Venice, 1860; d. Chicago, 1950) was considered
a dangerous socialist by Italian police authorities. He was secretary of a chamber
of labor in Intra (in Piemonte) and editor of its newspaper, before leaving for

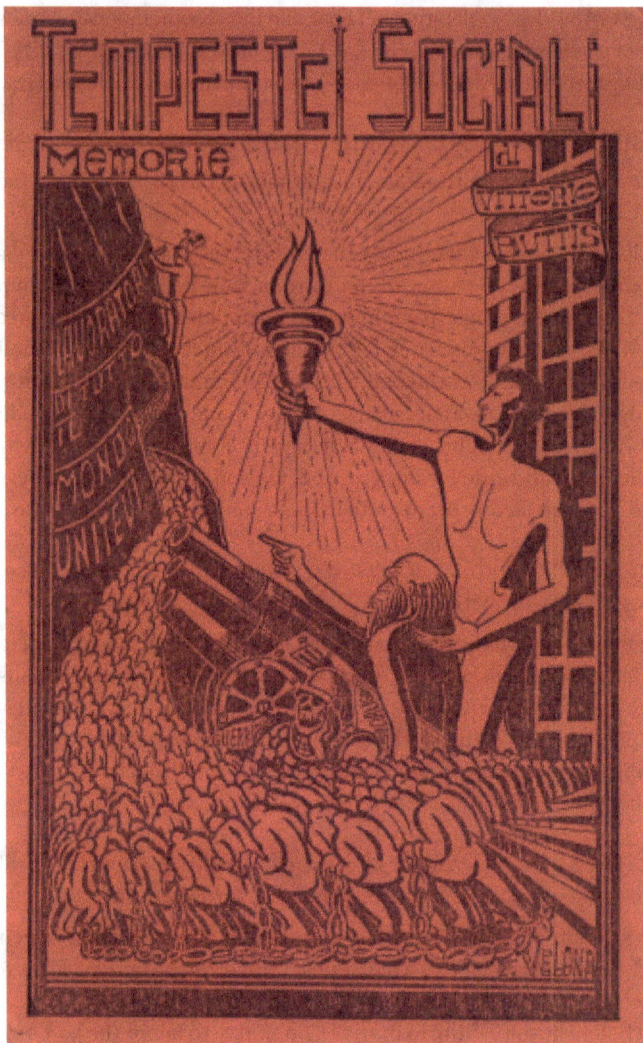

Brazil in 1911. Arriving in the U.S. (in 1915) he joined the Federazione Socialista Italiana of the Socialist Party of America, and in 1916 became editor of *La
Parola del Popolo* in Chicago. Though arrested in 1918 for his antiwar articles,
he was known as a voice of moderation and even as a censor of ideas he thought
too extreme; he did not support the Russian Revolution because he considered
Lenin too critical of international socialism. He helped run the soup kitchen for
striking workers in Lawrence in 1912, and wrote a daily column for *La Notizia* of
Boston, headed by Vincenzo Vacirca (cat. 34-35).

106 ⁑ E[gidio] Clemente and E[milio] Grandinetti. *Cinquantesimo Anniversario 1908–1958. La Parola del Popolo. Rivista Bimestrale. Year 50th* [Fiftieth Anniversary 1908-1958. The Word of the People. Bimonthly magazine], vol. 9, no. 37, December 1958-January 1959. Chicago: La Parola del Popolo Publishing, 1959.

This is a large format, 336-page commemorative edition for the 50th anniversary of the magazine *La Parola del Popolo*. Its pages contain many illustrations by the leading leftist illustrator, Fort Velona (cat. 65, 105), and large black and white photographs of leading anti-fascist scholar Gaetano Salvemini and of Giacomo Battistoni (cat. 116), as well as of the objects of the "*ommagios*" [homages] to several influential radicals. Of the several articles, titles include "Il movimento socialista democratic e la 'Parola,'" (The democratic socialist movement and La "Parola"), "Storia del movimento socialista rivoluzionario italiano" (History of the Italian revolutionary socialist movement) by Mario De Ciampis (cat. 98), and homages to, among others, "Eugenio" V. Debs (written by Carmelo Zito), Carlo Tresca (written by Arturo Giovannitti), and Alberico Molinari (written by Tomasso Toselli).

Fort Velona's summary of the history of this important organ of Italian socialists shows the parallel growth of the Italian socialist movement in the U.S. and the newspaper that was its banner: after a period of name changes from *La Parola dei Socialisti*, its name in 1908, in a vain attempt to evade postal authorities' efforts to prevent sending subscribers copies of the newspaper of the fledgling Federazione Socialista Italiana (*La Fiaccola* and *L'Avanti!* were two others), and following the ending of World War I, when postal suppression relaxed, the former *La Parola dei Socialisti* (see, *e.g.*, cat. 88) was reborn as *La Parola del Popolo* in 1920. From that time, when Egidio Clemente took over the renamed newspaper, publication continued uninterrupted until its final issue in 1982. Years after his editorship of *La Parola*, Clemente (b. Trieste, 1899; d. Chicago, ?) established his own imprint, which published Giovannitti's Italian poems in 1957 (cat. 64) and again, posthumously, in 1962, in a commemorative edition of "Collected Poems" of the English-language poems of the perfectly bi-lingual Giovannitti (cat. 113).

SOCIALIST AND COMMUNIST

107 ⁑ Flavio Venanzi. *Scritti politici e letterarii* [Political and literary writings]. New York: Venanzi Memorial Committee, 1921.

With a book cover design by sculptor Onorio Ruotolo, and an introduction by Giovannitti, this work is a compilation of the writings of Venanzi (b. Rome, 1882; d. New York, 1920), who was *Il Proletario*'s correspondent during the trial of Ettor,

Giovannitti and Caruso in 1912, during the Lawrence, Mass., textile mill strike, and an influential member of the Federazione Socialista Italiana. These literary and political essays, gathered after his death in 1920 at age 37, which probably resulted from pneumonia, were not filler material: like his friend, Giovannitti, Venanzi was a voracious reader and writer who produced as many articles and essays on art and literature (including the classical Dante, Boccaccio, Ariosto, as well as more modern writers such as Foscolo, Leopardi and D'Annunzio) as he did on political subjects. By reading to her from Dante, Venanzi taught Italian to Helen Keller, who wrote an introduction to Giovannitti's *Arrows in the Gale*.

During the debate on whether Italy should enter World War I, Venanzi was a leading neutralist. He was also among those members of the FSI and the I.W.W. who embraced communism, and who, on November 6, 1921, organized the Federazione dei Lavoratori Italiani d'America, a section of the American Labor Alliance, located on East 10th Street in Manhattan, which aimed at "uniting all avant-garde elements of the Italian subversive movement in the U.S." [12]

108 ⊹ Anonymous. *Mussolineide: Poema antifascista e di rivendicazione sociale* [The Mussoliniad: An antifacist poem of social demands]. [N.p.: n.p.], [*ca.* 1930s].

This anonymous work, an elegantly written and substantial (nearly 300 pages) mock-epic in *terza rima* of sixteen cantos, about the life and work of Mussolini, bears signs of more communist than either socialist or anarchist views of the author. Its citation to the evil deeds of the Americans, Rockefeller and Ford, as capitalist devils – in effect, as collaborators of Mussolini – matches a communist point of view of the international capitalist conspiracy, but does not mark the work necessarily as an American one. *Mussolineide* was most likely published in Italy or elsewhere in Europe, since publication of such a tract in America in the late '20s or early '30s would hardly have to have been done anonymously – witness Armando Borghi's freedom to publish *Mussolini in camicia* in New York in 1927 (cat. 56) with his name attached to the work, something that would have been unthinkable in Italy.

ANTI-CLERICALISM

L'Asino

One example of the Italian imprint and one of the U.S. imprints of this important illustrated review (1892–1925) are on display here. Started in Rome by Guido Podrecca (who about 25 years later turned to fascism) and Gabriele Galantara (1865–1937, who under the *nom d'artiste*, Rata Langa, was the principal cartoonist of the magazine), *L'Asino* (The Donkey) was best known for its virulent anti-clerical expression and colorful political illustrations. Claiming a circulation of about 100,000, the magazine won international admiration in the early 20th century. It was widely distributed among Italians in the United States by an Italian bookstore that still exists, S. F. Vanni, then of 548 West Broadway in Manhattan. Not surprisingly, given its popularity, the magazine earned the hatred of the Church, as the observation of one priest visiting an Italian community in Ybor City, Florida in 1905, suggests. He informed his superiors that Italians there were largely indifferent to religion, as "every week about 70 copies of the most infidel, anarchical and lascivious paper published in Italy are distributed among them." [13]

In 1908, a papal nuncio in Washington took action that led to denial of entry of *L'Asino* into the U.S., on the grounds that it contained pornographic material, at the same time that police raided Vanni's and arrested the owner. A new edition, still containing Rata Langa's vivid cartoons and caricatures, was promptly issued by the U.S.-based "Asino Publishing Company," whose offices are noted in the masthead of the U.S. imprint (cat. 110) as being located at 548 West Broadway in Manhattan – the location of Vanni's bookstore. Note that it is denoted as "Anno II" (Year 2) of the new series – now published in the U.S. – that began in 1908. *L'Asino*, still largely composed in Italy even after publication in the U.S. began, was permanently closed down by the Fascist Party in 1925.

109 ❧ Guido Podrecca and Gabriele Galantara. *L'Asino* [The Donkey] Anno XIV. No. 2, January 8, 1905. Roma: L'Asino, 1905.

As with all issues of *L'Asino*, this one features bright, full-color front and rear cover (and interior black-and-white) political and anti-clerical cartoons. The motto of the newspaper, carried on the masthead, *L'Asino è il popolo, utile, paziente e bastonato*, reflect the magazine's premise that like the donkey, "the people [are] hardworking, patient and mistreated." The front cover illustrates four people on the same seesaw; a fat banker sits on one end with bags of money, while a priest, a poor man, and a policeman are held up in the air on the other. More disturbing, the rear cover is a drawing of a fat monk with a lecherous facial expression holding a cowed child in his hands. The caption sarcastically states, in Italian, "The training of your sons is in good hands!"

110 ❧ Guido Podrecca and Gabriele Galantara. *L'Asino.* Anno II. No. 48, November 28, 1909. New York: Asino Publishing Co., 1909.

This American edition of *L'Asino*, in the second year of the new series begun in New York in 1908, contains an advertisement for Nicoletti Bros. publishers (cat. 8, 15, 18) as well as an English-Italian dictionary (*Il Millhouse*, which refers to the 1600-page, two-volume *New English and Italian Dictionary*, a popular

CAT. 109

CAT. 109

CAT. 110

Italian-English dictionary compiled by John Millhouse and originally published in New York in 1849 by D. Appleton & Co.). It was offered for sale here by A. De Martino at his "Complete Bookstore" two years prior to the first Società Libraria Italiana imprint (cat. 136, 140) produced on Mulberry Street and many years before De Martino's pro-Fascist Party leanings would have made advertising in *L'Asino* unthinkable.

III ⊹ Pulvio Zocchi. *Sprazzi di luce: Pennellate di propaganda anticlericale* [Flashes of Light: Brush-strokes of Anti-Clerical Propaganda]. New York: [Federazione Socialista Italiana?], 1910. Second edition.

The recto of the final leaf displays an ad for *Il Proletario*, published by the Federazione Socialista Italiana in New York; it is possible that the federation also published this pamphlet, with its preface by Giovannitti. Pulvio Zocchi and Filippo Corridoni were leaders of major worker struggles in 1912–13 in Italy led by the Unione Italian Sindacale (1912-1925). Vividly anti-clerical, this polemic contains almost ghoulish portraits of predatory priests, whose mellifluous and caressing voices hide their slipperiness and evil designs.

The unscrupulousness of priests is apparent from that most sacred of first rites, baptism, which Zocchi calls "the first act of the comedy" that is religion (23). "The mother feels the joy of a new life entering the earth, full of joy, hopes, worries and aspirations. But the priest doesn't think this way; he keeps watch. He has no scruples. He's the friend of the parents and the spiritual confessor of the mother, sometimes also the physical one. [The father is proud, he thinks he knows the score]. . . . But the priest is cunning. He works in the shadows. Just like the Jesuits" (23).

Giovannitti might have felt some ambivalence in implicitly blessing this scathing attack on the clergy, of which he was one (albeit a Protestant minister, not a Catholic priest). Unlike the case with Tresca and most of the other radicals, Giovannitti's political beliefs did not include overt anti-clericalism or a rejection of Christian principles; indeed, some of his poetry reflects religious overtones.

ARTURO GIOVANNITTI

112 ⊹ Portrait of Giovannitti, from "Syndicalism – the Creed of Force."
In *The Independent* (New York), October 30, 1913, 209-211.

Arturo M. Giovannitti (b. Campobasso, 1884; d. New York, 1959) immigrated to Montreal at 17, where he became a Protestant pastor; he then moved to Pennsylvania, preaching predominantly to miners. In Springfield, Mass., his interest in socialism began. In 1905, he arrived in New York, where he joined the

Federazione Socialista Italiana. He participated in the 1912 textile strike in Lawrence, Mass., where 25,000 workers went on strike, half of them women, who developed the slogan, "We want bread and roses too," that gave its name to that strike (cat. 148). It was there that Giovannitti was accused falsely of homicide and arrested, along with Joseph Ettor and Joseph Caruso. Put on the stand in the legendary trial at Salem, he delivered an apologia, in English, that became famous and was published several times, in Italian as well (cat. 115), and which identified him as a charismatic leader.

In prison, meanwhile, Giovannitti had composed "The Walker," which appeared in 1912 in *The Atlantic Monthly* and which was compared favorably to Oscar Wilde's *The Ballad of Reading Gaol.* Giovannitti, who became the director of *Il Proletario* in September 1909, was reconfirmed by the Utica congress in April 1911. When the poet was arrested, the paper was temporarily run by Edmondo Rossoni; after he got out of jail, Giovannitti remained as director until the summer of 1913, when he was replaced by Flavio Venanzi and later, once again by Rossoni. Highly esteemed in the milieu of the political and intellectual left, and eminent proponent of the I.W.W., Giovannitti contributed to *The Masses* and *The Liberator;* founded and directed *Il Fuoco;* and was at the same time included in histories and anthologies of American poetry, for example, as compiled by Louis Untermeyer. After 1920, he was among the organizers of the committee for the defense of Sacco and Vanzetti, one of the acknowledged leaders of the anti-fascist movement, in the leadership of AFANA, and a member of the committee formed after the assassination of his friend Carlo Tresca (cat. 125-26).

A complex intellectual figure, perennially astride two worlds, and equally comfortable in both English and Italian, Giovannitti is the rare case of an Italian American writer who, despite the extraordinary reception accorded him within the American literary culture, never abandoned the ambiance of the Italian community. His English-language poems were often translated into Italian, or even Sicilian dialect.

Giovannitti had the gift of a charisma equal to Tresca's and had a similar capacity to cut through the divisions of the left. Because he was dear to both the anarchists and the more moderate trade-unionists, everybody tried after his death to consider him one of their own. Giovannitti was not a fighter like Tresca. Rather, he was a poet, an orator, a man who knew how to confer a metapolitical, almost messianic depth to the fortunes of the labor movement.

113 ⨝ Arturo Giovannitti. *The Collected Poems of Arturo Giovannitti.*
Chicago: E. Clemente & Sons, 1962. Introduction by Norman Thomas.

Giovannitti was working on this collection of his English poems at the time of his death in 1959. This work, which follows his collection of Italian poems published in 1957, *Quando Canta Il Gallo* (cat. 64), was posthumously published by his friends and family, and a rare effort by Egidio Clemente to publish a work in English. Giovannitti's revolt against the cruelty, poverty and ignorance of mankind, and his championing of noble ideals of brotherhood, were frequent themes.

114⊹ [Industrial Workers of the World]. *Unionismo industriale e trade-unionismo: Può un socialista e industrialista far parte dell'A.F. of L.? Resoconto stenografico del contradittorio tra Joseph J. Ettor ed Arturo Caroti tenutosi a New York il 26 Marzo 1911.* [Industrial unionism and trade unionism: Can a socialist and industrialist belong to the A[merican] F[ederation] of L[abor]? Stenographic account of the debate between Joseph J. Ettor and Arthur Caroti held in New York on the 26th of March 1911]. Chicago: Industrial Workers of the World, 1911.

In the year following this "debate" between the revolutionary trade unions of the I.W.W. (and the Federazione) and the reformist A.F. of L., Joseph Ettor became one of the leaders of the Lawrence "Bread and Roses" strike of 1912 (see cat. 148). It was fateful that Giovannitti, who later joined Ettor and Joseph Caruso in that strike, would write the preface to the record of this debate. Arturo Caroti had long been the administrator of *Il Proletario* and the FSI's official propagandist in 1904-05, as well as a strong partisan of Tresca personally and politically, admiring the latter as a "man of action, courageous to the point of recklessness . . . always in the front lines of the proletarian struggle. . . ."[14]
    This is Mario De Ciampis's personal copy, with his name is written at the top of the front wrapper (see cat. 97-98, 103, 106).

115⊹ Arturo Giovannitti, G[iovanni] Gianformaggio, and Emma Goldman. *Pagine scelte* [Selected Works]. Brooklyn: Libreria dell'I.W.W., 1930.

This work contains Giovannitti's speech (entitled *"Davanti ai Giurati di Salem, Massachusetts"* [Before the Jurors of Salem, Mass.]) in 1912 to the jurors in the trial at which he, Joseph Ettor and Joseph Caruso were accused of the murder of Anna Lo Pizzo. Lo Pizzo was killed during the Lawrence millworkers strike in 1912, an event memorialized in Ralph Fasanella's painting (cat. 148). The jurors rightly believed the defense that the police were instead responsible, and the arrest of strike leaders Giovannitti and Ettor, in particular, was a pretext to make them unavailable to lead the crippling strike. The work also includes *L'Evoluzione del Pensiero* (The Evolution of Thought) of Giovanni Gianformaggio (1859-1901) and Emma Goldman's *Sindacalismo: Lo spettro del capitalismo* (Syndicalism: The spectre of capitalism), with a preface by Giovannitti.

CARLO TRESCA

Carlo Tresca (b. Sulmona, Italy, 1879; d. New York, 1943) was the radical left's most complex and fascinating character, a powerful thinker, charismatic orator and rabble rouser, ladies' man and a warm friend who never forgot the human dimension of people whatever their politics. In a two-part profile in *The New Yorker* in 1934, Max Eastman described Tresca, since Eugene Debs' death, as "the most universally esteemed and respected man in the revolutionary movement."[15] Eastman also noted Tresca's charisma, that if only he had learned English, "he would have been one of the biggest men in the history of American labor."[16] Eastman included Tresca as one of his profiles in his 1942 *Heroes I Have Known: Twelve Who Lived Greatly*, drawn in part from the earlier profile in *The New Yorker*.

Italian American radicals for the most part put aside their factionalism to join in the fight against fascism: among the founding members of the Anti-Fascist Alliance of North America, AFANA, were, besides Carlo Tresca, Giuseppe Cannata and Arturo Giovannitti. This generally unified purpose did not prevent the Galleanisti from finding fault even with Tresca's leadership role in anti-fascism. Tresca's popularity earned him a lifetime of enmity from Luigi Galleani during much of the latter's American period (1903–1919) and from Galleani's followers (the Galleanisti) after the latter's deportation from the U.S. to Italy in 1919.

Tresca's political views cannot be easily summarized, and they changed over time. Rather, their evolution, especially in the U.S., to which he immigrated in 1904, is described by the leading Tresca scholar, Nunzio Pernicone, as shifting over the course of some nine years: from revolutionary socialism to revolutionary syndicalism in 1905, at which time he became its leading Italian proponent and practitioner, to anarcho-syndicalism by 1913. These transitions resulted most likely from three related factors: ideological considerations, the need for independence demanded by his personality, and his natural propensity for direct action in labor struggles and the fight against capitalism.

The focus on union organizing was especially anathema to the Galleanisti anarchists, who rejected any organized form of anarchism. Galleani and his followers became obsessed with destroying Tresca's reputation. Like Galleani and most of the radicals, Tresca was also a virulent anti-cleric, a stance that began in his birthplace of Sulmona, and which continued unabated in the U.S. His articles in *L'Avvenire,* accusing priests of various crimes, led to his persecution by the Church, which enhanced Tresca's reputation as a *mangiaprete* ("priest-eater," *i.e.,* rabid anti-cleric).

116 ⊹ Carlo Tresca to Giacomo Battistoni, autograph letter signed. New York, [*ca.* 1920].

Tresca's holograph letter to Giacomo Battistoni, the leader of the Italian branch of the Socialist Party in Buffalo, offered to give a talk in Buffalo sometime in December of 1919 or 1920, during one of Tresca's *giri di propaganda* (propaganda tours). Buffalo was not some remote outpost of socialism included only incidentally on those tours: only two years before, October 7-9, 1917, it had been the situs of the first National Congress of the FSI. Tresca inquires in this letter about what topic Battistoni would like him to speak: "would an anti-religious talk please you? — I have to know right away." Tresca's offer was probably irresistible: he was known to be particularly effective in leaving workers in a state of emotional frenzy and with the desire to hear him speak again as soon as possible: in an earlier such tour, in the California wineries in 1915, when company guards tried to expel him, several hundred workers deterred them, demanding to hear him speak.

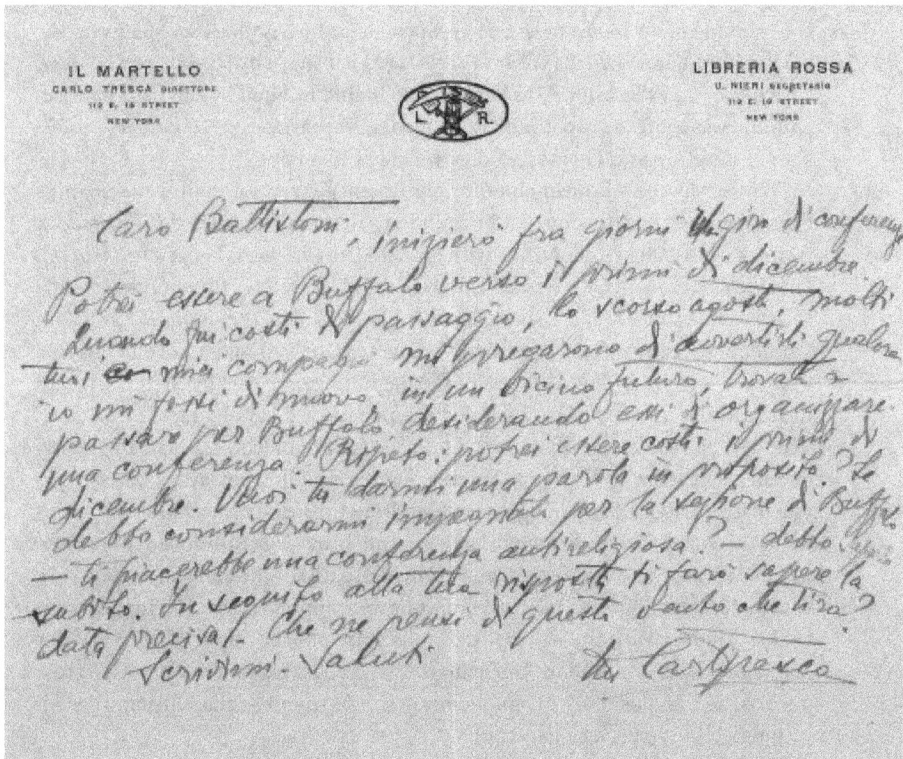

117 ⨳ Pietro Troilo to Nicola Mastrorilli, autograph letter signed. Hoboken, June 30, 1919, on Italian Interstate Federation letterhead.

This holograph letter is from Pietro Troilo, executive ssecretary of the Italian Interstate Federation, which is, as the letterhead indicates, the section of the "Socialist Part [sic]" covering New York, New Jersey and Pennsylvania, to Nicola Mastrorilli, president of the Buffalo section of the Federation, the same section that Tresca offered to visit to give a talk to in one of his *giri di propaganda* (cat. 116). This letter discusses the pending dispute, so important to socialists of both New Jersey and New York, between the Interstate Federation and and the National Federation that Troilo expects to be cleared up at the very important next Congress of the Italian Interstate Federation of the Socialist Party of New York and New Jersey on July 27, 1919.

118 ⨳ Carlo Tresca. *Il Martello. Rivista Popolare di Lettere, Scienze ed Arte.* [The Hammer. Popular Review of Letters, Science and the Arts]. New York: Carlo Tresca, 1918–19. Twenty issues bound in one volume.

One volume of 20 issues of the newspaper-magazine *Il Martello*, spanning the period from January 1918 (Volume 3, No. 1) to February 1919 (Volume 4, No. 3), with a few issues lacking. This volume was bound by hand by Augusto Lentricchia and was a gift to me of Frank Lentricchia, Katherine Everett Gilbert Professor of Literature and Theater Studies at Duke University.

Tresca was the editor-in-chief (or equivalent) at several radical newspapers over his career, but the one that he founded and ran for decades — *Il Martello* — is the one most closely identified with him, and he with it. As befits a *"rivista popolare di lettere-scienze ed arte,"* the issues of *Il Martello* in this volume include several short stories (and an occasional column, *Cronache Femminili*), by Clara Palumbo Vacirca, wife of Vincenzo Vacirca (cat. 34-35) and a novella entitled *Come era nel principio* (As it was in the beginning), written by Arturo Giovannitti (cat. 64, 113-115). Also included are poems or essays by Efrem Bartoletti (cat. 76), Flavio Venanzi (cat. 107), Ludovico Caminita (cat. 24, 40), and nearly one in every issue by Vincenzo Vacirca. Tresca's political essays, a description of a British Labour Party congress held in June 1918, and an account of how difficult the Post Office makes sending issues timely by post (November 16, 1918, p. 16) also appear. The tag "True translation filed with the post master at New York City on [date] as required by the act of Congress, approved Oct. 6th, 1917, known as the 'Trading with the Enemy Act'" was systematically appended to articles originally written in Italian, German or Russian, during an era when Congress gave to the U.S. Post Office tremendous power to suppress anarchist and socialist publications (see, *e.g.*, cat. 106).

Tresca founded *Il Martello* in 1917, and he directed it (with some interruptions due to poor finances) until his assassination in 1943. As is evident from the broad range of writing genres noted above, *Il Martello* was not a traditional Italian anarchist newspaper or a "movement" publication in the specific way that *La Questione Sociale* (edited by Ludovico Caminita and by Galleani briefly) was for anarcho-syndicalists, or the *Cronaca Sovversiva* and *L'Adunata dei Refrattari* were for anti-organizationist anarchist communists like Galleani and his followers (cat. 51-55, 92). Rather, *Il Martello* was too eclectic and unorthodox, like Tresca himself, to be classified according to conventional typology — "You can't label him. You can't classify him," said Eastman in *The New Yorker* profile.[17] The personal affection that Tresca's friends and colleagues had for him infuriated the more cerebral Galleani and his ultra-loyal founders, who unfairly attacked Tresca personally when they were unable to do so doctrinally.

That a reader of a review like *Il Martello* would lovingly gather issues into a homemade binding, beginning only a year after the founding of *Il Martello* in 1917, is a measure of the affection that Tresca's followers felt for him and everything he did. An immigrant from Morollo, south of Rome, Augusto Lentricchia settled in Utica in the first decade of the 20th century, where he worked for the New York Central Railroad, from which he was fired several times for trying to organize other railroad workers to radical causes. Lentricchia was also a poet who wrote about radical issues; one of his poems was published in *Il Martello*. His bound diaries containing his poetry were donated by Professor Frank Lentricchia to the Italian American Collection at the State University of New York at Stony Brook.

Lentricchia met Tresca when the latter came through Utica to counsel draft resistance during World War I, and may have met him there earlier, in 1911, at the national congress of the U.S. Federazione Socialista Italiana (founded in New York City in 1910, and directly affiliated with the Socialist Party of America), which took place in Utica on April 2-4, 1911. Tresca, who was the Pennsylvania section's delegate, played an important role at the congress, aligning himself with the revolutionary syndicalists of the far left who were in the ascendancy from the parliamentary socialists. Tresca later wrote about the Utica congress, in particular, of the transformation of the FSI from "evangelical propaganda for the masses" into a "vanguard revolutionary party." The opportunity to demonstrate this tactical shift to direct action came soon after with the textile workers' Bread and Roses strike of January 11-March 12, 1912 in Lawrence, Massachusetts (cat. 148).

119 ⊁ Carlo Tresca. *L'attentato a Mussolini, ovvero Il segreto di Pulcinella* [The attempt on Mussolini, or The secret of Pulcinella]. New York: Casa Editrice Il Martello, 1925.

Carlo Tresca
L'ATTENTATO A MUSSOLINI
ovvero
IL SEGRETO DI PULCINELLA

When the premiere performance of this play, based on actual historical circumstances — namely, a staged *attentato*, or attempt (to assassinate Mussolini) — was announced, the Fascist Party ambassador to the U.S. asked the State Department, which considered anarchists like Tresca to be troublesome "Reds," to prevent the performance from taking place. FBI agents and Bomb Squad officials invaded the Central Opera House in New York City on opening night, Sunday, December 13, 1925, and stopped the opening curtain on the specious grounds that the performance would violate New York's Sunday "Blue Laws."

Tresca took the stage, faulted the government's prohibition for acting at the behest of Mussolini, whose fascist dictatorship, he declaimed, was in the thrall of high-finance capitalism. The New York press, which normally disapproved of anarchists like Tresca, expressed sympathy for the anti-fascists, raising questions as to why a foreign government was being placated by American authorities in this way. The claimed attempt on Mussolini's life was the pretext for the repressive "emergency laws" in Italy of November 1926.

120 ⊁ Luigi Fabbri. *Le dittature: Contro la libertà dei popoli* [Dictatorships: against the freedom of the people]. New York: Il Martello Publishing Co., [*ca.* 1920s].

The verso of the cover of this pamphlet states "(Tradotto dal supplemento de 'La Protesta' di Buenos Aires)" (translated from the supplement of "La Protesta" of Buenos Aires). *La Protesta* is an Argentine anarchist newspaper still in publication. The final paragraph of Fabbri's essay ends with the statement, "Enough of dictatorship and tyranny; the revolution has finally come!" Fabbri (b. Ancona, 1877; d. Montevideo, 1935) was a close comrade of Errico Malatesta, the godfather of Italian anarchism, in Ancona in Italy, and later became his biographer. In fact, many of Carlo Tresca's articles were reprints of anarchist writings and doctrines of Malatesta, Fabbri, and Pietro Gori.

Fabbri was briefly considered as a possible replacement for Tresca as editor of *Il Martello*: however, Fabbri lived in Montevideo, in Uruguay, at that time, and nothing came of the effort. After suspensions of the newspaper due to poor finances, it resumed publication in 1934 with a new office and new infusion of cash, probably from the newest woman in his life, Margaret DeSilver. It was also starting at this time, whether coincidentally or not, that issues of *Il Martello* opened more in English than in Italian, as did the entire last page; that this change occurred at the same time that Tresca began drafting his autobiography in English (and that *Il Progresso Italo Americano* began a similar practice) is noteworthy, as Martino Marazzi points out, in the gradual "Americanization" of a man who remained resolutely Italian.

121 ⚜ Max Nettlau. *Errico Malatesta*. New York: Casa Editrice Il Martello, [1922].

Nettlau (b. Neuwaldegg [Vienna], 1865; d. Amsterdam, 1944) was a German anarchist and historian who met Malatesta in London, and remained friends for the rest of their lives. Realizing that the history of anarchists would be lost as the first generation began to pass away, he planned on interviewing them and writing their biographies. This 304-page biography of Malatesta is comprised of 20 chapters documenting the most important events in Malatesta's life. Another of Nettlau's works is on exhibit here, published in Barre (cat. 94).

122a ⚜ Eugene Lyons. *The Life and Death of Sacco and Vanzetti*. New York: International Publishers, 1927.

122b ⚜ Eugene Lyons. *Vita e morte di Sacco e Vanzetti*. New York: Il Martello Publishing Co., 1928.

This, the most dramatic, galvanizing (until their execution) and dispiriting historical event of the era involving Italian anarchists led to mass demonstrations in Paris, London and elsewhere around the world protesting the injustice of the executions of two immigrant Italians for their political activities. This would result in a nearly "instant" (post-execution) biography of those two men, who became the most famous of anarchists, written and published first in English, and then translated and published by Tresca's press in the following year.

123a ❧ *Salviamo Due Innocenti!* [Let us save two innocent men!]. Handbill, [1921].

An early call to arms, in year two of an eight-year process, to all Italians to help save two innocent men, wrongly accused of murder during the robbery in South Braintree, Mass., of the Slater & Morrill Co. paymaster.

123b ❧ *"Shall Sacco and Vanzetti Die July 10 1927?"* The Official Bulletin of the Sacco-Vanzetti Defense Committee of Boston, Massachusetts. April 1927.

Issued only a few months prior to their execution, this four-page bulletin summarizes the evidence of Sacco and Vanzetti's innocence, recounting the efforts of the Committee to "knock on every door" to obtain justice for the defendants, including a new trial, accusing prosecutor Katzmann of violating his duty to see justice done (*i.e.*, not to convict the defendants), and decrying the failure to consider the recent sworn confession of another that he, not Sacco and Vanzetti, was the robber.

124 ❧ *Athos Terzani, Accusato falsamente di omicidio / Athos Terzani, Facing trial for murder.* Handbill, Philadelphia: Anti-Fascist United Front, [1933]. Recto printed in Italian, verso in English.

This handbill announces a mass meeting in support of Athos Terzani's innocence. The English text states: "Athos Terzani, Facing trial for murder on the false story of 'General' Art J. Smith of the Khaki Shirts, will put his case before the people of Philadelphia at a Mass Meeting Friday, November 24, at 8 P.M." Speakers included Giovannitti and Tresca, among the leading Italians. Norman Thomas, co-chairman of the Terzani Defense Committee with Roger Baldwin, organized by Tresca, was also a speaker; his work eventually led to Terzani's exoneration at trial the following month.

A cab driver, Terzani was a young anti-fascist follower of Tresca's who was falsely accused of the murder of another anti-fascist, Antonio Fierro, at a rally of the fascist Khaki Shirts of America held in Astoria, Queens, on July 14, 1933. The rally was held a few months before a fascist "March on Washington" planned for Columbus Day, 1933, ostensibly to overthrow the government and establish a fascist dictatorship. Tresca had quickly organized a counter-rally, with the headline in that morning's *La Stampa Libera* sounding his exhortation: "MOBILITAZIONE ANTIFASCISTA! [ANTI-FASCIST MOBILIZATION!]."

The murder had been preceded by the clubbing to unconsciousness of Fort Velona, the noted illustrator (cat. 65, 105), for crying out "Morte a Mussolini!" upon hearing "Il Duce"'s name praised. Charged with murder in the second degree in a politically-charged indictment by the Queens district attorney, Terzani was released on $15,000 bail. The leader of the legal team was the brilliant Arthur Garfield Hays. At Terzani's trial from December 11-13, several ex-Khaki

Shirts identified a Khaki Shirts bodyguard as Fierro's shooter. Terzani was found not guilty by a jury in 32 minutes; shortly afterward, Terzani and his fiancé were married at a victory celebration, with Norman Thomas as best man, and Tresca's new companion, Margaret DeSilver, as matron of honor.

125⊹ Norman Thomas. *Who Killed Carlo Tresca?* New York: Tresca Memorial Committee, 1945.

126 ⊹ Norman Thomas. *Chi uccise Carlo Tresca?* New York: Tresca Memorial Committee, 1947.

The covers of these pamphlets also note "Forwards by Arturo Giovannitti and John Dos Passos" and "Con prefazione di Arturo Giovannitti e John Dos Passos." The goal was to incite readers to "stir the authorities out of their lethargy in the Tresca situation," urging them to contact Manhattan district attorney Frank S. Hogan and the newly appointed police commissioner to undertake a new and independent investigation. (The Italian version, issued two years later, lacks this exhortation at the end, probably because it was no longer timely.) As Giovannitti asks in his preface, "Who had any reason to have Carlo murdered? . . . For this man was everybody's friend, tutor, and counselor; he really loved everybody from the derelict and the destitute up to the teacher, the healer, even the man of affairs. . . . He was a friend of the policeman who arrested him scores of times, of the District Attorney who denounced him as an enemy of society but ate and drank at his table, the jailer who locked him up for interminable days. . . ."

Tresca's attacks on Mussolini were almost surely responsible for his assassination (under circumstances that remain mysterious to this day). One evening in 1943 — the same year in which Mussolini was deposed — upon leaving the office of his newspaper, *Il Martello* in Union Square, Tresca was gunned down. Some say it was on direct orders from Mussolini because of Tresca's unrelenting polemics against him; others, such as union leader (and leading anti-communist) Luigi Antonini, blamed the Communists, and in particular, former Tresca colleague, with whom Tresca had become disenchanted, Vittorio Vidali (known in America as Enea Sormente). The more likely culprit was the then young hitman, Carmine Galante, possibly on orders from Generoso Pope, the pro-Mussolini publisher of *Il Progresso Italo-Americano*, the largest circulation and longest-lived Italian-language daily.

The Tresca Memorial Committee included A. Philip Randolph, Edmund Wilson and John Dewey, as well as its chair, Norman Thomas, the perennial Socialist Party candidate for president. This pamphlet, far more common in its English version than in the Italian one, was circulated with the exhortation that "those who believe with us that political murder in the United States must not go unpunished . . . help circulate this pamphlet widely . . . we have no thought of placing the guilt in the Tresca assassination at the door of any specific organization or individual," but it is clear that Tresca's assassination obsessed many who loved him.

127 ꙮ [Industrial Workers of the World]. *Lavoratori! Il noto conferenziere italiano Edmondo Rossoni di New York, che à fatto parecchi giri di propaganda in tutte le colonie de Nord-America, parlerà in questa città il giorno* [Workers! The noted lecturer, Edmondo Rossoni of New York, who has made several propaganda trips in all the [Italian] colonies of North America, will speak in this city on the day of ---, beginning at 8 pm, on the topic 'The Battles of Work.' Handbill, [New York?]: [Industrial Workers of the World], [*ca.* 1911].

This handbill, *ca.* 1911, when Rossoni was the official propagandist of the New York-based Federazione Socialista Italiana, as well as an editor of *Il Proletario*, was used during *giri di propaganda* (propaganda trips) by which charismatic leaders like Rossoni or Tresca traveled across the Italian communities scattered across the U.S. to deliver speeches or engage in political debates. Such tours were crucial in spreading revolutionary ideas among Italians in the industrial and mining areas of northeastern and midwestern states, and even as far west as California wineries, and reinforcing transnational ties among radical groups. The date and location – apparently, the talk was always given at 8 pm – would be filled in to reflect the upcoming talk, and urged Italians with the following exhortation:

> Given the skill and the war-like spirit of the orator, no one will want to miss it. Italians, attend in mass, for your instruction, and out of feelings of brotherhood and international solidarity that ought to inspire you to hear a sincere and enthusiastic word in defense of the rights of the people.

Like many leftists, Rossoni was deported from the United States, returning to Italy in 1917. Though seemingly a turncoat, when appointed head of the CNCS, the fascist labor federation, Rossoni eventually alienated the Fascist Party leadership; by late 1927, Mussolini warned him about his "subversive" behavior and in 1928 stripped him of his power. Nevertheless, he gained a cabinet position as minister of agriculture and forests by 1935, and voted to remove Mussolini as prime minister in July 1943. Though sentenced to death both by a Fascist Party tribunal and by the provisional Italian government established in 1943, he lived (in Canada) to see his sentence rescinded in 1952.

Who supported the Fascist Party regime in the U.S.? There was a small core of active fascist supporters, with the two magazines that vied for primacy with Mussolini as organs of fascism in America: Agostino de Biasi's *Il Carroccio* (cat. 29), which published from 1915 until 1935, with a circulation of about 10,000–12,000, and Domenico Trombetta's *Il Grido della Stirpe* (The Cry of the Race), which became the largest circulation pro-fascist periodical at about 30,000 at its height in the mid-late 1920s, dropping to about 5,000 in the late 1930s as Italian Americans soured on Mussolini.

Both fascist and therefore anti-fascist activities were not confined to New York, Chicago and other big cities. By the early 1920s, Fascist Party cells in the United States were present in Buffalo, Albany, Rochester and Syracuse. Opposing Mussolini united Italians of the left, so that anarchists put aside their internal differences to work together, and with the Italian socialists, in this effort.

128 ❧ [CPUSA]. *A Basso* [sic] *con Mussolini e il fascismo!... A Basso La Guerra – Defendere L'Itopia!!!* [Down with Mussolini and fascism! Down with War - Defend Ethiopia!!!]. Handbill, New York: Communist Party [CPUSA], [n.d.]. "Elmira NY CP 1935" handwritten at bottom edge.

That this typewritten, rather than printed, handbill was prepared locally is suggested by the mistake ("A Basso" should be "Abasso") that one was less likely to see in a nationally prepared handbill like the Rossoni (cat. 127). This particular handbill was used to incite Italians to show their opposition to the Italian adventure in Ethiopia, calling them to rallies in August 1935, in both Elmira and Ithaca in upstate New York.

129 ❧ Dott. Gaetano F. Lisanti. *La crisi sociale da Cristo a Mussolini* [The social crisis from Christ to Mussolini]. New York: Cocce Bros., 1933.

In this 24-page pamphlet, Lisanti, who in 1916 authored a standard Italian-English dictionary published by the Società Libraria Italiana, praises fascism, though noting its differences from Christianity. Lisanti declared that fascism has substituted for Christ's exhortation to "Love your neighbor as you love yourself," the "political imperative of deductive reason: 'Act so as to cooperate for the common good,'" promoting the political relation between capital and work for creating a social equilibrium, just as Christianity proclaimed the moral relation between riches and poverty in order to create social equilibrium.

Lisanti seems an unlikely candidate to have become a Black Shirt or Khaki Shirt (*i.e.*, a militant fascist) rather than the philosophical fascist as seen in a work like this one, much as Renzo Novatore (cat. 90) was more a philosophical anarchist rather than a man of action (much less violent action). Fascism is "the affirmation of historical determinism," to navigate safely between the Scylla of Socialism and the Charybdis of Communism, in Lisanti's view.

130 ❧ Rosario Di Vita. *I nostri fiori alla patria* [Our flowers for the homeland]. New York: Società Tipografica Italiana, 1924.

Di Vita (b.Palermo, 1880; d. New York, 1939), who immigrated to America in 1905 or 1906, directed several literary newspapers and founded the Cenacolo Artistico Letterario Vincenzo De Simone. He also published several volumes of poetry, generally in the Sicilian dialect. *I nostri fiori* is a collection of poems by others of homage to Italy, either as "la patria" (the fatherland) or as "soave madre gentile" (kind, sweet mother), with an occasional expression of hope that fascism would prevail. But his nationalistic fervor later moved him to the hard right, and in 1933 Di Vita later published a massive, 12-volume work dedicated to "Il Duce," the *Raccolte del Decennale,* an exhaustive, detailed documentation of all published works in the two Americas pertaining to fascism.

131 ❧ Domenico Trombetta. *Pervertimento: L'antifascismo di Carlo Fama* [Depravity: the anti-fascism of Carlo Fama]. New York: Libreria del Grido della Stirpe, [1930].

Trombetta (b. Aquila, 1885; d. New York, *ca.* 1950s) was a freelance journalist who immigrated to the U.S. in 1903. He began his journalistic career at the leftist *L'Italia Nostra* (Our Italy), a weekly interventionist paper founded by Edmondo Rossoni. Changing political stripes at the same time as Rossoni but without the latter's ambivalent feelings, in 1923 Trombetta founded the violently polemical fascist bi-weekly *Il Grido della Stirpe* and its circulation more than doubled that of de Biasi's politically similar *Il Carroccio. Il Grido* was sued repeatedly for libel, from which Trombetta, who eventually became a leading voice of Italian American fascism, usually escaped unscathed. While "pervertimento" can mean more broadly "corruption" or "depravity," Trombetta also, rather speculatively, calls Fama (at p. 127) "pervertito," a pervert and a degenerate. Fama, a respected medical doctor, Presbyterian minister and Republican Party supporter, was a particularly effective and unusual anti-fascist: as one of the few whose anti-fascism did not arise from a radical or labor militancy, he had a respectability that gave special credibility to his charges about fascist activities.

132 ❧ Vittorio E. De Fiori; Guido Podrecca. *Mussolini. Il fascismo.* New York: Italy Publishing Co., 1923.

De Fiori (b. Venezia, 1890; active 1910s-1940s) knew Mussolini "intimamente" from contact during readings and from the time that Mussolini was expelled from the Socialist Party in Italy. Podrecca, co-founder of *L'Asino* (cat. 109-110), later turned to fascism, returning to Italy after several years in the U.S. during his "conversion." To Podrecca's work, Agostino de Biasi wrote a personal preface, praising the steadfast support of Podrecca for fascism following his youthful fling with socialism. De Biasi's Il Carroccio Publishing Company printed these two works in one volume.

Earlier, in 1915, De Fiori left Milan to go to Barre, when Luigi Galleani was situated there, in order to take on the role of secretary of the Cooperative Union. In 1916, when another newspaper he worked for, the *Rinascenza Italica*, merged with *Il Messagero* in Paterson, De Fiori moved to New York to direct the new newspaper, the first and only one in America to publish Mussolini's war diaries. In 1921-1922, De Fiori was involved in organizing in New York the first Fascist Party cell outside of Italy. In 1928, Dutton published his *Mussolini — the Man of Destiny*.

133* [Benito] Mussolini, [Librero] Tancredi and [Gustavo] Hervé. *Dio e patria nel pensiero dei rinnegati* [God and country in the thoughts of the renegades]. New York: [n.p.], [*ca.* 1924-25]. Second edition.

This work reproduces, first, the record of a debate on March 25, 1904 (and Mussolini's preface thereto, dated July 1904), in Lausanne (Lossana), Switzerland between the then virulently anti-clerical young socialist Mussolini, already known for his violent oratory and animal vitality, and the evangelist Taglialatella over the existence of God, in which Mussolini affirmed his belief in the absurdity of the concept of God. The editors republished the record of this debate twenty years later — after Mussolini became Italy's prime minister, but probably before he became "Il Duce" in 1925 — to reflect a favorite radical theme about the once anti-clerical Mussolini: that in consolidating his power and distancing himself from his early socialist and anti-clerical roots, he embraced the Church and capitalism, and in so doing became a "*voltagabbana*" (turncoat) to his origins. The second essay recounts a religious debate between Tancredi and a priest in Providence, R.I., on December 11, 1910, subsequent to the first edition, and the third is a translation of a French political philosopher's argument about the "lies" of patriotism.

It was at the time and place of the 1904 debate that Carlo Tresca met Mussolini, who chided the older Tresca for "not being revolutionary" enough, according to Tresca in his autobiography: it is difficult to imagine anything more ironic, given their later histories, than that Mussolini could have said at any time that Tresca "was not sufficiently imbued with the spirit of revolt."[18]

This undated work calls itself a "second edition" at "the distance of twenty years" from its first appearance in print. Indeed, it would have been virtually impossible to print or publish it in Italy, if it was in fact 1924, for by that time, Mussolini had managed to pass legislation to gag the press.

THE SOCIETÀ LIBRARIA ITALIANA, THE ITALIAN BOOK COMPANY

We know far more about the Società Libraria Italiana, or the Italian Book Company, than about the Cocce Press, Nicoletti Bros., Frugone & Balletto or any of the other Italian-language publishers. The company is noted in the 1938 *The Italians of New York* as having "one of the most important wholesale and retail Italian books shops in the city." No standard reference sources describe the company or its founders, Francesco Tocci and Antonio De Martino. Tocci, who had previously published several authors at his Emporium Press (cat. 5, 16), was the IBC's first president.

We know the most, however, about Antonio De Martino, originally the treasurer of the company and later its proprietor and possibly sole owner for decades, well into the 1950s. De Martino successfully transformed the Società Libraria Italiana into the robust, successful and − above all − diversified publishing phenomenon, the Italian Book Company. De Martino was a savvy businessman who bought copyright protections wherever he could (*e.g.*, cat. 135b, 143b); and he did not hesitate to sue those who, in his view, infringed on the IBC's copyright, as the legal papers of the company reveal difficult legal issues on which U.S. and Italian copyright law differed. Correspondence reveals that the scope of copyright protection that De Martino seems to have bargained for was never as clear as he claimed. De Martino asserted the most expansive reservations of rights, and vigorously defended copyright infringement charges against him.

Two essays written decades after this company had been established are enlightening. The first is a kind of puff piece in *Il Progresso Italo-Americano* of February 10, 1956 − this was in the Generoso Pope era of that newspaper, long after Carlo Barsotti had died − that celebrated the sailing of De Martino's ship from New York. He took this, his 53rd Atlantic crossing to his native Italy, "to enrich this bookstore with all the newest and most interesting publications that see the light of day in Italy" in order to develop an unrivaled collection for his American public, and to be able to offer the most complete and varied collection, all in Italian.[19] His trips, the article emphasizes, were not pleasure trips, but excursions of bibliographic research that enhanced his flourishing book business.

Review of the business records suggests that De Martino arranged book deals and translation deals with leading Italian authors, or, alternatively, he developed book distribution arrangements with Italian publishers such as Bemporad & Figli of Milan. This ensured that, much as Lorenzo Da Ponte had done nearly a century before in importing and distributing Italian imprints in the United States, new political, economic, social and literary ideas from Italy were made available to at least that part of the American public who could read Italian. And by also publishing Italian lessons in book form for a native English-speaking audience as he did, De Martino encouraged creation of a class of new readers of Italian (*e.g.*, cat. 6, 7).

From a more sophisticated source of information, we have an essay from the accomplished fiction writer, Italo Stanco (né Ettore Moffa), writing in *Divagando*, an elegant and important, large-circulation Italophone weekly cultural journal. Stanco praised De Martino as someone who was a "pioneer" who "refined the crude minds of the humbler Italian immigrants of more than a half-century ago," immigrants who lived "in the mean dens of the Five Points, of Mott, Mulberry and Elizabeth Streets."[20] Starting with a small, hidden stall squeezed between many others, according to Stanco, De Martino took the Italian Book Company to the glory of the large emporium it occupied at 145-47 Mulberry Street by the time Stanco wrote. The "indefatigable bookseller-editor" De Martino possessed literary and artistic properties of "thousands" of works of every type, from novels to songs, and the records of the company bear this out. To obtain many of these properties, De Martino "commuted" between New York and his beloved native Naples — 53 crossings, as of three years later, make that claim no exaggeration — where he stayed anywhere from two to thirteen months, from news accounts.

Both the 1956 story in *Il Progresso Italo-Americano* and the Stanco essay of several years earlier make it clear that De Martino was recognized then as an important figure in New York's Italian American community at large, not merely among the smaller Italian-language book-scribbling crowd. The types of works published by the Italian Book Company included not only the serious literature from both Italy and America, but also an extensive series of full-length (as well as pamphlet-sized) gardening and cook books, *e.g.*, a 250-page illustrated *Arte del casaro* (The Art of the Dairyman) and a three-volume illustrated work, *Orticultura moderna*, all of which were advertised in Aiello's *La cucina casareccia napoletana pei golosi e buongustai* (cat. 139). In addition, the IBC sold kitchen gadgets, such as espresso makers (such as Moka Express) and other cooking utensils, at least by the time the IBC had moved into its capacious headquarters at 145-147 Mulberry Street, pictures of which adorn the Stanco article. And to help a native Italian-speaking immigrant learn to read and write English, the Italian Book Company continued a line of language courses, in book form by Alfonso Arbib-Costa, that founder Tocci had started in his Emporium Press days, to help Italians learn English (cat. 5).

134 |✦ *Uncle Sam is ready to bury the chief of the barbarians / Uncle Sam è pronto a seppellire il capo dei barbari.* Chromolithograph poster, 27 x 31". New York: Italian Book Company, 1918.

UNCLE SAM IS READY TO BURY THE CHIEF OF THE BARBARIANS

UNCLE SAM È PRONTO A SEPPELLIRE IL CAPO DEI BARBARI

CAT. 134

This stunning lithograph is one of a series of three that were produced by the Società Libraria Italiana in 1918, all of which relate to the actual or impending defeat of the German Kaiser that would end World War I. The captions at the top and bottom about Uncle Sam seem perfect for this bi-lingual publisher. This particular chromolithograph states (alone among the three) in the lower left corner, "5007 © 1918 ITALIAN BOOK CO. NEW YORK" and in the lower right corner, in effect the same caption, "TUTTI I DIRITTI RISERVATI [ALL RIGHTS RESERVED] SOCIETÀ LIBRARIA ITALIANA – NEW YORK."

The Smithsonian describes these rare works of ephemera as produced in America to persuade Italian Americans to sign up for the draft during World War I; it was perhaps to counter the draft resistance urged by Tresca and Galleani, among others, during their propaganda tours. The posters may also have been meant to persuade the U.S. government that the majority of Italian Americans supported the war effort.

135a ✦ Bernardino Ciambelli. *I sotterranei di New York* [The Undergrounds of New York]. New York: Società Libraria Italiana, 1915.

This novel is the 16th of 19 or 20 that Ciambelli authored over a long and productive career.

135b ✦ Assignment of rights to publication by Ciambelli to the Società Libraria Italiana of *I sotteranie di New-York*, May 28, 1915. Photocopy.

136 ✦ A[ntonio] De Martino. *Tripoli italiana: La guerra italo-turca. Le nostre prime vittorie.* New York: Società Libraria Italiana, 1911.

De Martino lost no time in rooting for Italy's colonialist ventures: after all, a state of war, as is noted early on, was only declared against Turkey by Italy on September 29, 1911, the year of publication of this work. *Tripoli italiana* reflects the patriotic spirit felt by most Italians living in America, which reflected itself in support for Italy's several imperialistic (and usually disastrous) adventures in Africa.

As would be the case with the Italian war with Austria (cat. 42), the Company wasted no time publishing a nationalist promotion of Italian actions in the same year the war ended, 1918. This one concerned the war between Italy and Turkey over Tripoli, bordered on the west by Tunisia and on the east by Egypt. This unthinking patriotic fervor was in obvious contrast to the radicals, who opposed such ventures (see, *e.g.*, cat. 128).

137 ✦ Franco Bello. *Casanova: Memorie d'avventure amorose* [Casanova: Recollections of amorous adventures]. New York: Italian Book Company, 1944.

The fascination of many with the "avventure amorose" of one of the great pleasure seekers and serial seducers (of the wives and daughters of important subjects of French King Louis XV) in European history was apparently true in 1940s America among Italians. Casanova and Da Ponte (cat. 1) were great friends and competitors as ladies' men, and at least one meeting of the two while Cassanova was writing his *Memoirs* has been reported, in which Da Ponte introduced his own wife to Casanova as his mistress, to save face. This meeting occurred some years before Da Ponte actually came to America, where he wrote and published his own memoirs.

As is sometimes the case with books published by the Company, the information on the cover and title page do not match. Here the title on the cover, which is mostly a photo of a bewigged Casanova in a garden with one of his conquests states, "*Casanova* | *Idolo di tutte le donne*"; this subtitle, "Idol of all women," does not appear on the title page and may have been an afterthought based on another work of the publisher: the rear cover announces a new release entitled

Vita Amorosa di Valentino, with a photo of the great Italian movie idol who, at least in films, was a modern day Casanova, and a text that reads, in Italian, "There needs no explanation for this new publication of the Italian Book Company. The life of the adventurous hero of the screen, idol of women, incomparable artist, his triumphs, his loves, his tragic ending are a subject that will thrill and enthrall any reader, female or male." The work was available "in an elegant edition" in both a paperback ($1) and a hardbound ($2) version. Of Franco Bello, we know that he published a play in Milan in 1915, *Oberdan, il martire di Trieste: Dramma patriottico in 5 atti* (Oberdan, the martyr of Trieste: Patriotic drama in 5 acts).

The fascination with Casanova continues unabated to this day: the French state displayed the original manuscript of his memoirs and other writings for the first time at the Bibliothèque Nationale de France for a few months, beginning in November 2011, to long lines of visitors.

138 ❧ Benito Mussolini. *John Huss the Veracious.* New York: Italian Book Company, 1939.

One of the relatively few works published by the company in English, presumably to reach Italian Americans not so fluent in Italian as the publisher's usual readers. From the photo (shot from below) of Mussolini on the cover, not an image of the ostensible subject of the book, we already realize that the publisher thought the author more important than the book's subject. Indeed, the publisher describes this as a youthful work of Mussolini about the 14th-15th century Bohemian heretic, one in which the dictator's "luminous genius is shown," adding that this work shows Mussolini's early perception that "the Italians of tomorrow will not be as the Italians of yesterday," as Italy is "in a process of formation," with the "powerful propulsion of his will power," by which Mussolini has "changed the face of Italy, reconstructing the Second Empire of Rome."[21]

139 ❧ Rosa Aiello. *La cucina casareccia napoletana pei golosi e buongustai* [The homecooking Neapolitan kitchen for gourmands and gourmets]. New York: Italian Book Company, [*ca.* 1940s].

The title page of this copy is stamped "E. Rossi & Co., Imported Novelties and Housewares," then located at 191 Grand Street in Manhattan's Little Italy. (See cat. 142b–c for photos of the exterior and interior of E. Rossi's shop.) The Italian Book Company also published a now much-coveted and rare cookbook in English, *The Italian Cook Book: The Art of Eating Well/ Practical Recipes of the Italian Cuisine . . . Compiled by Mrs. Maria Gentile* (1919).

140 ⟨+ Antonio De Martino and Umberto Fragasso. *Il libro delle erbe: Medicinali e magiche di A. De Martino e Umberto Fragasso, compilato su varie opera di botanica medica.* [The book of medicinal and magical herbs, of A. De Martino and Umberto Fragasso, compiled from various works of Medical Botanica]. New York: Italian Book Company, 1946.

As noted with regard to cat. 137 above, the Società Libraria Italiana often employed a different title on a cover (here, *Erbario Figurato* [Illustrated Herbarium]) from that given on the title page. In addition to an alphabetically arranged and illustrated guide to herbs, there is advice on how to live a long life, gain weight or lose weight, avoid constipation and the like, all or nearly all from one Dottore T. E. Cutter, another possible target, like Dr. Collins at a much earlier time, of *La Follia*'s exposés of quack doctors servicing the immigrant community.

141 ⟨+ Casa Genarelli. *Autunno napoletano: Raccolta dei versi delle canzone antiche di grande successo* [Neapolitan Autumn: Collection of the verses of ancient popular songs]. New York: Italian Book Company, 1930.

This 16-page booklet contains verses to 34 songs about Naples, the sheet music for which is apparently for sale at the Casa Gennarelli of Naples, which also sells musical instruments advertised here.

Photographs

142a ⟨+ Interior of Tocci's Emporium Press, the predecessor to Società Libraria Italiana, *ca.* 1906 [from one of the photos in Tocci's self-description, in cat. 50].

142b ⟨+ Exterior view of E. Rossi's Bookstore, 191 Grand Street, Manhattan, *ca.* 1940s.

142c ⟨+ Interior of E. Rossi's Bookstore, 191 Grand Street, Manhattan, *ca.* 1940s.

143a ⟨+ Duchessa X. *L'assassinio della Contessa Trigona* [The Assassination of the Contessa Trigona]. New York: Italian Book Company, 1944.

Vincenzo Paternò del Cugno, a Sicilian baron who was always short on money, killed his lover, the Countess Giulia, in Rome in March 1911, when she refused to give him any more money and broke off the relationship. Married to Count Trigona, the Countess was a member of the Sicilian nobility, a lady in waiting to the Queen of Italy who was in Rome attending to the queen when she met with Paternò one last time, in a seedy hotel. Her sister was married to Tomasi di Lampedusa, whose one work *Il gattopardo* (The Leopard) — a signal landmark in Italian literary history — itself centered on the decline of the ancient Sicilian nobility.

Not surprisingly, when he got out of prison thirty years later, Paternò was once again broke. Having somehow learned about the publication in the U.S., thirty years after the fact, of a book about his murder of the Contessa, Paternò tried to cash in on it: he wrote to De Martino first to tell him that some details of the murder were incorrect. But it soon became clear that a little help getting back on his feet again would go a long way: the last letter in the series is Paternò's thank you to De Martino for a new suit and other gifts. Given the origins of his affair with the Contessa and the murder in Sicilian nobility, the denouement of Paternò's life story in his haggling over money with "his" publisher, an Italian immigrant, in America seems fitting.

While the Società Libraria Italiana thrived on its books and records imported from Italy, and supported some of the good and not so good Italian language American originals, as time wore on over the many decades of its publishing history, the company published more material in English, and helped make Americans of the immigrants, with its readers and dictionaries, its guides for writing letters, in English as well as in Italian. In that sense, it participated in the more common movement of assimilation: teaching immigrants how to become American. Following are some of the efforts by others to help the Italians assimilate.

143b ⊁ Copyright renewal registration (1945) for *L'assassinio della Contessa Trigona*.

Antonio De Martino was clever enough to obtain, on behalf of the company, the copyright to tell this story as early as 1912, although there is no evidence of the book's actual publication in the thirty years before the 1944 edition on display here. There is also no evidence as to whether the pseudonym (Duchessa X) of the nominal author was anyone other than the enterprising De Martino himself.

———————

GUIDES FOR ITALIAN AMERICANS

Eager to transform Italian-language readers and speakers into Americans, such "American" groups as the Immigrant Education Society and the Daughters of the American Revolution published guides for immigrants, in some cases in both Italian and English.

144a ⊁ Cav[aliere] John Foster Carr. *Guida degli Stati Uniti per l'immigrante Italiano* [Guide to the United States for the immigrant Italian]. New York: Doubleday, Page & Co., 1910. Second edition.

Edited by the Società delle figlie della Rivoluzione Americana. Sezione di Connecticut (Daughters of the American Revolution, Connecticut Section). This copy was printed in the same year of publication as the first. A folded map of the United States is laid down in rear cover. In the third edition (1913), also in my collection, readers are directed on the cover (where "Doubleday, Page & Company" had appeared in the earlier editions) "*Per Ordinazioni ed Informazioni*" (For orders and information) to turn to the Immigrant Education Society on Fifth Avenue in New York, and in the frontispiece, President William Howard Taft has been dispatched in favor of a portrait of President Woodrow Wilson.

A practical guide, this work told immigrants the names of American states and cities, how to find work, spend money, travel, and even, summing up on the last page, how to comport oneself in public: "Speak in a low voice. TRY NOT TO GESTICULATE TOO MUCH WHEN SPEAKING, AND DON'T GET EXCITED DURING DISCUSSIONS. TAKE CARE ABOUT YOUR PERSONAL APPEARANCE . . . DON'T ABUSE LIQUOR. BE PROUD OF YOUR HOMELAND AND YOUR FAMILY. Never change your name, unless absolutely necessary to simplify it for American pronunciation. . . . The best opportunities for the immigrant are not in New York but in the interior of the country. BY FOLLOWING THESE WARNINGS YOU WILL BE RESPECTED AND WELL-RECEIVED IN AMERICA."

144b ⊁ John Foster Carr. *Guide to the United States for the Immigrant Italian.* Garden City: Doubleday, Page & Co., 1911.

Like the Italian original, "published under the Auspices of the CONNECTICUT DAUGHTERS OF THE AMERICAN REVOLUTION"; the frontispiece: President William Howard Taft. Map of the U.S., also in this edition, laid down in rear cover. The title page also indicates that the work is "a nearly literal translation of the Italian version."

Carr, who spoke and wrote Italian fluently, is said to have translated his own Italian-language original into English. Evidently, even those Italian immigrants who had learned a sufficient amount of English to read a guide to the country they were adopting, temporarily or more likely permanently, still needed to be advised "don't get excited during discussions" and to "try not to gesticulate too much."

145 ✠ J. J. Zmrhal. *A Primer of Civics, English and Italian: Manuale di Cittadinanza* [Citizenship Manual] *designed for the guidance of the Immigrant*. Chicago: The Illinois Society of the Colonial Dames of America, 1918.

The author, a Bohemian immigrant to the United States, began this series with an English-Bohemian version published in 1912, then English only (1912), English-Polish (1914), and English-Lithuanian (1915), just prior to this English-Italian version in 1918. The order mirrors in descending order the size of the respective immigrant community of Chicago.

The foreward closes with a letter addressed (in facing pages, English on the left, Italian on the right, as with the remainder of the work) to "Dear Friends" reading it, asking, among other things, rather less respectfully than Carr did: "Is it too much to ask, while so much has been done for you that you do something in return, that you help others as you have been helped, that you love and respect the Land of Liberty you have chosen for your new home?" As the name implies, the *Primer of Civics* explains the organization and operation of the federal, state and city of Chicago governments.

146 ✠ Elizabeth C. Barney Buel, compiler. *Manuale degli Stati Uniti: Istruzioni ad uso degli immigranti e stranieri*. [Manual of the United States: Instructions for the use of immigrants and foreigners]. Washington, D.C.: Società Nazione Figlie della Rivoluzione Americana/The National Society, Daughters of the American Revolution, 1930. Sixth edition.

Not the sixth Italian edition, but translated from the sixth English edition (1930), this work notes in Italian on the verso of the cover that it was printed in English "and in the following foreign languages," listing 17 languages, mostly European.

Similar to Carr's work but without Carr's sympathy for Italians perhaps, after explaining that there are laws in America to protect working people, it stresses the importance of learning English, "the language spoken in the U.S. It is very important that you learn it. You need it to obtain work," etc. Perhaps somewhat oversimplifying the case, it advises that "You can learn English easily. In evening classes you can learn to speak and write it. You'll feel happier if you do. Your children will respect you more [if you do]. How to Learn English. The English language is a beautiful one...." One wonders if the Italian writers in this exhibition would "feel happier if" they learned English. The Manual encouraged readers to use public libraries, and indeed, the Italians did. Figures kept of library usage by the New York Public Library reflect that of all immigrant groups, only Jewish immigrants used the libraries in greater numbers.

147a |+ Handbill announcing an appearance of Farfariello (Eduardo Migliac-
cio) at the Academy of Music, 26 Ashland Place and Lafayette Avenue, Brooklyn,
NY, to take place on March 13, 1938; 7½" x 10 ⁵/₈". 147a-c and 148 are from the
collection of Emelise Aleandri.

147b |+ Handbill announcing a performance of *I Dieci Comandamenti
di Carlo Garuffi* at the Majestic Theatre, 651 Fulton Street, Brooklyn, May
15, 1938; 6½" x 10½". Facsimile.

147c |+ Handbill for an appearance by Ria Rosa at Fleisher Auditorium (Broad
& Pine Sts.) in Philadelphia, March 11, 1937; 6 ⁵/₈" x 12".

———————

148 |+ Ralph Fasanella. The Great Strike – Lawrence, 1912. Signed print of
a 1978 painting; 20" x 28".

Fasanella (b. The Bronx, 1914; d. Hastings, N.Y., 1997) was a labor organizer and
painter. For years, the original 1978 painting of this print of the great Lawrence,
Mass. strike of 1912 (see cat. 96, 105, 107, 112, 114, 115), purchased by labor
unions, hung in the Labor and Education Subcommittee Hearing Room in the
Rayburn Office building in Washington, D.C., but was removed by Republican
House staffers in 1994. His paintings focus on men and women at work, in union
halls, strikes, sit-ins and baseball games (one of which hangs in the Baseball Hall
of Fame in Cooperstown), and include a May Day demonstration and one of an
Italian American family scene ("Family Supper") that hangs in the Ellis Island
Museum. Another, of subway riders, hangs at the 53rd Street and Fifth Avenue,
Manhattan, subway stop.

149 |+ Lawrence Ferlinghetti. *The Old Italians Dying.* One of 50 copies of
a mimeographed poem, inscribed to Neeli Cherkovski, 1976.

Ferlinghetti (b. Yonkers, 1919) is best known for *A Coney Island of the Mind*
(San Francisco, 1958), the best-selling collection of poetry of all time, and for
co-founding San Francisco's City Lights Bookstore in 1953 and starting the City
Lights publishing arm two years later. He is also known for publishing the Beat
poets: upon hearing the premier performance by Allen Ginsberg of his *Howl*,
Ferlinghetti offered to publish it. This led to Ferlinghetti's infamous prosecution on obscenity charges, of which he was acquitted after trial in 1957. Besides
the Beats, City Lights published Kenneth Rexroth, William Carlos Williams and

other notables. A philosophical anarchist himself, Ferlinghetti sold Italian anarchist newspapers, perhaps including those on display in this exhibition, at the City Lights Bookstore to the old Italians of North Beach, on whose decline and passing this 1976 poem elegiacally reflects. Ferlinghetti is published in Italy by City Lights Italia. Cherkovski (b. Santa Monica, 1945, né Nelson Cherry) is a poet and biographer of Ferlinghetti and of Charles Bukowski.

150 ⚔ Letterio Calapai. *Eight-Thirty Express.* Woodcut, 1943. Edition of 50; signed, titled and numbered in pencil; 5¼" x 8½".

Calapai (b. Boston, 1902; d. Glencoe, Ill., 1993), child of Sicilian immigrants, studied at the Boston School of Fine Arts and Crafts, and at the School of Art and Beaux Arts Institute of Design in New York, worked in the Mural Division of the WPA, and was active in furthering unionism in the arts. He also taught at the New School and founded the Intaglio Workshop of Advanced Printmaking in New York in 1960. His works hang in museums in Italy and Israel, India and Australia, as well as in France and the U.S.

151 ⚔ Valenti Angelo. *The Subway.* Two-color woodblock print, 1952; 13½" x 10".

Valenti Angelo (b. Massarosa, Tuscany, 1897; d. San Francisco, 1982) was an engraver, printmaker, illustrator and graphic artist. He decorated or illustrated about 250 books during his career, including a series that he wrote for the Viking Press, the first one of which, *Nino*, was a Newbery Honor children's book in 1939. In 1976, the Book Club of California, in San Francisco, published a handsome volume of his work (part of my collection), *Valenti Angelo: Author, Illustrator, Printer.*

1. Giuseppe Prezzolini, *I trapiantati* [The uprooted]. Milano: Longanesi, 1963 (item 669, p. 238).

2. Franca Bernabei, "Little Italy's Eugène Sue: The Novels of Bernardino Ciambelli," in Boelhower and Pallone, eds. *Adjusting Sites. New Essays in Italian American Studies*, Forum Italicum - Fililibrary Series, no. 16, 1999 (item 766).

3. Martino Marazzi, *Voices of Italian America*. Madison: Fairleigh Dickinson University Press, 2005 (item 499, p. 65).

4. Menotti Pellegrino, *I misteri di New York*. New York: Tipografia Italiana Unione De Luca & Benedetti, 1903 (item 189, p. 5).

5. *Time*, December 7, 1925.

6. Marazzi, *Voices of Italian America*, (item 499, p. 32).

7. *The Anarchist's Cookbook*, a bomb-making manual published in 1971, may be considered a kind of homage to Galleani's work.

8. Marazzi, *Voices of Italian America* (item 499, p. 131).

9. Leonard Covello, *The Social Background of the Italo-American School Child*. Leiden, Neth.: E. J. Brill, 1967 (item 520).

10. "Pane al pane e vino al vino," *Corriere della Sera*, March 30, 1941, reprinted in *Scrittori inglesi e americani*, vol. 2 (Milan: il Saggiatore, 1968), p. 330.

11. Michael Miller Topp, *Those Without a Country: The Political Culture of Italian American Syndicalists*. Minneapolis: University of Minnesota Press, 2001 (item 505, pp. 160-161).

12. *Alba Nova* (New Dawn), October/November 1921, p. 4.

13. Gary R. Mormino and George E. Pozzetta, *The Immigrant World of Ybor City: Italians and Their Latin Neighbors in Tampa, 1885–1985*. Urbana: University of Illinois Press, 1987, p. 215.

14. Arturo Caroti, *Per Carlo Tresca* (Milan, 1916), p. 28.

15. Eastman, "Profiles - Troublemaker I." *The New Yorker*, September 15, 1934, p. 31.

16. "Profiles - Troublemaker II." *The New Yorker*, September 22, 1934, p. 27.

17. Eastman, "Profiles," September 15, 1934, p. 31.

18. Carlo Tresca, *The Autobiography of Carlo Tresca* (ed. Nunzio Pernicone). New York: John J. Calandra Italian American Institute, 2003 (item 433 at p. 68).

19. *Il Progresso*, February 10, 1956.

20. *Divagando*, September 16, 1953, p. 26.

21. Mussolini, *John Huss the Veracious*. New York: Italian Book Company, 1939 (cat. 138, p. 8, "Publisher's Preface").

Bibliography

ITALIAN-LANGUAGE AMERICAN IMPRINTS

(1830-1945) AND RELATED WORKS

INTRODUCTION

The scope of this bibliography is generally described in its title. Readers looking for a particular Italian-language author should refer to both parts of Section I. While the distinction between political and creative writing is generally useful, some of the most important writers cannot be easily classified as exclusively belonging to one category or the other (*e.g.*, Pallavicini, Caminita, Cordiferro). Secondary works are classified according to subject matter or, in a few selected cases, by the name of a key author, for easy reference for readers who wish to locate quickly secondary materials on specific writers.

For primary works, this bibliography is comprehensive. The starting point was the bibliography prepared by Francesco Durante ("Durante") (see especially volume 2 of *Italoamericana* (2005) (item 474)), much of which was used prior to its publication in 2005, with permission, in my first bibliography (Gardaphé-Periconi (2000) (item 481)). Since 2005, I have supplemented Durante's groundbreaking achievement with works that I have acquired copies of, or reviewed in libraries (especially the New York Public Library, which is particularly rich in this material) and on-line catalogues of the holdings of American and Italian libraries, works not available to Durante at the time of the preparation of his bibliography. For secondary works, this bibliography does not purport to be complete, especially as to recent scholarly articles or Ph.D theses in general. The term "and related works" includes, as in the exhibition, some primary (as well as many secondary) works issued outside the U.S. by Italian publishers.

Key to reference notations and symbols:

> *Cat.*: catalogue number of the work in the exhibition catalogue portion of this work
>
> item no.: cross reference to another entry in this bibliography
>
> +: in the Periconi collection

I. PRIMARY WORKS

A ✦ IMAGINATIVE AND OTHER WORKS: POETRY, FICTION, HISTORY AND BIOGRAPHY

1. Altavilla, Corrado. *Gente lontana*. Milano: Edizioni Medici Domus, 1938. *Cat. 73.*

2. Anonymous. *In memoria della Rev[erendissi]ma Francesca Saverio Cabrini: fondatrice e Superiora Generale delle missionarie del S. Cuore del Gesù, volata al cielo in Chicago il 22 Dicembre 1917.* New York: A. Bernasconi, 1918, xvi, 463 pp.; Roma: Scuola Tipografia Salesiana, 1918, xvi, 381 pp. *Cat. 43.*

3. Aquilano, Baldo. *L'Ordine Figli d'Italia in America.* New York: Società Tipografica Italiana, 1925. *Cat. 37.*

4. Arbib-Costa, Alfonso. *Advanced Italian Lessons.* New York: Italian Book Company, 1914. *Cat. 7.*

5. ———. *Italian Lessons.* New York: Italian Book Company, 1914. *Cat. 6.*

6. ———. *Lezione graduate di lingua inglese.* New York: Francesco Tocci, 1906. *Cat. 5.*

7. Bachi, Pietro. *A Grammar of the Italian Language.* Boston: Charles C. Little and James Brown, 1838. Simultaneously published in London by Richard James Kennett. *Cat. 4.*

8. Baucia, Camillo. *I miei ragli. Raccolta di sonnetti.* New York: Nicoletti Bros., 1909. *Cat. 15.*

9. Bello, Franco. *Casanova: Memorie d'avventure amorose.* New York: Italian Book Company, 1944. *Cat. 137.*

10. Bello, Vincenzo. *Rose e spine. Versi.* New York: Bagnasco Press, [n.d.].

11. Bernardy, Amy A. *America vissuta.* Torino: Fratelli Bocca, 1911. *Cat. 69.*

12. ———. "Attraverso la 'Piccola Italia' di Boston." In *Gli Italiani negli Stati Uniti d'America* (1906), 167-174 (item 164).

13. ———. "Contributi italiani alla formazione degli Stati Uniti d'America." *Il Giornale di Politica e Letteratura* (Roma) 18 (January-February 1942): 20-39.

14. ———. "Emigrazione di lungo corso." *La Lega Navale* (June 1907).

15. ———. *Italia randagia attraverso gli Stati Uniti.* Torino: Fratelli Bocca, 1913.+

16. ———. *Paese che vai. Il mondo come l'ho visto io.* Firenze: Le Monnier, 1923.

17. ———. "Perché gli italiani si addensano nelle città americane." In Sheridan,

Gl'italiani negli Stati Uniti (1909), 33-40 (item 574).

18.   Bosi, Alfredo. *Cinquant'anni di vita italiana in America*. New York: Bagnasco Press, 1921. *Cat. 32*.

19.   Branchi, Eugenio Camillo. *Così parlò Mister Nature. Fatti e impressioni di un italiano in America*. Bologna: Licinio Cappelli, 1953.+

20.   ———. "Dagoes." In *Novelle Transatlantiche*. Bologna: Licinio Cappelli, 1927.

21.   ———. "Hold Up!" *Il Carroccio* 24, no. 8 (August 1926).+

22.   ———."L'opera del fiorentino Carlo Bellini." *La Nazione* (Firenze) (July 26, 1928).

23.   ———. *Il primato degli italiani nella storia e nella civiltà americana*. Bologna: Licino Cappelli, 1924.

24.   ———. "Sarete mia, Laura." *Il Carroccio* 23, no. 1 (January 1926).

25.   Buel, Elizabeth C. Barney. *Manuale degli Stati Uniti: Istruzione ad uso degli immigranti e stranieri*. Wash., D.C.: Società Nazione Figlie della Rivoluzione Americana/National Society, Daughters of the American Revolution, 1930. *Cat. 146*.

26.   Cadicamo, Giuseppe. *Canidio. Scena romana*. Corigliano Calabro: Tipografia Letteraria, 1886.

27.   ———. *I Daitjas. Poemetto novo*. Corigliano Calabro: Tipografia Letteraria, 1885. Second edition: Roma: Tipografia Centenari, 1886.

28.   ———. *Davidica. Nova lirica*. New York: Emporium Press, 1910.

29.   ———. *Davvero è morta? Ode patriottica*. Milano: Fratelli Treves, 1877.

30.   ———. *Dèlia, romanza orientale*. Milano: Fratelli Treves, 1875.

31.   ———."A Giuseppe Giacosa." *L'Eco d'Italia* (November 8, 1891).

32.   ———. *Mascah e Marsiglia. Io triumphe!* Milano: Fratelli Treves, 1881.

33.   ———. *Natura ed arte (da* Les feuilles d'automne *di V. Hugo). Versione a fantasia libera. Versi*. Corigliano Calabro: Tipografia Letteraria, 1886.

34.   ———. *La necropoli monumentale di Sibari scoperta dall'ingegnere Cav. Saverio Cavallari. Impressioni e studii*. Milano: Tipografia Letteraria, 1879.

35.   ———. *Rosmunda*. New York: Nicoletti Bros., 1915.

36.   ———. *Tennysoniae: "Nothing will die," "All things will die," Versione libera*. New York: Francesco Tocci, 1909. *Cat. 16*.

37.   ———. *Visione epitalamica*. New York: Emporium Press, 1906.

38.   ———. *Il voto d'una derelitta. Storia bulgara*. Milano: Fratelli Treves, 1877.

39. Calitri, Antonio. *Canti del Nord-America.* Roma: Alberto Stock, 1925.

40. Carnovale, Luigi. *Esortazione ai direttori dei giornali italo-americani, a gli emigrati italiani tutti, per commemorare degnamente negli Stati Uniti d'America il sesto centenario della morte di Dante.* Chicago: [n.p.], 1921.

41. ———. *Il giornalismo degli emigrati italiani nel Nord America.* Chicago: Casa Editrice del giornale "L'Italia," 1909. *Cat. 63.*

42. ———. *Il secentenario dantesco 1321–1921 negli Stati Uniti d'America suprema purissima gloriosa imperitura affermazione di italianità intellettuale spirituale morale.* Chicago: Blakely-Oswald Printing Co., 1924.

43. ———. *Soltanto l'eliminazione della neutralità potrà subito e per sempre impedire le guerre.* Chicago: Italian-American Publishing Co., 1920.+

44. ———. *Il supremo ideale umano raggiunto.* Chicago: [n.p.], 1926+

45. Carr, John Foster. *Guida degli Stati Uniti per l'immigrante italiano.* Garden City: Doubleday, Page & Co., 1910. *Cat. 144a.*

46. ———. *Guide to the United States for the Immigrant Italian.* Garden City: Doubleday, Page & Co., 1911. *Cat. 144b.*

47. Caruso, Enrico. *Caricatures in four parts / Caricature in quattro parti.* New York: La Follia di New York, 1908. *Cat. 30.*

48. Cavallaro, Luigi. *Pionieri ed eroi della storia americana.* New York: Frugone, Balletto & Pellegatti, 1907. *Cat. 31.*

49. Cecchi, Emilio. *America amara.* Firenze: G. C. Sansoni, 1940. *Cat. 75.*

50. Cennerazzo, Armando. *'A cirinara: Monologo drammatico siciliano.* New York: V. Foti, [1924?].

51. ———. *La canzona della Madonna, dramma.* New York: A. Cennerazzo Prod., 1936.

52. ———. *I figli abbandonati, di Francesco Mastriani.* New York: Eloquent Press, 1934.

53. ———. *Odio e vendetta: Scene napoletane in un atto.* New York: Commercial Printing Co., 1914.

54. ———. *Poesie napoletane. Volume primo.* Napoli: Ciro Russo, 1949. *Cat. 77.*

55. ———. *Rose rosse e rose gialle: Nuove poesie napoletane.* Napoli: A. Guida, 1957.

56. ———. *Senza mamma – Senza perdono (seguito a "Senza mamma") – Povera canzona. Tre lavori drammatici ricavati dalle canzoni omonime di Francesco Pennino.* New York: Francesco Pennino – Italian Book Company, 1931.

57. Cennerazzo, Armando and G. Vitrone. *Rapitori di fanciulli, ovvero La mano nera. scene coloniali in un atto.* Manuscript dated 1912. In the Biblioteca Lucchesi Palli, Cennerazzo Collection, Napoli.

58. Ciambelli, Bernardino. "L'Aeroplano Fantasma. Romanzo contemporaneo." *La Follia di New York* (September 24, 1911 and thereafter). In parts.

59. ———. *Amore, lussuria e morte, ovvero Il processo di Antonio Bianco.* New York: Frugone & Balletto, 1894.

60. ———. "L'arcibanchettone." *La Follia di New York* (February 19, 1911).

61. ———. *La bella Biellese, ovvero Il mistero di Columbus Avenue.* New York: Frugone & Balletto, 1894.

62. ———. "La città nera ovvero I misteri di Chicago." *L'Italia–Giornale del Popolo* (Chicago) (July 15, 1893 and thereafter). Published in parts (never completed).

63 ———. "Columbus Day." In *Gli Italiani negli Stati Uniti d'America* (1906), 153-155 (item 164). *Cat. 50.*

64. ———. *I delitti dei bosses (cosidetti padroni).* New York: Frugone & Balletto, 1895.

65. ———. "Il delitto di Coney Island, ovvero La vendetta della zingara." *La Follia di New York* (1906-8). In parts.

66. ———. *I drammi dell'emigrazione, seguito ai Misteri.* New York: Frugone & Balletto,1893.

67. ———. *Fiori d'arancio, o La moglie del barbiere.* New York: Frugone & Balletto, 1893.

68. ———. *Il martire del dovere, ovvero Giuseppe Petrosino. Dramma in quattro atti.* Napoli: Pironti, 2009.

69. ———. *I misteri della polizia di New York. Il delitto di Water Street.* New York: Frugone & Balletto, 1895.

70. ———. *I misteri di Bleecker Street.* New York: Frugone & Balletto, 1899.

71. ———. "I misteri di Harlem, ovvero La bella di Elizabeth Street." *La Follia di New York* (January 16, 1910 to September 17, 1911). In 89 parts.

72. ———. *I misteri di Mulberry.* New York: Frugone & Balletto, 1893.

73. ———. "Il Natale di Caino." *La Follia di New York* (December 19, 1926).

74. ———. "Il Natale di Abele e quello di Caino." *La Follia di New York* (December 18, 1927).

75. ———. "Il Natale di un eroe." *La Follia di New York* (December 23, 1928).

76. ———. *I sotterranei di New York.* New York: Società Libraria Italiana, 1915. *Cat. 135a.*

77. ———. "La Strage degli Innocenti, ossia I delitti di un medico." *La Follia di New York* (August 20, 1908–October 31, 1909). In 57 parts.

78. ———. *Il terremoto in Sicilia e Calabria*. New York: Florence Publishing Co., 1909.

79. ———. *La trovatella di Mulberry Street, ovvero La stella dei Cinque Punti.* New York: Società Libraria Italiana, 1919. *Cat. 10.*

80. ———. *I viaggi*. New York: Società Libraria Italiana, 1915.

81. ———. *World's Fare, ovvero Suicidio con l'elettricità.* New York: Frugone & Balletto, 1893.

82. Cianfarra, Camillo. "Arti e Mestieri." In *Gli Italiani negli Stati Uniti d'America* (1906), 73–78 (item 164).

83. ———. *Il diario di un emigrato*. New York: Tipografia dell' Araldo Italiano, 1904.

84. ———. "Le Industrie." In *Gli Italiani negli Stati Uniti d'America* (1906), 67–72 (item 164).

85. Collins, Professor E. C., M.D. *Guida alla salute: Il come prevenire le malattie, come curarle, come riguadagnare la salute, estesa descrizione delle cause, sintomi, e trattamento di tutte le malattie del corpo umano con un capitolo sul matrimonio e la vita sessuale.* New York: E. C. Collins / New York Medical Institute, 1904. *Cat. 47.*

86. Cordiferro, Riccardo [Alessandro Sisca]. *A Giacomo Leopardi: Per il centenario della sua morte.* New York: Scipio di Dario, 1938.

87. ———. *Canzone d'a guerra*. New York: Società Libraria Italiana, 1917.

88. ———. *Ermete novelli*. New York: Manhattan Printing Co., 1919.

89. ———. *Gabriele D'Annunzio nella vita e nell'arte.* New York: Cocce Bros., 1938. *Cat. 41*

90. ———. *Giuseppina Terranova, ovvero L'onore vendicato, dramma in quattro atti.* New York: Nicoletti Bros., [1906].

91. ———. *Mater Doloroso, dramma in un atto.* Brooklyn: Union Press, 1933.

92. ———. *'O ritorno d'a guerra, dramma napoletano in un atto.* New York: La Follia di New York, 1928.

93. ———. *Ode alla Calabria*. Buenos Aires: La Voce dei Calabresi, 1933. *Cat. 72.*

94. ———. *L'onore perduto*. New York: [n.p.], 1901.

95. ———. *Il pezzente. Monologo in versi.* New York: Coccè Bros., 1895.

96. ———. *Il poema dell'amore, liriche.* [N.p.]: [n.p.], 1928.

97. ———. *Poesie scelte.* Campobasso: Edizioni Pungolo Verde, 1967.

98. ———. *Il prete attraverso la storia.* Barre, Vt.: Circolo di Studi Sociali, 1915.

99. ———. *Il prisco cavaliere.* Brooklyn: F. Sparacino, [*ca.* 1924]. *Cat. 22b.*

100. ———. *Scugnizzo. Poemetto napoletano.* New York: Coccè Press, 1924.

101. ———. *Singhiozzi e sogghigni.* New York: L'Araldo Italiano, 1910.

102. ———. *Gli stornelli della guerra.* New York: Società Libraria Italiana, 1917.

103. ———. *La vendetta. Lirica in versi liberi.* New York: La Follia di New York, [*ca.* 1933]. *Cat. 22a.*

104. ——— and Giuseppe Valvo. *Brindisi ed augurii per ogni occasione.* New York: Società Libraria Italiana, 1917. *Cat. 45–46.*

105. Crespi, Cesare. *Fascismo, masnadieri antichi e moderni.* San Francisco: [n.p.], 1943.+

106. ———. *In attesa della pace.* [Cal.]: [n.p.], 1946.

107. ———. *Per intenderci meglio.* San Francisco: The Author, 1947.

108. ———. *Per la libertà! (dalle mie conversazione col conte Carlo di Rudio, complice de Felice Orsini).* San Francisco: Canessa Print Co., 1913.

109. ———. *San Francisco e la sua catastrofe.* San Francisco: Tipografia Internationale, 1906. *Cat. 62.*

110. ———. *La stirpe martoriata. Spigolature storiche e brevi commenti.* San Francisco: Lanson & Garfinkel, 1944.

111. ———. *Il tallone di ferro.* San Francisco: Gene's Print Shop, 1939.+

112. ———. *Tempra italiana, dramma in quattro atti.* San Francisco: Tipografia Lanson & Lauray, [1912?].

113. Da Ponte, Lorenzo. *Memorie di Lorenzo Da Ponte da Ceneda in tre volume. Scritte da esso. Seconda edizione corretta, ampliata e accresciuta d'un intero volume.* New York: Pubblicate dall'autore, Gray & Bunce, 1829 (vol. 1); Pubblicate da Lorenzo Da Ponte, G. F. Bunce, Stampatori, 1829 (vol. 2); John H. Turney, Stampatori, 1830 (vol. 3).

114. ———. *Poesie varie di Lorenza* [sic] *da Ponte.* New York: Pubblicate dall'autore, 1830. Second edition. *Cat. 1.*

115. ———. *Storia compendiosa della vita di Lorenzo Da Ponte.* New York: I. Riley, 1807.

116. ———. *Storia della lingua e letteratura Italiana in New-York.* New York: Gray e Bunce Stampatori, 1827.

117. De Gaudenzi, Angelo. *Nuovissima grammatica accelerata: Italiana-inglese ed enciclopedia popolare con pronunzia. Divisa in 11 parti.* New York: Italian Book Company, [ca. 1944]. *Cat. 9.*

118. De Martino, A[ntonio]. *Tripoli italiana: La guerra italo-turca. Le nostre prime vittorie.* New York: Società Libraria Italiana, 1911. *Cat. 136.*

119. De Martino, Antonio and Umberto Fragasso. *Il libro delle erbe: Medicinali e magiche di A. De Martino e Umberto Fragasso, compilato su varie opera di botanica medica.* New York: Italian Book Company, 1946. *Cat. 140.*

120. De Rosalia, Giovanni. *Il duello di Nofrio. Farsa.* New York: Italian Book Company, 1918.

121. ———. *Nofrio ai bagni. Farsa.* New York: Italian Book Company, 1918.

122. ———. *Nofrio al telefono. Farsa.* New York: Italian Book Company, 1918.

123. ———. *Nofrio in pericolo. Farsa.* New York: Italian Book Company, 1918.

124. ———. *Lu socialisimu e lu ciarlatanu. Scherzi poetici.* New York: Società Libraria Italiana, [1916].

125. Del Giudice, Giuseppe. *Canti della sorgente. Italiam laeto clamore salutant.* New York: Bronx Standard Press, 1928; Torino, Roma: M. E. Marinetti, 1928.

126. Di Vita, Rosario. *Chiantu di Galiota: Sceneggiata siciliana in 3 parti.* New York: V. Grassi & Co., 1925.

127. ———. "Corruzioni di vocaboli inglesi sicilianizzati." *Rivista Italiana di Letteratura Dialettale*, Year III, no. 3 (1931).

128. ———. *Fiori d'oltremare.* Milano: Edizioni Siculorum Gymnasium, 1934.

129. ———. *Matri; esito del consorso — poetico siciliano d'America sotto gli auspici del Po'T' 'U Cuntu: New York, N.Y.: febbraio 1932.* Palermo: Po' T' 'U Cuntu, 1932.

130. ———. *I nostri fiori alla patria.* New York: Società Tipografica Italiana, 1924. *Cat. 130.*

131. ———. *Perle azzurre.* Genova: Milanta, 1922.

132. ———. *Prime stille.* New York: Società Tipografica Italiana, 1915.

133. ———. *Scenette umoristiche e drammatiche.* New York: Tipografia V. Grassi & Co., 1926.

134. ———. *Vuci d'oltrimari.* Milano: Edizioni Siculorum Gymnasium, 1934.

135. Duchessa X. *L'Assassinio della Contessa Trigona.* New York: Italian Book Company, 1944. *Cat. 143a.*

136. Ferrazzano, Tony. "'Na Serenata llaica helle!..." In *Raccolta di canzoni – Macchiette e duetti coloniali.* New York: Società Libraria Italiana, 1911.

137. ———. *Nuove canzoni popolari sulla guerra italo-turca e su Trento e Trieste*. New York: Società Libraria Italiana, 1911.

138. ———. *Nuove canzoni sulla guerra italo-austriaca*. New York: Società Libraria Italiana, 1916.

139. ———. *Poesie umoristiche sulla guerra fra l'Italia e l'Austria*. New York: Società Libraria Italiana, 1915.

140. Fiaschetti, Michele. "Caccia grossa." *Corriere d'America* (New York) (January 19-31, 1926).

141. ———. "Le due sorelle." Retitled "La prova del fuoco." *Corriere d'America* (New York) (February 19-27, 1926).

142. ———. *Gioco duro* (ed. Martino Marazzi). Cava de' Tirreni: Avagliano, 2003.+

143. ———. "La lotteria della morte." *Corriere d'America* (New York) (March 6, 1926).

144. ———. *The Man They Couldn't Escape: The Adventures of Detective Fiaschetti of the Italian Squad as Told to Prosper Buranelli by Michael Fiaschetti*. London: Selwyn & Blount, 1928, reprinted as: *You Gotta Be Rough: The Adventures of Detective Fiaschetti of the Italian Squad as Told to Prosper Buranelli by Michael Fiaschetti*. Garden City: Doubleday, Doran & Co., 1930; New York: A. L. Burt, 1930.+

145. ———. "Il mistero della perla." *Corriere d'America* (New York) (March 14-?, 1926).

146. ———. "La scomparsa del sepolto." *Corriere d'America* (New York) (March 12-16, 1926).

147. ———. "Le spie e i confidenti." *Corriere d'America* (New York) (May 5-June 14, 1926).

148. ———. "Le tre veglie." *Corriere d'America* (New York) (February 10, 1926).

149. Flamma, Ario. *Dramas*. New York: Ario Flamma, 1909.+

150. ———. *Fiamme: Dramma in un atto. Memorie di un suicida*. New York: Ario Flamma, 1911. *Cat. 25*.

151. ———. *Fiorello La Guardia*. New York: Worthy Printing, 1934. *Cat. 38*.

152. ———. *Flames and Other Plays*. New York: Stage Publishing Co., 1928.+

153. ———. *Foglie nel turbine, commedia in tre atti – Don Luca Sperante, dramma in un atto*. Wilkes-Barre: Modern Publishing Co., 1923.

154. ———. *Italiani di America: Enciclopedia biografica*. New York: Casa Editrice Cocce Bros., 1936. *Cat. 39*.

155. ———. *Italiani di America: Enciclopedia biografica*, Volume II. New York: Casa Editrice S. F. Vanni, 1941.

156. ———. *Italiani di America: Enciclopedia biografica*, Volume III. New York: Coccè Press, 1949.+

157. ———. *Piccole anime, dramma in tre atti*. New York: Italian Press Publishing Association, 1912.

158. Fontana, Ferdinando. "Dario Papa." *Il Progresso Italo-Americano* (New York) (January 19, 1882).

159. Fusco, Nicola. *Le variazioni*. New York: Il Carroccio Publishing Co., 1916. *Cat. 19*.

160. Gentile, Maria. *The Italian Cook Book: The Art of Eating Well*. New York: Italian Book Company, 1919.+

161. Giacometti, Paolo. *Cristoforo Colombo alla scoperta dell'America*. New York: Società Libraria Italiana/Teatro Italiano, [n.d.].

162. Hapgood, Hutchins. "The Foreign Stage in New York: III The Italian Theatre." *The Bookman* 11 (August 1900): 545-553.

163. Italian American Directory Co. *1905 Italian American Directory: Guida generale per il commercio Italo Americano / General guide for the Italian American trade*. New York: Italian American Directory Co., 1905. *Cat. 49*.

164. Italian American Directory Co. *Gli italiani negli Stati Uniti d'America*. New York: Italian American Directory Co., 1906. *Cat. 50*

165. Lalli, Franco. *Fireflies*. Translated by Giulietta Talamini. New York: E. P. Dutton & Co., 1925.+

166. ———. *La prima santa d'America*. Brooklyn: Fortuna Publishing Co., 1944. *Cat. 44*.

167. Lisanti, Gaetano F. *Dizionario moderno italiano-inglese*. New York: Società Libraria Italiana, 1916.

168. Livingston, Arthur. "La Merica Sanemagogna." *The Romanic Review* 9, no. 2 (April-June 1918): 206-226.

169. Longfellow, Henry Wadsworth. Da H[enry] W[adsworth] Longfellow. *Saggi de novellieri Italiani d'ogni secolo, tratti dà più celebri scrittori, con brevi notizie intorno alla vita di ciascheduno*. Boston: Presso Grey e Bowen, 1832. *Cat. 3*.

170. Marinoni, Antonio. *An Elementary Grammar of the Italian Language*. New York: W. R. Jenkins Co., 1911.

171. ———. *An Italian Reader*. Philadelphia: David McKay/Brentano's, 1923.

172. Mennella, Federico. *Le canzonei de l'ora*. New York: Edizioni Sirena, 1945.+

173. ———. *Napule d'Aiere*. New York: Cocce Press, 1944.+

174.   ———. *Partenopea. Poesie napoletana.* Napoli: Ciro Russo, [1945].

175.   ———. *Rapsodia napoletana.* New York: Cocce Press, 1944. *Cat. 23.*

176.   Migliaccio, Eduardo (Farfariello). "Bacilogia." *La Follia di New York* (April 14, 1945). Short story.

177.   ———. "Il Bacio di Mezzanotte." *La Follia di New York* (February 1, 1945). Short story.

178.   ———. "Don Leopoldo. Annunziatore radiofonico, chiaroveggente, grafologo, astrologo, e altre sciocchezze." *La Follia di New York* (January 15, 1946). Short story.

179.   ———. "Padre Taliano." *Il Carroccio* (New York) 16, no. 2 (August 1922): 220-223.

180.   Molinari, Giovanni. *Raccolta di discorsi per ogni occasione.* New York: Società Libraria Italiana, 1917. *Cat. 45-46.*

181.   Mortara, Vincenzo. *Amore e fede, commedia in 4 atti.* New York: Nicoletti Bros., 1911.

182.   ———. *Momento fatale! Dramma in 4 atti.* New York: Nicoletti Bros., 1914.

183.   Mussolini, Benito. *John Huss the Veracious.* New York: Italian Book Company, 1939. *Cat. 138.*

184.   Novasio, Pietro, Franco Lalli and Elisa Odabella. *La strada della gioia.* New York: Liberal Press, 1946. *Cat. 48.*

185.   Pallavicini, Paolo. *L'amante delle tre croci. Romanzo. Seguito a "Per le vie del mondo."* San Francisco: L'Italia Press Co., 1923.

186.   ———. *La carezza divina.* Milano: Sonzogno, 1939.

187.   ———. *La casa del peccato. Dramma in tre atti.* San Francisco: L'Italia Press Co., 1931. Translated by Nino Ghio as *The House of Sin*; typescript in San Francisco Public Library.

188.   ———. *La figlia de Nennè. Dramma in quatro atti.* New York: Italian Press Publ. Assoc., 1914.

189.   ———. *La guerra italo-austriaca (1915-1919).* New York: Società Libraria Italiana, 1919. *Cat. 42.*

190.   ———. *Lascia che piova. Commedia in tre atti*, 1929. Manuscript in San Francisco Public Library.

191.   ———. *Nella terra del sogno. Radiodramma in 24 episodi.* San Francisco: L'Italia Press Co., [1933?].

192.   ———. *Nix, il figlio dell'austriaco.* New York: Società Libraria Italiana - Italian Book Company, 1920.

193. ———. *Per le vie del mondo.* Milano: Sonzogno, 1933. *Cat. 70.*

194. ———. *Quando Berta filava. Romanzo.* San Francisco: L'Italia Press Co., 1923.

195. ———. *Tutto il dolore, tutto l'amore: Romanzo d'ambiente italo-americano.* L'Italia Press Co., 1926. *Cat. 61.*

196. ———. *Il ventaglio di Aquileia.* Firenze: Salani, 1917.

197. Pane, Michele. *Le poesie* (eds. Giuseppe Falcone and Antonio Piromalli). Soveria Mannelli: Rubbettino, 1987.

198. Papa, Dario. *La donna in America e la donna in Italia.* Milano: Aliprandi, 1895.

199. ———. *Il giornalismo. Rivista estera ed italiana.* Verona: Franchini, 1880.

200. Papa, Dario and Ferdinando Fontana. *New-York.* Milano: Giuseppe Galli, 1884. *Cat. 67.*

201. Pecorini, Alberto. *Grammatica-encyclopedia italiana-inglese.* New York: Nicoletti Bros., 1911. *Cat. 8.*

202. Pellegrino, Menotti. *I misteri di New York.* New York: Tipografia Italiana U. De Luca & Benedetti, 1903.

203. ———. *I tre cavalieri di Trinacria.* New York: Menotti Pellegrino, 1929. *Cat. 11.*

204. Picchianti, Silvio. *La madre triestina. Dramma in un atto. Episodio tragico della guerra europea.* New York: Frugone, Balletto and Pellegatti, 1908.

205. ———. *La "Montanina." Melodramma in 3 atti. Musica di Salvatore Iodice.* [*ca.* 1930s]. Spiralbound typescript. *Cat. 26*

206. ———. *Nostalgie. Versi.* Chicago: Galbraith Press, 1908.

207. ———. *Ombre russe: Melodramma in 4 atti e 4 sceni.* New York: E. F. Kalmus, 1929.

208. ———. *Le trecce d'Isabella. Dramma in un atto. Episodio tragico della invasion austriaca in Italia.* New York: Società Libraria Italiana, 1919.

209. ———. *Tribunali domestici.* Napoli: Biblioteca Lucchesi Palli, Raccolta Cennerazzo, C566, [n.d.].

210. ———. *L'zio d'America.* [N.p.]: [n.p.], [n.d.].

211. Piesco, Saverio. *Il rosso bagliore d'Oriente ovvero "Rasputin." Dramma con prologo e tre atti.* [N.p.]: [n.p.], 1920.

212. Preziosi, Giovanni. *Gl'italiani negli Stati Uniti del Nord.* Milano: Libreria Editrice Milanese, 1909.

213. Pucelli, Rodolfo. *L'addio dell'emigrante (Polimetri in cinque lingue con prefazione in latino dell'autore).* Trieste: [n.p.], 1928.

214.   ———. *Anthology of Italian and Italo-American Poetry*. Boston: Bruce Humphries, 1954.

215.   ———. *Canti all'aria aperta*. Trieste: Susmel Co., 1921.

216.   ———. *Canti d'oltreoceano*. New York: Edizione A. Nicoletti, 1938.

217.   ———. *La canzone d'Aquileia*. Isola d'Istria: [n.p.], 1918.

218.   ——— (trans.). *Comments by Italian Writers on the "New Universal Order," Commenti di Scrittori italiani sul "Nuovo Ordine Universale."* New York: Coccè Press, 1950.+

219.   ———. *Ellis Island (poemetto polimetrico)*. New York: [n.p.], 1928.

220.   ———. *Lungo il cammino*. Milano: Gastaldi Editore, 1950.

221.   ———. *Poesie vecchie e nuove*. New York: Creative Printing, V. Grassi, 1947.

222.   ———. *Sonetti biografici di italo-americani*. Milano: Gastaldi Editore, 1950.

223.   ———. *Verso i'ignoto (Liriche)*. Milano: Gastaldi Editore, 1955.

224.   Pucciu, Calicchiu [Calogero Puccio]. *Cusuzzi. Poesie siciliane in tre voll: I cusuzzi; II storia di 'na lira d'argentu; III Sturnetti siciliani*. Brooklyn: Tipografia Ed. F. Sparacino, 1922.

225.   ———. *Fogghi di Lauru. Centu ritratti d'omini illustri. Sonetti siciliani*. Preface by Rosario Ingargiola. Brooklyn: Tipografia Ed. F. Sparacino, 1923.

226.   ———. *La Pruittedda. Poema in dialettu sicilianu*. Brooklyn: Tipografia Ed. F. Sparacino, [n.d.].

227.   ———. *Rimasugghi*. Brooklyn: Tipografia Ed. F. Sparacino, [1925].

228.   ———. *Lu sonnu di Monsignuri X: Poimettu in lingua siciliana*. Brooklyn: Tipografia Italiana del Rinascimento, 1912. *Cat. 17*.

229.   ———. *Triateuco: Poesie siciliane*. New York: Gutenberg Printery, 1909.

230.   Ricciardi, Francesco. *La distruzione dei Cristiani in Cina, con Pulcinella impalato vivo e lottatore con un orso e un orangtane. Commedia in quattro atti*. Manuscript in the Biblioteca Lucchesi Palli, Raccolta Cennerazzo, Napoli, C14, 1902.

231.   ———. *Pulcinella condannato alla sedia elettrica. Commedia in tre atti*. Manuscript in the Biblioteca Lucchesi Palli, Raccolta Cennerazzo, Napoli, C12, [1898?].

232.   ———. *Pulecenella a Nuova York, ovvero Nu buordo puosto a rummore da Pulecenella e da n'americano. Commedia in tre atti*. Manuscript in the Biblioteca Lucchesi Palli, Raccolta Cennerazzo, Napoli, C31, [n.d.].

233.   Rosati, Angelo. *Parole, parole, parole...!* Hazleton, Pa.: Union Printing Co., 1925.

234. Rossi, Adolfo. *Un italiano in America*. Milano: Fratelli Treves, 1892. New edition (Milano: Casa Editrice La Cisalpina, 1899). *Cat. 68*.

235. ———. "La mano d'opera Italiana negli Stati Unitei." In *Gli italiani negli Stati Uniti d'America* (1906), 18-26 (item 164).

236. ———. *Nel paese dei dollari (tre anni a New York)*. In appendice: *Alberto Mario a New York*. Milano: Max Kantorowicz, 1893.

237. ———. "Per la tutela degli italiani negli Stati Uniti." *Bollettino dell'Emigrazione*, no. 16, (1904). Letter of Inspector Adolfo Rossi, written to the Commissioner's office for emigration in the course of his mission in the United States of (North) America.

238. Roversi, Luigi. *Luigi Palma di Cesnola e il Metropolitan Museum of Art di New York*. New York: Metropolitan Museum of Art, 1898. *Cat. 33a*.

239. ———. *Ricordi canavesani. Luigi Palma di Cesnola a Rivarolo Canavese e a Cesnola*. New York: [n.p.], 1901.

240. Ruotolo, Onorio. *Accordi e dissonanze*. Milano: Convivio Letterario, 1958.+

241. ———. *Convito d'amore (poemetto)*. New York: Casa Editrice La Lucerna, 1949.

242. ———. *Geremidade al bambino Gesu*. New York: Casa Editrice La Lucerna, 1948.

243. ———. *Il mio primo maestro (poemetto)*. New York: Casa Editrice La Lucerna, 1948.

244. ———. *Mother America*. New York: [n.p.], 1926.

245. ———. *Nel fuoco del rimorso*. New York: Casa Editrice La Lucerna, 1949.

246. Salvo, Carlo. *Ali vibranti*. New York: [n.p.], [n.d.].

247. ———. *Barbari e liberatori*. New York: Società Tipografica Italiana, 1917.

248. ———. *Fiamme alitur*. New York: Nicoletti Bros., 1916. *Cat. 18*.

249. ———. *Fiamme spente*. New York: Società Tipografica Italiana, [n.d.].

250. ———. *Ritmi*. New York: Helenson Press, 1948.

251. ———. *Lo sbarco di Marsala*. New York: Società Tipografica Italiana, [n.d.].

252. ———. *Trittico di gloria*. New York: Società Tipografica Italiana, [n.d.].

253. ———. *The Unknown Soldier*. Brooklyn: Union Press, 1939.

254. ———. *Verso l'America*. New York: Società Tipografica Italiana, [n.d.].

255. Seneca, Pasquale. *Il Presidente Scopetta, ovvero La Società della Madonna della Pace*. Philadelphia: [n.p.], 1927. *Cat. 66*.

256. Siciliani, Colonnello Domenico. *Fra gli italiani degli Stati Uniti D'America, luglio-settembre 1921*. Roma: Stabilimento Poligrafico per l'amministrazione della guerra, 1922.+

257. Sisca, Francesco. *Lu ciucciu. Poema in dialetto calabrese*. New York: Tipografia Sisca & Sons, 1913. *Cat. 21*.

258. St. John, Vincent. *L'I.W.W.: La sua storia, struttura e metodi*. Brooklyn: Laboratori Industriali del Mondo, [*ca.* 1919]. *Cat. 100*.

259. Stanco, Italo. "L'Amica del Kaiser." *La Follia di New York* (December 22, 1918–December 21, 1919).

260. ———. *Il diavolo biondo*. New York: Nicoletti Bros., 1916; using "J. Cansado," with the title *Lady Ryton, il diavolo biondo*). In episodes, *La Follia di New York* (1914).

261. ———. *Dopo la colpa*. New York: Fratelli Nicoletti, 1913.

262. ———. "Il nemico del bene." *La Follia di New York* (July 5, 1914–August 8, 1915).

263. ———. *La penna italiana. Paralipomeni*. Napoli: Stabilimento Tipografico degli Editori Fratelli Tornese, 1902.

264. ———. "Le piovre di New York." *Corriere d'America* (1925–1926), then in *La Follia di New York* (October 1, 1944–November 1, 1949).

265. ———. "Reginetta di fuoco." *Corriere d'America* (1931), then with the title "La Figlia del Dittatore" in *La Follia di New York* (November 15, 1949–March 1, 1953).

266. ———. "I rettili d'oro." *La Follia di New York* (September 26, 1915–December 9, 1917) (also appears in *Divagando* from July 2, 1952–July 22, 1953).

267. ———. "Sull'oceano." *La Follia di New York* (December 23, 1917–November 3, 1918).

268. ———. *Sull' oceano*. New York: Tipografia ed. L. Scarlino, 1921.

269. Cansado, J. [Italo Stanco]. "Il Re della Pampa." *La Follia di New York* (September 24, 1911).

270. Tarchiani, Alberto. "I disertori." *Il Cittadino-The Citizen* (New York) (September 25, 1915).

271. ———. "I disertori e il patrio governo." *Il Cittadino-The Citizen* (New York) (October 28, 1915).

272. ———. "La doppia cittadinanza." *Il Cittadino-The Citizen* (New York) (November 25, 1915).

273.   ———. "Gli imbelli, i bruti e i traditori." *Il Cittadino-The Citizen* (New York) (August 12, 1915).

274.   ———. "Né stranieri, né americani." *Il Cittadino-The Citizen* (New York) (December 9, 1915).

275.   Teresi, Matteo. *Con la patria nel cuore. La mia propaganda fra gli emigranti.* Palermo: D'Antoni, 1925. *Cat. 71.*

276.   ———. *Love and Health: The Problem of Better Breeding for the Human Family.* New York: Shakespeare Press, 1914.+

277.   ———. *Il sogno di un emigrato.* Rochester: Pioneer Print and Pub. Co., 1932.

278.   ———. *L'ultima menzogna religiosa - La democrazia cristiana.* Palermo: Tipografia Coop. Fra Gli Operai, 1905; New York: Luigi Florio Press, 1910.

279.   ——— and Dr. Salvatore S. Romano (trans.). *Love Lights the Way.* Cleveland: L'Araldo Publishing Co., 1948.+

280.   Varvaro, Pietro G. *Anima rerum.* Firenze: G. Barbèra, Ed., 1946.+

281.   ———. *S[an]. Giovanino.* New York: [n.p.], 1943. *Cat. 20.*

282.   Ventura, Luigi Donato. "Biographical Reminiscences." In Adelaide Ristori, *Memoirs and Artistic Studies.* New York: Doubleday, Page & Co., 1907.

283.   ———. "Christmas in Two Lands." *Overland Monthly and Out West Magazine* (San Francisco) 34, no. 204 (December 1899): 502-506.

284.   ———. *Coeur de Noel,* ill. by Mary G. Norris. San Francisco: Robertson, 1901.

285.   ———. "Mario." In *Stories Told For Revenue Only*, ed. John Joseph Conway. St. Paul: St. Paul Press Club, 1893.

286.   ———. "I negri d'America." *Cuore e Critica* Year III, no. 3, (February 20, 1889): 27-29.

287.   ———. "Peppino." In *Misfits and Remnants.* Boston: Ticknor & Co., 1886.

288.   ———. *Peppino.* New York: William R. Jenkins Co., 1889. In French.

289.   ———. *Peppino.* New York: William R. Jenkins Co., 1913. Reprinted in Sellers, *The Multilingual Anthology of American Literature* (2000) (item 669).

290.   ———. *Peppino, il lustrascarpe,* ed. M. Marazzi. Milano: FrancoAngeli, 2007. Original Italian text.+

291.   ———. "Una prefazione americana al 'Testa' di P. Mantegazza." *Cuore e Critica* Year II, no. 10 (September 1888): 151-153.

292.   ———. "Le scrittrici italiane giudicate in America." *Cuore e Critica* Year. II, no. 14 (November 1888): 217-220. Article reprinted from *The Chautauquan* of Meadville, Pennsylvania (July 1888).

293. Viola, Salvatore. *Il libro dei santi.* New York: Variety Bazaar & Italian Book, 1942. *Cat. 36.*

294. Zmrhal, J. J. *A Primer of Civics: English and Italian: Manuale di Cittadinanza designed for the guidance of the Immigrant.* Chicago: Illinois Society of the Colonial Dames of America, 1918. *Cat. 145.*

B ⊁ POLITICAL: ANARCHIST, SOCIALIST, SYNDICALIST, COMMUNIST, FASCIST AND ANTI-FASCIST

295. Agatodemon. *Dalla propaganda anticlericale alla propaganda antireligiosa.* Buffalo: Tipografia Cooperativa Italiana, 1909.

296. Anonymous. *Che cosa e L'I.W.W.?* Chicago: Industrial Workers of the World, 1923. *Cat. 97.*

297. ———. *Mussolineide: Poema antifascista e di rivendicazione sociale.* [N.p.]: [n.p.], [*ca.* 1930s]. *Cat. 108.*

298. ———. *I tre inni rossi.* West Hoboken: Clinton Printing Co., [n.d.].+

299. Barbato, Dr. N. *Scienza e fede.* Philadelphia: Social Printing Co., 1908.+

300. Bartoletti, Efrem. *Documenti e poesie* [cd-rom]. Costacciaro (Perugina), 1999.

301. ———. *Un' escursione all caverna di Monte Cucco.* Fabriano: Tipografia Economica, 1924.

302. ———. *Evocazioni e ricordi.* Bergamo: La Nuova Italia Letteraria, 1959.

303. ———. *Nel sogno d'oltretomba: antico libero.* Scranton: [n.p.], 1931.

304. ———. *Nostalgie proletarie. Raccolta di canti poetici e di inni rivoluzionari.* Brooklyn: Libreria Editrice dei Lavoratori Industriali del Mondo, 1919.

305. ———. *Poesie. Alla scoperta delle nostre radici storiche*, ed. Martino Marazzi. Costacciaro: Comune di Costacciaro, 2001.

306. ———. *Riflessioni poetiche.* Milano: Gastaldi Editore, 1955. *Cat. 76.*

307. Biblioteca del Circolo di Sociali. *All'anarchia: Si arriverà passando per lo stato socialista?* Barre, Vt.: Cronaca Sovversiva, 1905. *Cat. 95.*

308. Borghi, Armando. *Gli anarchici e le alleanze antifasciste.* New York: Circolo operaio di cultura sociale, 1927.+

309. ———. *Anarchismo e sindacalismo.* Roma: Stab. Pol. Ed. Romano, 1922.+

310. ———. *Il banchetto dei cancri (dopo Matteotti).* New York: Libreria Editrice dei Lavoratori Industriali del Mondo, 1925. *Cat. 79b.*

311. ———. *Conferma anarchica (due anni in Italia).* Forlì: L'Aurora, 1949.

312.   ———. *Due bozzetti contro il fascismo. Dante processato all'inferno. Italiani che ascoltano la radio dall'America.* Newark: Biblioteca de L'Adunata dei Refrattari, [1943].

313.   ———. *Errico Malatesta in 60 anni di lotte anarchiche. Storia – critica – ricordi.* New York: Edizioni Sociali, 1933. *Cat. 79a.*

314.   ———. *Errico Malatesta.* Milano: Istituto Editoriale Italiano, 1947.

315.   ———. *Fernand Pelloutier nel sindacalismo.* Bologna: Azzoguidi, 1913; Brooklyn: Libreria Editrice Lavoratori del Mondo, [n.d.].

316.   ———. *L'Italia tra due Crispi.* Paris: Libreria Internazionale, 1924.

317.   ———. *Mezzo secolo di anarchia (1898–1945).* Napoli: Edizioni Scientifiche Italiane, 1954.+

318.   ———. *Mischia sociale (da . . . alla Cooper Union), con due lettere introduttive di Errico Malatesta.* Brooklyn: Edizioni Sociali, 1931.

319.   ———. *Mussolini in camicia.* New York: Edizioni Libertarie, 1927. British ed.: *Mussolini Red and Black:* London: Wishart Books, 1935; *Mussolini Red and Black,* New York, Freie Arbeiter Stimme, 1938, trans. from French ed., *Mussolini en Chemise* [Paris: Rieder, 1932], by Dorothy Daudley; with an epilogue: *Hitler: Mussolini's Disciple.* Bologna: Mammolo Zamboni, 1947. *Cat. 56–60.*

320.   ———. *Il nostro e l'altrui individualismo.* Brisighella: [n.p.], 1907.

321.   ———. *La rivoluzione mancata.* Milano: Azione Comune, 1964.

322.   ———. *Il tramonto di Bacunin.* Newark: Biblioteca de l'Adunata dei Refrattari, 1939.

323.   ———. *Vivere da anarchici. Antologia di scritti,* ed. Vittorio Emiliani. Bologna: Alfa, 1966.

324.   Braida, Albino. *La società proletaria.* Brooklyn: Libreria Editrice dei Lavoratori Industriali del Mondo, [*ca.* 1910s].+

325.   ——— and Giovanni Baldazzi. *L'unionismo industriale.* Brooklyn: Italian I.W.W. Pub. Bureau, [*ca.* 1917].

326.   Buttis, Vittorio. *Carceri e domicilio coatto a cura del Comitato Veneziano per l'abolizione del domicilio coatto.* Venezia: Tondelli, 1897.

327.   ———. *Memorie di vita di tempeste sociali.* Chicago: Comitato "Vittorio Buttis," 1940. *Cat. 105.*

328.   Calvi, Giusto. *Dietro la maschera. Diario di Don Bruno.* Milano-Roma: Gastaldi Editore, 1949.

329.   ———. *Fanciullezza a Montefumo.* Castelluccio dei Sauri [Foggia]: Lampyris, 2006. With writings by Francesco Durante and Cosma Siani.

330. ———. *I senza patria. Note dal vero. Da New York a Napoli.* Valenza: L. Battezzati, 1901.

331. Calza, Gino. *Su la vena.* New York: Francesco Tocci, 1908.

332. Caminita, Ludovico. *Augusto Crovelli, romanzo.* New York: Stabilimento Tipografico Italia, 1927.

333. ———. *Che cosa è la religione.* Paterson: Libreria Sociologica; Chieti: Tipografia Ed. C. Di Sciullo, 1906.

334. ———. *I delinquenti.* Latrobe, Pa.: Editore Gruppo la demolizione, 1910.

335. ———. *Il diritto d'amare.* Philadephia: Social Printing Co., 1908.

336. ———. *L'educazione de' fanciulli; con una lettera del dott. O.D. Battendieri.* Philadelphia: Social Printing Co., 1908.

337. ———. *Free Country! Gli Stati Uniti sono un paese libero.* [N.p.]: [n.p.], 1917.

338. ———. *Nell'isola delle lagrime (Ellis Island).* New York: Stabilimento Tipografico Italia, 1924.

339. ———. *In Nuova York.* Scranton: Il Minatore Publishing Co., 1936.

340. ———. *Obici: Biografia.* New York: Tipografia editrice Scarlino, 1943. *Cat. 40.*

341. ———. *Sonata elegiaca: Dramma.* Brooklyn: Tartamella, 1921. *Cat. 24.*

342. C[annata], G[iuseppe]. *La tattica sindacalista in America.* Brooklyn: Libreria dei Lavoratori Industriali del Mondo, [1921]. *Cat. 101.*

343. ———. *La tecnica industriale e la rivoluzione proletaria.* Brooklyn: Libreria dei Lavoratori Industriali del Mondo, 1922. *Cat. 102.*

344. Ciancabilla, Giuseppe. *Fiori di maggio.* New York: Ruffo & Ciani, 1900.

345. ———. *Fired by the Ideal: Italian American Anarchist Responses to Czolgosz's Killing of McKinley.* London: Kate Sharpley Library, 2002.+

346. ———, trans. *Tolstoismo e anarchismo: Rapporto presentato al Congresso Operaio Rivoluzionario Internazionale di Parigi dal Gruppo degli Studenti Socialisti Rivoluzionarii Internazionalisti di Parigi.* Barre, Vt.: Biblioteca Circolo Studi Sociali, 1900. *Cat. 93.*

347. Comitato dei Gruppi Riuniti. *Rivoluzione e controrivoluzione: Manifesto dei militanti e dei Gruppi Anarchici Riuniti del Nordamerica.* New York: Galilei Club, 1944. *Cat. 91.*

348. Damiani, Gigi. *Attorno ad una vita (Niccolò Converti).* Newark: L'Adunata dei Refrattari, 1940.

349. ———. *La bottega: Scene della ricostruzione fascista, drama in due atti.* Detroit: Libreria Autonoma, 1927. *Cat. 84.*

350. ———. *Carlo Marx e Bacunin in Spagna.* Newark: L'Adunata dei Refrattari, 1939.

351. ———. *Cristo e Bonnot.* Chicago: Germinal, 1927.

352. ———. *Del delitto e delle pene nella società di domani.* Newark: Biblioteca de L'Adunata dei Refrattari, 1930.

353. ———. *Rampogne. Versi d'un ribello.* Torino: Gruppo Editoriale Anarchichi Piemontesi, 1946.

354. ———. *Razzismo e anarchismo.* Newark: Biblioteca de L'Adunata dei Refrattari, 1939.

355. ———. *Saggio su di una concezione filosofica dell'anarchismo.* Pistoia: Fondazione-Archivio, Famiglia Berneri, 1991. Originally published in *L'Adunata dei Refrattrari.+*

356. ———. *Stato e commune.* Newark: Biblioteca de L'Adunata dei Refrattari, 1946.

357. ——— *Viva Rambolot! Bozzetto in un atto.* Newark: Biblioteca de L'Adunata dei Refrattari, [ca. 1930s]. *Cat. 86.*

358. Simplicio [Gigi Damiani]. *"Fecondità." Commedia sociale in due atti.* Newark: Biblioteca de L'Adunata dei Refrattari, 1928. *Cat. 85.*

359. ———. *Sgraffi.* Newark: Biblioteca de L'Adunata dei Refrattari, 1946. *Cat. 87.*

360. D'Andrea, Virgilia. *Due conferenze: Chi siamo e cosa vogliamo. Patria e religione.* Newark: Biblioteca de L'Adunata dei Refrattari, 1947. *Cat. 82.*

361. ———. *L'ora di Maramaldo.* Brooklyn: Lavoratori Industriali del Mondo, 1925.

362. ———. *Richiamo all'anarchia. Protesta e proposta anarchica in otto conferenze pronunciate in terra d'esilio durante la dominazione fascista.* Cesena: L'Antistato, 1947.

363. ———. *Torce nella notte.* New York: [n.p.], 1933.

364. ———. *Tormento.* Milano: Tipografia E. Zerboni, 1922; republished Paris: La Fraternelle, 1929.

365. de Biasi, Agostino. *La battaglia dell'Italia negli Stati Uniti. Articoli e note polemiche.* New York: Il Carroccio Publishing Co., 1927.

366. De Fiori, Vittorio E. *Mussolini.* New York: Italy Publishing Co., 1923. Published together with Podrecca's *Il fascismo*, q.v. item 422. *Cat. 132.*

367. ———. "Socialismo italiano negli Stati Uniti." *Rassegna di politica e storia* 14, nos. 159, 160, 161 (1968) and 15, nos. 171, 172 (1969).

368. Ebert, Justus. *L'I. W. W. nella teoria e nella pratica.* Chicago: Industrial Workers of the World, [ca. 1922]. *Cat. 99.*

369. Fabbri, Luigi. *Le dittature contro la libertà dei popoli*. New York: Il Martello Publishing Co., [*ca.* 1920s]. *Cat. 120*.

370. ———. *Malatesta: L'uomo e il pensiero*. Naples: Ediz. RL, 1951.

371. Faggi, Angelo. *Uno storico processo di classe: I precedenti e lo svolgimento del processo dell'I.W.W. a Chicago*. Chicago: Industrial Workers of the World, [*ca.* 1918?]. *Cat. 96*.

372. Fichera, Filippo. *Il Duce e il fascismo nei canti dialettali d'Italia*. Milano: Edizione del "Convivio Letterario," 1937.

373. [Galleani, Luigi]. *Verso il comunismo*. Barre, Vt.: Cronaca Sovversiva, 1904. *Cat. 92*.

374. Mentana [Luigi Galleani]. *Faccia a faccia col nemico: Cronache giudiziarie dell'anarchismo militante*. East Boston: Edizione del Gruppo Autonomo, 1914. *Cat. 52*.

375. ———. *Madri d'Italia (per Augusto Masetti)*. Lynn, Mass.: Cronaca Sovversiva, 1913. *Cat. 51*.

376. Galleani, Luigi. *Una battaglia*. Roma: Biblioteca de L'Adunata dei Refrattari, 1947. *Cat. 55*.

377. ———. *Contro la guerra, contro la pace, per la rivoluzione*: Newark: Biblioteca de L'Adunata dei Refrattari, 1927.+

378. ———. *La fine dell'anarchismo?* Newark: Vecchi lettori di Cronaca Sovversiva, 1925. *Cat. 53*.

379. ———. *Mandateli lassù*. Cesena: Edizioni l'Antistato, 1954.

380. ———. *Medaglioni. Aneliti e singulti*. Newark: Biblioteca de L'Adunata dei Refrattari, 1935.+

381. ———. *Medaglioni. Figure e figuri*. Newark: Biblioteca de L'Adunata dei Refrattari, 1930. *Cat. 54*.

382. ———. *Metodi della lotta socialista*. Roma: Biblioteca de L'Adunata dei Refrattari, 1972.

383. Giantino [Alibrando Giovannetti]. *Unionismo industriale e sindacalismo*. Brooklyn: Casa ed. Lavoratori Industriali, [1923]. *Cat. 103*.

384. Giovannitti, Arturo. *Arrows in the Gale*. Riverside, Conn.: Hillacre Press, 1914.+

385. ———. *The Cage*. Riverside, Conn.: Hillacre Press, 1914.+

386. ———. *Il camminante ("The walker")*. Translation by Onorio Ruotolo. New York: Morgillo, 1950.

387. ———. *The Collected Poems of Arturo Giovannitti*. Chicago: E. Clemente &

Sons, 1962. Introduction by Norman Thomas. *Cat. 113.*

388. ———. *Come era nel principio (tenebre rosse). Dramma in 3 atti.* Brooklyn: Libreria Editrice dei Lavoratori Industriali del Mondo, 1918.

389. ———. *Ettor and Giovannitti Before the Jury at Salem, Massachusetts, November 23, 1912.* Chicago: Industrial Workers of the World, 1912.

390. ———. *Parole e sangue.* New York: Labor Press, 1938. Reprint edited by Martino Marazzi, with essays of Joseph Tusiani. Isernia: Iannone, 2005.

391. ———. *Quando canta il gallo.* Chicago: E. Clemente & Sons, 1957. *Cat. 64.*

392. ———. "Syndicalism - the Creed of Force." *The Independent* (New York), (October 30, 1913): 209-211. *Cat. 112.*

393. Giovannitti, A., G. Gianformaggio, and E. Goldman. *Pagine scelte.* Brooklyn: Libreria Editrice I.W.W., 1930. *Cat. 115.*

394. Giovannitti, Arturo and Onorio Ruotolo. *Rimane salda la fede.* New York: [n.p.], 1943.

395. Gori, Pietro. *Prigioni. Versi. Al popolo ed a quanti combattono per l'umanesimo.* Chicago: Libreria Sociale, [n.d.].

396. ———. *Primo Maggio: Bozzetto drammatico in un atto.* Barre, Vt.: Salvatore Pallavicini Editore, 1896.

397. ———. *Senza patria.* Brooklyn: Club "L'Avanti!," 1915. Third Italian edition. (Republished in item 398,Vol. II).

398. ———. *Scritti scelti.* Cesena: Edizione L'Antistato, 1968.

399. Haywood, William D. *Speech of Wm. D. Haywood on the case of Ettor and Giovannitti.* Lawrence, Mass.: Ettor-Giovannitti Defense Committee, 1912.+

400. [Industrial Workers of the World.] *Unionismo industriale e trade-unionismo: Può un socialista e industrialista far parte dell'A.F. of L.? Resoconto stenografico del contradittorio tra Joseph J. Ettor ed Arturo Caroti tenutosi a New York il 26 Marzo 1911.* Chicago: Industrial Workers of the World, 1911. *Cat. 114.*

401. Ingargiola, Rosario. "'Gente lontana' di Corrado Altavilla." *La Follia di New York* (December 11, 1938).

402. ———. *Io canto la vita e la morte!* New York: Il Carroccio Publishing Co., 1923.

403. ———. *Il primato della civiltà italiana.* Brooklyn: Union Press, 1930.

404. Ingrao, Vincenzo. *Italia: Poemetto di rivendicazione.* New York: Società Tipografica Italiana, 1923.

405. Kampf, Leopoldo. *La vigilia: Dramma in tre atti.* East Boston: Edizione del Gruppo Autonomo, 1917. *Cat. 83.*

406. Lisanti, Dott. Gaetano F. *La crisi sociale da Cristo a Mussolini*. New York: Cocce Bros., 1933. *Cat. 129.*

407. Lyons, Eugene. *Vita e morte di Sacco e Vanzetti*. New York: Il Martello Publishing Co., 1928. *Cat. 122b.*

408. Malatesta, Errico. *Al caffè: Conversazioni dal vero*. Paterson, N.J.: Libreria Sociologica, [ca. 1910]. *Cat. 81.*

409. ———. *A Talk between Two Workers*. [Oakland, CA]: [Man!], [1933].+

410. ———, Max Nettlau and Luigi Galleani. *Organizzazione e anarchia*. Paris: L. Chauvet, 1925.+

411. Meledandri, Enrico. *La crisi del socialismo*. Chicago: Il Proletario, [1922]. *Cat. 104.*

412. Merlino, Francesco Saverio. *Perché siamo anarchici?* New York: [n.p.], 1893.

413. Molinari, Alberico. *Discorsi brevi*. Chicago: Libreria Sociale, 1909. Contains writings appearing in *L'Ascesa del Proletariato* between 1908 and 1909.

414. ———. *I martiri di Chicago. Episodio storico ai primi albori del movimento rivoluzionario presente*. Chicago: Italian Labor Publishing Co., 1910.

415. ———. *Le teorie di Cesare Lombroso: Spiegati agli operai*. Chicago: Libreria Sociale, 1920.

416. Montana, Vanni B. *Amarostico. Testimonianze euro-americane*. Livorno: U. Bastogi Editore, 1975.

417. Mussolini, [Benito], [Librero] Tancredi and [Gustavo] Hervé. *Dio e patria nel pensiero dei rinnegati*. New York: [n.p.], [ca. 1924-25]. Second edition. *Cat. 133.*

418. Nettlau, Max. *La responsabilità e la solidarietà nella lotta operaia: Rapporto letto alla "Freedom Discussion Group" il 5 Dicembre 1899*. Barre, Vt.: Casa ed. L'Azione, 1913. First Italian edition. *Cat. 94.*

419. ———. *Errico Malatesta*. New York: Casa Editrice Il Martello, [1922]. *Cat. 121.*

420. Novatore, Renzo. *Verso il nulla creatore*. West New York, N.J.: Virginio De Martin, 1939. *Cat. 90.*

421. [La Parola dei Socialisti]. *La morale di Arlecchino*. Chicago: Tipografia "la Parola" [dei Socialisti], [ca. 1910]. *Cat. 88.*

422. Podrecca, Guido. *Il fascismo*. New York: Italy Publishing Co., 1923. Published as second work commencing at p. [177] together with De Fiori's *Mussolini*, q.v. item 366. *Cat. 132.*

423. Gold O'Bay [Tintino Rasi]. *Quaderno No. 1. La grande rivoluzione in marcia*. Newark: Gruppi Riuniti dell'Antracite, 1940. *Cat. 89a.*

424. ———. *Quaderno No. 2. Le basi della società e del diritto*. Newark: Gruppi Riuniti dell'Antracite, 1940. *Cat. 89b.*

425. ———. *Quaderno No. 3. La produzione: Le sue basi, i suoi mezzi, le sue funzioni, i suoi scopi*. Newark: Gruppi Riuniti dell'Antracite, 1942. *Cat. 89c.*

426. Rossi, Carlo. *In the Dungeons of Mussolini*. New York: Italian Patronati to Aid the Political Prisoners of Italy, 1936.+

427. Roudine, Vittorio. *Max Stirner: (Un refrattario)*. East Boston: Edizione del Gruppo Autonomo, 1914. *Cat. 80.*

428. Sacco, Nicola. "Nicola Sacco (Note autobiografiche)." *L'Agitazione* (organ of the Defense Committee) (Boston), December 1920. Republished in *La Controcorrente*, Boston, 10, no. 2 (August 1948).

429. Saudino, Domenico. *Fra i roseti di Eros: Saggio populare di sociologia genetica*. Chicago: Avanti!, 1918.

430. ———. *Sotto il segno del littorio: La genesi del fascismo*. Chicago: Libreria Sociale, 1933. *Cat. 65.*

431. Schiavina, Raffaele. *Sacco e Vanzetti – Cause e fini di un delitto di stato*. Paris: Jean Bucco, 1927.

432. St. John, Vincent. *L'I.W.W.: La sua storia, struttura e metodi*. Brooklyn: Lavoratori Industriali del Mondo, [ca. 1919]. *Cat. 100.*

433. Taddei, Ezio. *Alberi e casolari*. New York: Edizioni in Esilio, 1943. *Cat. 13.*

434. ———. *C'è posta per voi, Mr. Brown!* Roma: Edizioni di Cultura Sociale, 1953.

435. ———. "I crimini del titismo. Vittorio Poccecai (Biografia d'un evaso dall'inferno di Tito)." *Il Lavoratore*, Trieste, New Series, Year VIII, no. 1048 (1952).

436. ———. "De Gasperi consiglia gli italiani ad emigrare." *Propaganda* (supplement in no. 47). [n.d.].

437. ———. *La fabbrica parla*. Milano: Milano Sera, 1950.+

438. ———. *Hanno assassinato i Rosenberg!* [N.p.]: [n.p.], 1953.

439. ———. *Ho rinunciato alla libertà*. Milano: Le edizioni sociali, 1950.+

440. ———. "Michele Esposito." *raccontanovelle*, nos. 2 – 8/9 (1956).

441. ———. *Parole collettive*. New York: S.E.A. [Società Editrice Americana], 1941. *Cat. 14.*

442. ———. *Il pino e la rufola*. New York: Edizioni in Esilio, 1944. *Cat. 12.*

443. ———. *Le porte dell'Inferno*. Roma: Mengarelli, 1945.

444. ———. "Potente." In *Il secondo risorgimento d'Italia*. [N.p.]: Centro Editoriale

d'Iniziativa, 1955.

445. ———. *Il quinto Vangelo*. Roma: Mengarelli, 1951 (then Vicenza: Edizioni della Locusta, 1970).

446. ———. *Rotaia*. Torino: Einaudi, 1946.

447. ———. "Salviamo i Rosenberg," ed., The Italian Committee to Save the Rosenbergs. *Il Seme* (supplement to no. 1), Year 5, [n.d.].

448. ———. *L'uomo che cammina*. New York: Edizioni L'Esule, 1940.

449. Thomas, Norman. *Chi uccise Carlo Tresca?* New York: Tresca Memorial Committee, 1947. *Cat. 126.*

450. Tresca, Carlo. *L'attentato a Mussolini, ovvero Il segreto di Pulcinella*. New York: Casa Editrice Il Martello, 1925. *Cat. 119.*

451. ———. *The Autobiography of Carlo Tresca*, ed. Nunzio Pernicone. New York: John J. Calandra Italian American Institute, 2003.+

452. ———. *Le falangi rosse al lavoro. La rivolta degli schiavi*. New York: Biblioteca Rossa, 1920.

453. ———. *Il vendicatore. Dramma antifascista*. New York: Il Martello, [n.d.].

454. Trombetta, Domenico. *Pervertimento: L'antifascismo di Carlo Fama*. New York: Libreria del Grido della Stirpe, 1931. *Cat. 131.*

455. Vacirca, Clara. *Cupido fra le camicie nere*. New York: La Strada Publishing Co., 1938.

456. Vacirca, Vincenzo. *La crisi americana*. New York: La Strada Publishing Co., 1940.

457. ———. *Figlia: Dramma*. New York: [n.p.], 1918.

458. ———. *L'Italia e la guerra*. Boston: Alessi, 1915.

459. ———. *Madre. Dramma antifascista in quattro atti*. Chicago: Italian Labor Publishing Co., 1931.

460. ———. *Mussolini. Storia d'un cadavere*. New York: La Strada Publishing Co., 1942. *Cat. 35.*

461. ———. "Il Rogo." *Il Solco*, Year I, no. 1 (January 1927) to Year II, no. 5 (May 1928).

462. ———. *La Russia in fiamme (22 mesi di rivoluzione)*. New York: Casa Editrice "I Giovani," 1919. *Cat. 34.*

463. Valentini, Girolamo. *Eugenio V. Debs: Apostolo del socialismo. Con "Sogno del prigioniero 9653" poema allegorico di Arturo Giovannitti*. Chicago: Italian Labor Publishing Co., [n.d.].

464. Valentini, Ernesto. *Il ricatto. Eccola, la giustizia! Rivelazioni e documenti.* Torino: Tipografia Silvestrelli e Cappelletto, 1924.

465. Venanzi, Flavio. *La nuova Russia (documenti storici)*. New York: Biblioteca Rossa, 1918.

466. ———. *Scritti politici e letterari.* New York: Venanzi Memorial Committee, 1921. *Cat. 107.*

467. Zocchi, Pulvio. *Sprazzi di luce: Pennelate di propaganda anticlericale.* New York: [n.p.], 1910. *Cat. 111.*

II. SECONDARY WORKS

A ╠ ITALIAN AMERICAN LIFE LIVED IN ITALIAN

468. Bencivenni, Marcella. *Italian Immigrant Radical Culture: The Idealism of the Sovversivi in the United States 1890–1940*. New York: New York University Press, 2011.+

469. Calabrese, Omar, ed. *Modern Italy: Images and History of a National Identity*, vol. 2. Milano: Electa Ed., 1983.+

470. Cannistraro, Philip V. *Blackshirts in Little Italy*. West Lafayette, Ind.: Bordighera Press, 1999.+

471. ——— and Gerald Meyer, eds. *The Lost World of Italian-American Radicalism*. New York: Praeger, 2003.+

472. D'Acierno, Pellegrino, ed. *The Italian American Heritage. A Companion to Literature and Arts*. New York: Garland Publishing, 1999.+

473. Durante, Francesco. *Italoamericana. Storia e letteratura degli italiani negli Stati Uniti. Vol. I. 1776–1880*. Milano: Mondadori, 2001.+

474. ———. *Italoamericana. Storia e letteratura degli italiani negli Stati Uniti. Vol. II. 1880–1943*. Milano: Mondadori, 2005.+

475. Federal Writers Project. *The Italians of New York*. New York: Random House, 1938.+

476. Federal Writers Project. *Gli Italiani di New York*. New York: Labor Press, 1939.+

477. Flamma, Ario. *Italiani di America*. New York: Cocce Press, 1936.+

478. Franzina, Emilio. *Dall'Arcadia in America: Attività letteraria ed emigrazione transoceanica in Italia (1850–1940)*. Torino: Fondazione Giovanni Agnelli, 1996.+

479. Fucilla, Joseph G. *The Teaching of Italian in the United States: A Documentary History*. New Brunswick: American Association of Teachers of Italian, 1967.+

480. Gabaccia, Donna and Fraser M. Ottanelli, eds. *Italian Workers of the World: Labor Migration and the Formation of Multiethnic States*. Urbana: University of Illinois, 2001.+

481. Gardaphé, Fred L. and James J. Periconi. *The Italian American Writers Association Bibliography of the Italian American Book*. Mount Vernon, N.Y.: Shea & Haarmann Publishing Co., 2000.+

482. Guglielmo, Jennifer. *Living the Revolution: Italian Women's Resistance and Radicalism in New York City, 1880–1945*. Chapel Hill: University of North Carolina Press, 2010.+

483. Haller, Hermann W. *Una lingua perduta e ritrovata. L'italiano degli italo-americani*. Firenze: La Nuova Italia, 1993.+

484. La Gumina, Salvatore J., Frank J. Cavaioli, Salvatore Primeggia and Joseph A. Varacalli, eds. *The Italian American Experience: An Encyclopedia*. New York: Garland Publishing, 2000.+

485. Marazzi, Martino. *A occhi aperti*. Milano: FrancoAngeli, 2011.+

486. ———. *Voices of Italian America. A History of Italian American Literature with a Critical Anthology*. Madison, N.J.: Fairleigh Dickinson University Press, 2005.+

487. Martelli, Sebastiano, ed. *Il sogno italo-americano. Realtà e immaginario dell'emigrazione negli Stati Uniti*. Atti del Convegno dell'Istituto "Suor Orsola Benincasa," Napoli, November 28-30, 1996. Napoli: Cuen, 1998.+

488. Pernicone, Nunzio. *Carlo Tresca: Portrait of a Rebel*. New York: Palgrave-Macmillan, 2005.+

489. ———. *Italian Anarchism: 1864–1892*. Princeton: Princeton University Press, 1993.+

490. Schiavo, Giovanni Ermenegildo, ed. *Italian-American Who's Who. A Biographical Dictionary of Italian-American Leaders*. New York/El Paso: Vigo Press (21 editions with updates), 1935-1967.+

491. Topp, Michael Miller. *Those Without a Country: The Political Culture of Italian American Syndicalists*. Minneapolis: University of Minnesota Press, 2001.+

B ╪ GENERAL HISTORY OF ITALIANS IN AMERICA

492. Adams, Joseph H. *In the Italian Quarter of New York*. New York: [n.p.], [1903]. (Facs. reprint in *Italians in the United States: A Repository of Rare Tracts and Miscellanea*. New York: Arno Press (NY Times Co.), 1975.)+

493. Anonymous. *[Constitution of] The Society for the Protection of Italian Immigrants*. New York: Powers & Stein Press, 1902.+

494. ———. *Consigli Agl'Immigranti / Advice for Immigrants*. [N.p.]: [n.p.], [1904]. (Facs. reprint in *Italians in the United States: A Repository of Rare Tracts and Miscellanea*. New York: Arno Press (NY Times Co.), 1975.)+

495. Benanti, Salvatore. *La secessione della "Sons of Italy Grand Lodge" — Studi polemici su diversi problemi degl'italiani in America*. New York: Colamco Press, 1926.

496. ———. *Studi critici di dinamica sociale*. New York: La Follia di New York, 1928.

497. Bevilacqua, Piero, Andreina De Clementi and Emilio Franzina, eds. *Storia dell'emigrazione italiana. Partenze*. Roma: Donzelli, 2001.

498. ———. *Storia dell'emigrazione italiana. Arrivi*. Roma: Donzelli, 2002.

499. Brandenburg, Broughton. *Imported Americans: The Story of the Experiences of a Disguised American and his Wife Studying the Immigration Question*. New York: Stokes, 1904.

500. Caporale, Rocco, ed. *The Italian Americans through the Generations. Proceedings of the Fifteenth Annual Conference of the American Italian Historical Association*. Staten Island: AIHA, 1986.+

501. Cinel, Dino. *From Italy to San Francisco: the Immigrant Experience*. Stanford: Stanford University Press, 1982.

502. ———. *The National Integration of Italian Return Migration*, 1870-1929. Cambridge: Cambridge University Press, 1904.

503. Colajanni, Napoleone. "La criminalità degli italiani negli Stati Uniti." In Sheridan, *Gl'italiani negli Stati Uniti* (1909), 117-192 (item 574).

504. ———. "I non desiderabili (The undesirables)." In Sheridan, *Gl'italiani negli Stati Uniti* (1909), 83-113 (item 574).

505. Corsi, Edward. *In the Shadow of Liberty*. New York: Macmillan Co., 1935.+

506. Covello, Leonard. *The Italians in America: A brief survey of a sociological research program of Italo-American communities*. New York: Casa Italiana Educational Bureau, 1934.

507. ———. *The Social Background of the Italo-American School Child*. Leiden: E. J. Brill, 1967.+

508. DiStasi, Lawrence. *Una Storia Segreta: The Secret History of the Italian American Evacuation and Internment during World War II*. Berkeley: Heyday Books, 2001.+

509. Dore, Grazia. *La democrazia italiana e l'emigrazione in America*. Brescia: Morcelliana, 1964.+

510. *Euroamericani. La popolazione di origine italiana negli Stati Uniti*, vol. 1. Torino: Edizioni della Fondazione Giovanni Agnelli, 1987.

511. Femminella, Francis X., ed. *Italian and Irish in America. Proceedings of the Sixteenth Annual Conference of the American Italian Historical Association*. Staten Island: AIHA, 1985.+

512. ———, ed. *Power and Class: The Italian-American Experience Today. Proceedings of the Fourth Annual Conference of the American Italian Historical*

Association. Staten Island: AIHA, 1973.+

513. Foerster, Robert E. *The Italian Emigration of Our Times*. Cambridge: Harvard University Press, 1919.+

514. Fox, Stephen. *Uncivil Liberties: Italian Americans Under Siege During World War II*. New York: Universal Publishers, 2000.

515. Franzina, Emilio. *Gli italiani al nuovo mondo. L'emigrazione italiana in America 1492–1942*. Milano: Mondadori, 1995.

516. Gambino, Richard. *Blood of My Blood. The Dilemma of the Italian Americans*. Garden City: Doubleday, 1974.+

517. Griel, Cecile L., M.D. *Il Bambino*. New York: YMCA, 1920.

518. ———. *I problemi della madre in un paese nuovo*. New York: YMCA, [1919]. (Facs. reprint in *Italians in the United States: A Repository of Rare Tracts and Miscellanea*. New York: Arno Press (NY Times Co.), 1975.)+

519. Guglielmo, Jennifer and Salvatore Salerno, eds. *Are Italians White? How Race is made in America*. New York: Routledge, 2003.+

520. Guglielmo, Thomas A. *White on Arrival: Italians, Race, Color, and Power in Chicago, 1890–1945*. New York: Oxford University Press, 2003.+

521. Higham, John. *Strangers in the Land: Patterns of American Nativism, 1860–1925*. Rutgers: Rutgers University Press, 1955.+

522. *Italia e Stati Uniti dall'indipendenza americana ad oggi (1776–1976). Atti del I Congresso Internazionale di Storia Americana (Genova, 26–29 May 1976)*. Genova: Tilgher, 1978.

523. *Gli italiani negli Stati Uniti. L'emigrazione e l'opera degli italiani negli Stati Uniti d'America. Atti del III Symposium di Studi Americani, Firenze 27–29 May 1969*. Firenze: Istituto di Studi Americani, Università degli Studi, 1972.+

524. Jacobson, Matthew Frye. *Whiteness of a Different Color: European Immigrants and the Alchemy of Race*. Cambridge: Harvard University Press, 1998.+

525. Juliani, Richard N. *Building Little Italy. Philadelphia's Italians Before Mass Migration*. University Park, PA: Pennsylvania State University Press, 1998.+

526. ———, ed. *The Family and Community Life of Italian Americans. Proceedings of the Thirteenth Annual Conference of the American Italian Historical Association*. Staten Island: AIHA, 1983.+

527. Juliani, Richard N. and Philip V. Cannistraro, eds. *Italian Americans: The Search for a Usable Past. Proceedings of the 19th Annual Conference of the American Italian Historical Association*. Staten Island: AIHA, 1989.+

528. Krase, Jerome and William Egelman, eds. *The Melting Pot and Beyond: Italian*

Americans in the Year 2000. Proceedings of the XVIII Annual Conference of the American Italian Historical Association. Providence, R.I. Nov. 7-9. 1985. Staten Island: AIHA, 1987.+

529. La Gumina, Salvatore J., ed. *Wop! A Documentary History of Anti-Italian Discrimination in the United States.* San Francisco: Straight Arrow Books, 1973.+

530. ———. *The Immigrants Speak. Italian Americans Tell Their Story.* New York: Center for Migration Studies, 1979.

531. Lord, Eliot, John J. D. Trenor and Samuel J. Barrows. *The Italian in America.* New York: Buck & Co., 1905.+

532. Luconi, Stefano. "Becoming Italian in the US: Through the Lens of Life Narratives." *Melus* 29, no. 3/4 (Fall 2004): 151-164.+

533. Lyell Earle, E. "Character Studies in New York's Foreign Quarters." *Catholic World* 68, no. 408 (March 1899): 782-793.

534. Maffi, Mario. *Nel mosaico della città. Differenze etniche e nuove culture in un quartiere di New York.* Milano: Feltrinelli, 1992. Trans. as *Gateway to the Promised Land. Ethnicity and Culture in New York's Lower East Side* (New York: New York University Press, 1995).

535. Mangano, Antonio. *Religious Work Among Italians in America.* Philadelphia: Board of Home Missions and Church Extension of the M[ethodist].E[piscopal] Church, 1917.

536. ———. *Sons of Italy. A Social and Religious Study of the Italians in America.* New York: Missionary Education Movement of the United States and Canada, 1917.

537. Mangione, Jerre and Ben Morreale. *La Storia. Five Centuries of the Italian American Experience.* New York: Harper Collins, 1992.+

538. Mariano, John Horace. *The Italian Contribution to American Democracy.* Boston: Christopher Publishing House, 1921.+

539. ———. *The Italian Immigrant and Our Courts.* Boston: Christopher Publishing House, 1925. (Facs. reprint, New York: Arno Press (NY Times Co.), 1975.)+

540. ———. *The Second Generation of Italians in New York City.* Boston: Christopher Publishing House, 1921.

541. Martellone, Anna Maria. *Una Little Italy nell'Atene d'America. La comunità italiana di Boston dal 1880 al 1920.* Napoli: Guida, 1975.

542. ———, ed. *La "questione" dell'immigrazione negli Stati Uniti.* Bologna: Il Mulino, 1980.

543. Mayor des Planches, Edmondo. *Attraverso gli Stati Uniti - per l'emigrazione*

italiana. Torino: Unione Tipografico-Editrice Torinese, 1913. *Cat. 78.*

544. ———. *Della convenienza che l'Italia artistica ed industriale partecipi all'esposizione di Saint Louis (Missouri).* Torino: Tipografia Roux e Viarengo, 1904.+

545. ———. "Gli Italiani in California." *Bollettino del Ministero degli Affari Esteri,* no. 284 (1904).

546. Moquin, Wayne and Charles Van Doren, eds. *A Documentary History of the Italian Americans.* New York: Praeger Publishers, 1974.+

547. Musmanno, Michael A. *The Story of the Italians in America.* Garden City: Doubleday, 1965.+

548. Pane, Remigio, ed. *Italian Americans in the Professions. Proceedings of the Twelfth Annual Conference of the American Italian Historical Association.* Staten Island: AIHA, 1983.

549. ———, Allon Schoener and A. Bartlett Giamatti. *The Italian Americans.* New York: Macmillan, 1987.

550. ———. "In Memoriam Giovanni Schiavo (1898-1983)." In Femminella, *Italian and Irish in America* (1985), 5-11 (item 511).

551. Pecorini, Alberto. *Gli americani nella vita moderna osservati da un italiano.* Milano: Fratelli Treves, 1909. *Cat. 74.*

552. ———. "The Italians in the United States." *The Forum,* no. 45 (January 1911): 15-29.

553. Riis, Jacob A. *How the Other Half Lives: Studies among the Tenements of New York.* New York: Charles Scribner's Sons, 1890.

554. ———. *The Making of an American.* New York: Grosset & Dunlap, 1901.+

555. Rimanelli, Marco and Sheryl L. Postman. *The 1891 New Orleans Lynchings and U.S.-Italians: A Look Back.* New York: Lang, 1992.

556. Salerno, Eric. *Rossi a Manhattan.* Roma: Quiritta, 2001.

557. Sartorio, Henry Charles. *Social and Religious Life of Italians in America,* with an Introduction by Dean George Hodges. Boston: Christopher, 1918.

558. Schiavo, Giovanni Ermenegildo. *Four Centuries of Italian-American History.* New York: Vigo Press, 1952.+

559. ———. *The Italians in Chicago.* Chicago: Vigo Press, 1928.

560. ———. *Italian-American History,* vol. I (*Italian Music and Musicians in America since 1757 — Dictionary of Musical Biography — Public Officials*). New York: Vigo Press, 1947. (Facs. reprint, New York, Arno Press (NY Times Co.), 1975.)+

561. ———. *Italian-American History*, vol. II, *The Italian Contribution to the Catholic Church in America*. New York: Vigo Press, 1949. (Facs. reprint, New York, Arno Press (NY Times Co.), 1975.)+

562. Scura, Antonio. *Gli albanesi in Italia e i loro canti tradizionali*. New York: Francesco Tocci, [1912].

563. Sensi-Isolani, Paola and Anthony Julian Tamburri, eds. *Italian Americans Celebrate Life. The Arts and Popular Culture. Selected Essays from the 22nd Annual Conference of the American Italian Historical Association*. Staten Island: AIHA, 1990.

564. Sheridan, Frank. "Italian, Slavic and Hungarian Unskilled Immigrant Laborers in the United States. *Bulletin of the Bureau of Labor, No. 72 (The American Immigration Library Series)*. Washington, D.C.: U.S. Government Printing Office, 1907.

565. Sheridan, Frank J., Amy A. Bernardy, Emily Fogg Meade and Napoleone Colajanni. *Gl'italiani negli Stati Uniti*, Roma-Napoli: Biblioteca della Rivista Popolare, 1909. (Facs. reprint in *Italians in the United States: A Repository of Rare Tracts and Miscellanea*. New York: Arno Press (NY Times Co.), 1975.)+

566. Sollors, Werner. *Beyond Ethnicity. Consent and Descent in American Culture*. New York: Oxford University Press, 1986.+

567. ———. "The Invention of Otherness: The Creation of 'Immigrant' and 'Indigenous' Identities." In Jean Cazemajou, ed., *L'immigration européenne aux Etats-Unis (1880–1910)*, Bordeaux: Presses Universitaires de Bordeaux, 1986.

568. Speranza, Gino Carlo. *The Diary of Gino Speranza*, 2 vols., ed. Florence Colgate Speranza. New York: Columbia University Press, 1941.

569. ———. *Race or Nation: A Conflict of Divided Loyalties*. Indianapolis: Bobbs-Merrill Co., 1925. (Facs. reprint, New York: Arno Press (NY Times Co.), 1975.)+

570. Strafile, Alfonso. *Memorande coloniale*. Philadelphia: La Forbice, 1911.+

571. Tamburri, Anthony. "To Hyphenate or Not To Hyphenate: The Italian/American Writer and 'Italianità.'" *Italian Journal* (1989): 37-42.

572. Tirabassi, Maddalena. *Amy Bernardy e l'emigrazione italiana negli Stati Uniti*. Torino: Quaderni della Fondazione Luigi Einaudi, 2005.

573. ———. *Ripensare la patria grande: gli scritti di Amy Allemand Bernardy sulle migrazioni italiani, 1900–1930*. Isernia: Iannone, 2005.

574. Tomasi, Silvano M. and Madeline H. Engel, eds. *The Italian Experience in the United States*. Staten Island: Center for Migration Studies, 1970.

575. Tori, Jacopo. *Il processo muto di Sacramento, California*. Brooklyn: Libreria

dei Lavoratori Industriali del Mondo, 1919.

576. Tropea, Joseph L., James E. Miller, and Cheryl Beattie-Repetti, eds. *Support and Struggle. Italian and Italian Americans in a Comparative Perspective. Proceedings of the Seventeenth Annual Conference of the American Italian Historical Association*. Staten Island: AIHA, 1986.+

577. Tua, Antonio. *Giovanni da Verrazzano alla corte di Francesco I. Dramma storico in quattro atti*. New York: Italian American Printing, 1913.

578. Valeri, Adolfo. *La "Mano Nera."* New York: Stamperia "Bolletino della Sera," 1905.

579. Vecoli, Rudolph J. "L'etnia, una dimensione trascurata della storia americana." In Martellone, *La "questione" dell'immigrazione negli Stati Uniti* (1980), 157-172 (item 542).

580. ———. "Fare la Merica: sogno o incubo?" In Martelli, *Il sogno italo-americano* (1998) (item 487).

581. ———. "Prelates and Peasants: Italian Immigrants and the Catholic Church." *Journal of Social History* 2 (Spring 1987): 216-278.

582. ———. "La ricerca di un'identità italo-americana: continuità e cambiamento." In *Gli italiani negli Stati Uniti* (1972), 217-243 (item 523).

583. Velinkonja, Joseph. "Family and Community: The Periodical Press and Italian Communities." In Juliani, *Family and Community Life of Italian Americans* (1983), 47-60 (item 526).

584. Villari, Luigi M. *Gli Stati Uniti d'America e l'emigrazione italiana*. Milano: Fratelli Treves, 1912.+

585. Wright, Frederick H. *The Italians in America*. New York: Missionary Education Movement of the U.S. and Canada, 1913. (Facs. reprint in *Italians in the United States: A Repository of Rare Tracts and Miscellanea*. New York: Arno Press (NY Times Co.), 1975.)+

586. Zucchi, John E. *The Little Slaves of the Harp. Italian Child Street Musicians in Nineteenth Century Paris, London and New York*. Montreal: McGill-Queen's University Press, 1992.+

C ⊁ LEARNING THE LANGUAGE

587. Carnevale, Nancy C. *A New Language, A New World: Italian Immigrants in the United States 1890-1945*. Urbana: University of Illinois, 2009.+

588. Corsi, Edward. "Il dialetto italo-americano." *Convivio Letterario*, Year 20, nos. 10-12 (1952): 61-62.

589. D'Ariano, Regina and Roy. *Italo-American Ballads Poems Lyrics and Melodies*, Parsons, W.V.: McClain Printing Co., 1976.

590. DeLuise, Alexandra. "The Italian Immigrant Reads: Evidence of Reading for Learning and Reading for Pleasure, 1890–1920s." *Italian Americana* 30, no. 1 (Winter 2012): 33-43.

591. Haller, Hermann W. "Italian Speech Varieties in the United States and Italian-American Lingua Franca." *Italica* 64, no. 3 (Fall 1987): 393-409.+

592. ———. "Verso un nuovo italiano. L'esperienza linguistica dell'insegnamento negli Stati Uniti." In Martelli, *Il sogno italo-americano* (1998), (item 487).

593. Sweet, May M. *Italian Books for American Libraries: A Supplement to the Italian Immigrant and His Reading*. Chicago: American Library Association, 1932.

594. ———. *The Italian Immigrant and His Reading*. Chicago: American Library Association, 1925.

595. Turano, Anthony M. "The Speech of Little Italy." *The American Mercury* 26, no. 103 (July 1932): 356-360.

D ᚦ IMAGINATIVE LITERATURE

596. Aiello, Rosa. *La cucina casareccia napoletana pei golosi e buongustai*. New York: Italian Book Company, [*ca.*1940s]. *Cat. 139*.

597. Aleandri, Emelise. *A History of Italian-American Theatre: 1900 to 1905*. A dissertation submitted to the Graduate Faculty in Theatre in partial fulfillment of the requirements for the degree of Doctor of Philosophy, City University of New York, 1983.

598. ———. *The Italian-American Immigrant Theatre of New York City*. Charleston, SC: Arcadia, 1999.+

599. ———. *The Italian-American Immigrant Theatre of New York City, 1746–1899*. Book 1, vols. 1-15. New York: Edward Mellen Press, 2006-2012.

600. ———. "Italian-American Theatre." In *Ethnic Theatre in the United States*, ed. Maxine Schwartz Seller. Westport, Conn.: Greenwood Press, 1983, 237-258.

601. Alfonsi, Ferdinando. *Poeti italo-americani/Italo-American Poets: Antologia bilingue/A Bilingual Anthology*. Catanzaro: Carello, 1985.+

602. ———. *Dictionary of Italian-American Poets*. New York: Peter Lang, 1989.+

603. Ballerini, Luigi and Fredi Chiappelli. "*Contributi espressivi delle scritture e parlate americo-italiane.*" In *L'espressivismo linguistico nella letteratura italiana. Atti del convegno di Roma, 16–18 January 1984*. Roma: Accademia nazionale dei Lincei, 1985.

604. Bandini Buti, A. *Dario Papa*. In *Aspetti e figure della pubblicistica repubblicana italiana. Atti del convegno organizzato dall'Associazione Mazziniana Italiana a Torino, 13-14 October 1961*. Genova-Milano-Torino: Associazione mazziniana italiana, 1962, 59 et seq.

605. Barolini, Helen, ed. *The Dream Book: An Anthology of Writings by Italian American Women*. New York: Schocken Books, 1985.+

606. Basile Green, Rose. *The Italian-American Novel: A Document of the Interaction of Two Cultures*. Madison, N.J. Fairleigh Dickinson University Press, 1974.+

607. Biagi, Ernest Louis. *The Purple Aster: A History of the Order Sons of Italy in America*. [New York]: Veritas Press, 1961.+

608. Boelhower, William. *Immigrant Autobiography in the United States (Four Versions of the Italian American Self)*. Verona: Essedue Edizioni, 1982.+

609. ——— and Rocco Pallone, eds. *Adjusting Sites. New Essays in Italian American Studies*, Forum Italicum - Fililibrary Series, no. 16. Stony Brook, N.Y.: Forum Italicum, 1999.

610. Cacioppo, Marina. "'Se i marciapiedi di questa strada potessero parlare'. Space, Class, and Identity in Three Italian-American Autobiographies." In Boelhower, ed., *Adjusting Sites* (1999) (item 609).

611. Caccioppo, Vincenzo. "La tragica fine di Calogero Puccio." *L'Araldo di Santa Margherita Belice*, no. 8, Year 1 (October 15, 1962).

612. Cammett, John M., ed. *The Italian American Novel. Proceedings of the Second Annual Conference of the American Italian Historical Association, October 25, 1969*. Staten Island: AIHA, 1969.

613. Castronovo, Valerio. *La stampa italiana dall'unità al fascismo*. Roma-Bari: Laterza, 1970.

614. Centro Pio Rajna. "La scrittura dell'emigrazione." In *Italiani e stranieri nella tradizione letteraria. Atti del convegno di Montepulciano, 8-10 ottobre 2007*. Roma: Salerno, 2009, 283-340.

615. Cocchi, Raffaele. "In Search of Italian-American Poetry in the USA." *In Their Own Words* 2, no. 1 (Winter 1984).

616. ———. "L'invenzione della letteratura italiana e italoamericana." *Altreitalie* no. 5 (April 7-13, 1991).

617. ———. "Selected Bibliography of Italian American Poetry." *Italian Americana* 10, no. 2 (Spring–Summer 1992).

618. Cunetto, Dominic J. *Italian Language Theatre Clubs in St. Louis, Missouri*

1910 to 1950. (M.A. thesis, Graduate Council of the University of Florida). University of Florida: Hillside Printing Co., 1960.

619.   Del Giudice, Luisa, ed. *Studies in Italian American Folklore*. Logan: Utah State University Press, 1993.+

620.   Deschamps, Bénédicte. "La letteratura d'appendice nei periodici italo-americani (1910-1935)." In Martelli, *Il sogno italo-americano* (1998) (item 487).+

621.   ———and Stefano Luconi. "The Publisher of the Foreign-Language Press as an Ethnic Leader? The Case of James V. Donnarumma and Boston's Italian-American Community in the Interwar Years." *Historical Journal of Massachusetts* 30, no. 2 (Summer 2002): 126-143.

622.   Di Pietro, Robert J. and Edward Ifkovic, eds. *Ethnic Perspectives in American Literature*. New York: Modern Language Association of America, 1983.

623.   Di Vita, Rosario, Damiano Bivona, Antonino Paolo Caruso, Salvatore Calcara, Leonardo Dia, Giacomo Di Bernardo, Germoglino Saggio and Giovanni Santacroce. *Omaggio del Cenacolo artistico letterario siciliano "Vincenzo De Simone" alla memoria di Giovanni De Rosalia*. New York: [n.p.], 1935.

624.   Durante, Francesco. "'Avventura' versus 'Flusso'. La letteratura come strumento per capire l'emigrazione." In Domenico Scafoglio, ed., *Le letterature popolari. Prospettive di ricerca e nuovi orizzonti teorico-metodologici. Atti del convegno di Fisciano-Ravello, 21-23 November 1997*. Napoli: Edizioni Scientifiche Italiane, 2001.

625.   ———. "'Farfariello': due 'macchiette coloniali.'" *Acoma – Rivista internazionale Di Studi Nordamericani*," no. 16 (Spring 1999): 54-60.

626.   ———. "Giunte ottocentesche al canone letterario italoamericano." In *Merica. Forme della cultura italoamericana*, ed. Nick Ceramella and Giuseppe Massara. Isernia: Cosmo Iannone, 2004, 31-39.

627.   ———. "Little Italy, la riscossa dei cafoni" (with three texts of Eduardo Migliaccio). *Il Mattino* (Naples) (March 12, 1993).

628.   ———. "Paisà. Anzi scrittore." *Il Mattino* (March 21, 1993).

629.   ———. "Partono i bastimenti. L'emigrazione e le esperienze della canzone napoletana in Usa." *Euros* 1 (January-February 1994).

630.   ———. "I poeti del 'sottobosco' italo-americano." In Mario Capasso and Enzo Puglia, ed. *Scritti di varia umanità in memoria di Benito Iezzi*. Sorrento: Franco Di Mauro, 1994.

631.   ———. "Viviani nella letteratura dell'emigrazione." In Marcello Andria, ed., *Viviani*. Napoli: Pironti, 2001.

632. "Esuli pensieri. Scritture migranti." *Storia e problemi contemporanei* 18, no. 38 (January–April 2005).

633. Falbo, Italo C. "Figure e scene del teatro popolare italiano a New York." Series of articles in *Il Progresso Italo-Americano* (May 3, 10, 17, 24, 31; June 7, 14, 21, 28; July 5, 12; September 13, 20, 1942).

634. Fant, Pietro Antonio (Marius). *Luigi Carnovale, l'eroe della italianità negli Stati Uniti d'America*. Roma: Tipografia delle Terme, 1927.

635. Fichera, Filippo. *Letteratura italoamericana*. Milano: Editrice Convivio Letterario, 1958.

636. Fontanella, Luigi. *La parola transfuga. Scrittori italiani in America*. Fiesole: Cadmo, 2003.+

637. ———. "Poeti emigrati ed emigranti poeti negli Stati Uniti." In Martelli, *Il sogno italo-americano* (1998) (item 487).

638. Fumagalli, Giuseppe. *La stampa periodica italiana all'estero. Indice dei periodici tutti in parte in lingua italiana, che si stampavano all'estero cioè fuori dei confini politici del Regno, negli anni 1905-1907. Preceduto da uno studio storico a cura di G.F.* Milano: Libreria Fratelli Bocca, 1909.

639. Gambino, Richard. "Wellsprings of Italian American Art: The Italian American Experience As Literalism, Myth, and Surrealism." *Italian Americana* 9, no. 1 (Fall–Winter 1990).

640. Gardaphé, Fred L. "Fact in Fiction: Oral Traditions and the Italian American Writer." In Krase, *The Melting Pot and Beyond* (1987): 165-174 (item 528).+

641. ———. *The Italian-American Writer. An Essay and an Annotated Checklist*. New York: Forkroads/Spencertown, 1995.+

642. ———. *Italian Signs, American Streets. The Evolution of Italian American Narrative*. Durham: Duke University Press, 1996.+

643. Grillo, Giacomo. *Pagine di un giornalista italo-americano*. Pisa: Giardini, 1971.

644. Haller, Herman W. *Tra Napoli e New York: Le macchiette italo-americane di Eduardo Migliaccio*. Roma: Bulzoni, 2006.+

645. Luconi, Stefano. "La stampa di lingua italiana negli Stati Uniti dalle origini ai giorni nostri." *Studi Emigrazione – Migration Studies* 46, no. 175 (July–September 2009): 547-567.

646. Marazzi, Martino. "I due Re di Harlem." *Belfagor* 58, no. 5 (September 2003): 533-550. Trans. 2006, "King of Harlem: Garibaldi Lapolla and Gennaro Accuci 'il Grande.'" In Aldo Bove and Giuseppe Massara, eds., *'Merica. A Conference on the Culture and Literature of Italians in North America*. Stony Brook, N.Y.:

Forum Italicum Publishing, pp. 190-210.

647.   ———. "Lacrime e libertà. Profilo di Ludovico Michele Caminita." *Nuova Prosa*, no. 50 (May 2009): 105-128.

648.   ———. *Misteri di Little Italy. Storie e testi della letteratura italoamericana*. Milano: FrancoAngeli, 2001.+

649.   Marchand, Jean-Jacques. *La letteratura dell'emigrazione. Gli scrittori di lingua italiana nel mondo*. Torino: Edizioni della Fondazione Giovanni Agnelli, 1991.

650.   ———. "Rappresentazioni letterarie dell'emigrazione italiana in California tra Ottocento e Novecento." *Forum Italicum* 43, no. 1 (Spring 2009): 155-191.

651.   Menarini, Alberto. *Ai margini della lingua*. Firenze: G. C. Sansoni, 1947.+

652.   Mencken, H. L. "Appendix: Non-English Dialects in American" [Sec. 2b. Italian]. In *The American Language. An Inquiry Into the Development of English in the United States*. New York: Alfred A. Knopf, 1936. Fourth edition.+

653.   Muscio, Giuliana. *Piccole Italie, grandi schermi. Scambi cinematografici tra Italia e Stati Uniti 1895-1945*. Roma: Bulzoni, 2004.

654.   Pandolfi, Vito. *Antologia del grande attore. Raccolta di memorie e di saggi dei grandi attori italiani dalla riforma goldoniana ad oggi*. Bari: Laterza, 1954.

655.   Park, Robert E. *The Immigrant Press and its Control*. New York: Harper & Bros., 1922.+

656.   Parker, Robert Allerton. "Farfariello, Most Popular Italian Impersonator, Who Scorns 'Big Time' For Ten-Cent Shows." *The New York Times* (January 4, 1914).

657.   Peragallo, Olga. *Italian-American Authors*. New York: S. F. Vanni, 1949.

658.   Prezzolini, Giuseppe. *Diario 1900-1941*. Milano: Rusconi, 1978.

659.   ———. "Scrittori italiani nel mondo - Stati Uniti, Autobiografia e romanzo." *La Gazzetta del Popolo* (December 19, 1934).

660.   ———. *I trapiantati*. Milano: Longanesi, 1963.+

661.   ———. "Voci di poeti nostri negli Stati Uniti." *La Gazzetta del Popolo* (December 12, 1943).

662.   Primeggia, Salvatore and Joseph A. Varacalli. "Pulcinella to Farfariello to Paone to Cooper to Uncle Floyd: a Socio-Historical Perspective on Southern Italian and Italian-American Comedy." *ECCSSA Journal* (Eastern Community College Social Science Association), 1, 5 (Winter 1988): 45-53.

663.   Ricciardi, Guglielmo. *Ricciardiana. Raccolta di scritti, racconti, memorie ecc. del veterano attore e scrittore Guglielmo Ricciardi*. New York: Eloquent Press, N. Morgillo, 1955.+

664. Rocca, Gabriele. "Rievocando il grande poeta calabrese [Michele Pane]." *La Parola del Popolo* (Chicago), *New Series*, no. 11 (July–September 1953).

665. Russo, Pietro. "La stampa periodica italo-americana." In *Gli Italiani negli Stati Uniti* (1972), 493-546 (item 523).+

666. Sanfilippo, Matteo. "Araldi d'Italia? Un quadro degli studi sulla stampa italiana d'emigrazione." *Studi Emigrazione – Migration Studies* 46, no. 175 (July–September 2009): 678-695.

667. Sogliuzzo, Richard. "Notes for a History of the Italian-American Theatre of New York." *Theatre Survey: The American Journal of Theatre History* 14, no. 2 (November 1973): 59-75.

668. Sollors, Werner. "Between Consent and Descent: Studying Ethnic Literature in the U.S.A." *In Their Own Words: European Journal of the American Ethnic Imagination* 1, no. 1 (1983).

669. ——— and Marc Shell, eds. *Multilingual America. Transnationalism, Ethnicity, and the Languages of American Literature.* New York: New York University Press, 1998.+

670. Sormani, Giuseppe. *Eco d'America.* Milano: Tipografia degli Operai, 1888.

671. Spataro, Pasquale, ed. *Poeti calabresi in America, antologia.* Bergamo: Nuova Italia Letteraria, 1957.+

672. Testi, Nicola. *Arpe, mandòle e pifferi (in tre tempi).* Milano: Gastaldi Editore, 1954.

673. Torlontano, Giuliano. "Alberto Tarchiani fra intransigenza e pragmatismo." In Varsori, *L'antifascismo italiano* (1984), 167-180 (item 750).

674. Traldi, Alberto. "La tematica dell'emigrazione nella narrativa italo-americana." *Comunità* 30 (1976): 176, 245-272.

675. Tusiani, Joseph. "Garibaldi in American Poetry." In Caporale, *Italian Americans through the Generations* (1986), 64-76 (item 500).

676. ———. "The Making of an Italian American Poet." In Pane, *Italian Americans in the Professions* (1983), 9-40 (item 548).

677. ———. *La parola antica. Autobiografia di un italo-americano (Parte III).* Fasano: Schena, 1992.

678. ———. *La parola difficile. Autobiografia di un italo-americano.* Fasano: Schena, 1988.+

679. ———. *La parola nuova. Autobiografia di un italo-americano (Parte II).* Fasano: Schena, 1991.+

680. Van Vechten, Carl. "A Night With Farfariello: Popular Bowery Entertainer Who

Impersonates Local Italian Types." *Theatre Magazine* 29 (January 1919): 32-34.

681. Vecoli, Rudolph J. "The Italian-American Literary Subculture. An Historical and Sociological Analysis." In Cammett, *The Italian American Novel* (1969), 6-10 (item 625).+

682. ———. "The Italian Immigrant Press and the Construction of Social Reality, 1850-1920." In James P. Danky and Wayne A. Wiegand, *Print Culture in a Diverse America*. Urbana: University of Ilinois Press, 1998, 17-33.

683. Viscusi, Robert. "Breaking the Silence: Strategic Imperatives for Italian American Culture," *VIA: Voices in Italian Americana*, I, 1 (Spring, 1990): 1-14.

684. ———. *Buried Caesars, and Other Secrets of Italian American Writing*. Albany: State University of New York Press, 2006.

685. ———. "*De vulgari eloquentia*: An Approach to the Language of Italian American Fiction," *Yale Italian Studies* I, no. 3 (Winter 1981): 21-38; reprinted in Frank M. Sorrentino and Jerome Krase, *The Review of Italian American Studies* (Lanham, Maryland: Lexington Books, 2000), 303-322.

686. ———. "The History of Italian American Literary Studies." In *Teaching Italian American Literature, Film, and Popular Culture*. Edvige Giunta and Kathleen McCormick, eds. New York: Modern Language Association, 2010.

687. ———. "La letteratura dell'emigrazione italiana negli Stati Uniti." In Marchand, *La letteratura dell'emigrazione* (1991), 125-137 (item 655).

688. Wilson, Edmund. "Alice Lloyd With Farfariello." *The New Republic* 44, 568 (October 21, 1925): 230.

E ✦ POLITICAL LITERATURE

689. *Alla memoria di Rosario Di Vita*. New York: Il Cenacolo Siciliano "Vincenzo De Simone," 1937.

690. *Anarchici e anarchia nel mondo contemporaneo. Atti del convegno promosso dalla Fondazione Luigi Einaudi (Torino 5,6,7 dicembre 1969)*. Torino: Fondazione Luigi Einaudi, 1971.

691. Andreasi, Anna Maria. "Anarchismo e sindacalismo nel pensiero di Armando Borghi (1907-1922)." In *Anarchici e anarchia nel mondo contemporaneo* (1971), 242-260 (item 690).

692. Avrich, Paul. *Anarchist Portraits*. Princeton: Princeton University Press, 1988.

693. ———. *Anarchist Voices: An Oral History of Anarchism in America*. Princeton: Princeton University Press, 1995.+

694. ———. *The Haymarket Tragedy*. Princeton: Princeton University Press, 1984.

695. Baker, John D. "Italian Anarchism and the American Dream – The View of John Dos Passos." In Vecoli, *Italian American Radicalism"* (1972), 30-39 (item 755).+

696. Bezza, Bruno. *Gli italiani fuori d'Italia: Gli emigrati italiani nei movimenti operai dei paesi d'adozione (1880-1940)*. Milano: Franco Angeli-Fondazione Brodolini, 1983.

697. Bock, Gisela, Paolo Carpignano and Bruno Ramirez. *La formazione dell'operaio massa negli USA 1898/1922*. Milano: Feltrinelli, 1976.

698. Buhle, Mary Jo, Paul Buhle and Dan Georgakas, eds. *Encyclopedia of the American Left*. New York: Garland Publishing, 1990.

699. Buhle, Mary Jo, Paul Buhle and Harvey J. Kaye, eds. *The American Radical*. New York: Routledge, 1994.

700. Carey, George. " 'La Questione Sociale' (an Anarchist Newspaper in Paterson, NJ (1895-1908))." In L. Tomasi, *The Italian in America* (1985), 289-297 (item 740).

701. Cartosio, Bruno. *Gli emigrati italiani e l'Industrial Workers of the World*. In Bezza, *Gli italiani fuori d'Italia* (1983), 359-395 (item 696).

702. Cerrito, Gino. "Sull'emigrazione anarchica italiana negli Stati Uniti d'America." *Volontà: Rivista anarchica bimestrale* (Pistoia) 22, no. 4 (July-August 1969).

703. Clemente, E[gidio] and E[milio] Grandinetti. *Cinquantesimo Anniversario 1908-1958. La Parola del Popolo. Rivista Bimestrale. Year 50th*, vol. 9, no. 37 (December 1958-January 1959). Chicago: La Parola del Popolo Publishing, 1959. *Cat. 106.*

704. Dadà, Adriana. "La stampa anarchica." In Varsori, *L'antifascismo italiano* (1984), 349-370 (item 750).

705. ———. "Stati Uniti." In Bettini Leonardo, ed., *Bibliografia dell'anarchismo, volume primo, tomo secondo: Periodici e numeri unici anarchici in lingua italiana pubblicati all'estero (1872-1971)*. Firenze: Crescita Politica, 1976.

706. D'Attilio, Robert. "Primo Maggio: Haymarket as Seen by Italian Anarchists in America," in David Roediger, ed., *Haymarket Scrapbook*. Chicago: Charles H. Kerr, 1986, 229-230.

707. ———. "La salute è in voi: The Anarchist Dimension." In Boston Public Library Staff, *Sacco-Vanzetti* (1982), 75-89 (item 788).

708. De Ciampis, Mario. "Storia del movimento socialista rivoluzionario italiano." Clemente, *Cinquantesimo Anniversario 1908-1958. La Parola del Popolo* (1959), 136-163 (item 703).

709. Deschamps, Bénédicte. "*Il Lavoro*, the Italian Voice of the Amalgamated, 1915-1932." *The Italian American Review* 8, no. 1 (Spring/Summer 2001): 85-120.

710. ———. "Feuilleton et presse sindacale italo-américaine: Le cas de *Velia, l'histoire d'une petite couturière* dans le journal *Giustizia* (1925-1928)." In Marie-Françoise Cachin, Diana Cooper Richet, Jean-Marie Collier and Claire Parfait, eds., *Au bonheur du feuilleton. Naissance et mutations d'un genre (Etats-Unis, Grande-Bretagne, XVIIIe-XXe siècles)*. Paris: Creaphis, 2007, 197-210.

711. Diggins, John P. *Mussolini and Fascism: The View from America*. Princeton: Princeton University Press, 1972.

712. Donini, Ambrogio. "L'Unità del Popolo" e "Lo Stato Operaio." In Varsori, *L'antifascismo italiano* (1984), 331-348 (item 750).

713. Dubofsky, Melvyn. "Italian Anarchism and the American Dream: a Comment." In Vecoli, *Italian American Radicalism* (1973), 52-55 (item 755).

714. Emiliani, Vittorio. *Gli anarchici*. Milano: Bompiani, 1973.

715. Fedeli, Ugo. *Giuseppe Ciancabilla*. Imola: Galeati, 1965.

716. Fenton, Edwin. *Immigrants and Unions, A Case Study: Italians and American Labor, 1870-1920*. Cambridge: Harvard University Press, 1957. (Facs. reprint, New York: Arno Press (NY Times Co.), 1975.)+

717. Ferraris, Luigi Vittorio. "L'assassinio di Umberto I e gli anarchici di Paterson." *Rassegna storica del Risorgimento* 55, no. 1 (January-March 1968): 47-64.

718. Fiori, Giuseppe. *L'anarchico Schirru, condannato a morte per l'intenzione di uccidere Mussolini*. Milano: Mondadori, 1983.

719. Franzina, Emilio and Matteo Sanfilippo. *Il fascismo e gli emigrati. La parabola dei Fasci italiani all'estero (1920-1943)*. Roma-Bari: Laterza, 2000.

720. Gambino, Richard. *Bread and Roses*. New York: Avon Books, 1983.

721. Gerson, Simon W. *Pete: The Story of Peter V. Cacchione, New York's First Communist Councilman*: New York: International Publishers, 1976. +

722. Javarone, Domenico. *Vita di scrittore (Ezio Taddei)*. Roma: Macchia, 1958.

723. Luconi, Stefano. *La "diplomazia parallela." Il regime fascista e la mobilitazione politica degli italo-americani*. Milano: FrancoAngeli, 2000.

724. ———and Guido Tintori. *L'ombra lunga del fascio: Canali di propaganda fascista per gli "italiani d'America."* Milano: M&B Publishing, 2004.

725. Masini, Pier Carlo. *Storia degli anarchici italiani da Bakunin a Malatesta (1862-1892)*. Milano: Rizzoli, 1969.

726. Molaschi, Carlo. *Pietro Gori*. Milano: Il Pensiero, 1959.

727. Molinari, Augusta. "I giornali delle comunità anarchiche italo-americane." *Movimento Operaio e Socialista* 2, *New Series*, nos. 1-2 (January-June 1981): 117-130.

728. ———."L'Internazionale a New York e gli internazionalisti italiani." In Giorgio Spini, *Italia e America dal Settecento all'età dell'imperialismo.* Venezia: Marsilio, 1976, 279-295.

729. Pacciardi, Randolfo. "L'antifascismo italiano negli Stati Uniti: Una testimonianza." In Varsori, *L'antifascismo italiano* (1984), 5-17 (item 750).

730. Padovano, Giorgio. "Appunti sulle origini e gli sviluppi dell'Office of War Information e della "Voce dell'America." In Varsori, *L'antifascismo italiano* (1984), 69-74 (item 750).

731. Pernicone, Nunzio. "Anarchism in Italy, 1872-1900." In Vecoli, *Italian American Radicalism* (1973), 1-29 (item 755).

732. ———. *Italian Anarchism, 1864-1892.* Princeton: Princeton University Press, 1993.+

733. Petacco, Arrigo. *L'anarchico che venne dall'America.* Milano: Mondadori, 1969.

734. Salomone, A. William. "The Italian Anarchists in America: Comment and Historical Reflections." In Vecoli, *Italian American Radicalism* (1973), 40-51 (item 755).+

735. Salvemini, Gaetano and Bruno Roselli. *L'Italia sotto il fascismo. I suoi aspetti economici, politici e morali discussi in contraddittorio dal prof. Gaetano Salvemini e dal prof. Bruno Roselli.* New York: Il Martello Publishing Co., [n.d.].

736. Tagliacozzo, Enzo. "Il gruppo de 'L'Italia libera' di New York tra il 1943 e il 1945." In Varsori, *L'antifascismo italiano* (1984), 371-384 (item 750).

737. Terranova, Lorenzo. "Vincenzo Vacirca, fulgida ed interessante figura del Socialismo umano e romantico." *La Parola del Popolo* (Chicago), *New Series*, no. 70 (December 1964-January 1965).

738. Testi, Arnaldo. "L'immagine degli Stati Uniti nella stampa socialista italiana (1886-1914)." In Giorgio Spini, *Italia e America dal Settecento all'età dell'imperialismo.* Venezia: Marsilio (1972), 313-347.

739. Tomasi, Lydio F., ed. *Italian Americans: New Perspectives in Italian Immigration and Ethnicity.* New York: Center for Migration Studies, 1985.

740. ———, ed. *The Italian in America: The Progressive View, 1891-1914.* Staten Island: Center for Migration Studies, 1978.

741. Torcellan, Nanda. "L'antifascismo negli USA: 'Il Mondo'." In Varsori, *L'antifascismo italiano* (1984), 315-330 (item 750).

742. Turcato, Davide. "Italian Anarchism as a Transnational Movement, 1885-1915." *International Review of Social History* 52, no. 3 (December 2007): 407-444.

743. Umbrella, Belfiore. "Ricordo di Ezio Taddei." *La Parola del Popolo* (Chicago), *New Series*, no. 83 (April-May 1967).

744. Tinghino, John J. *Edmondo Rossoni: From Revolutionary Syndicalism to Fascism*. New York: Peter Lang, 1991.

745. Tirabassi, Maddalena. "La Mazzini Society (1940-1946): un'associazione degli antifascisti italiani negli Stati Uniti." In Giorgio Spini, et al., *Italia e Stati Uniti dalla grande guerra ad oggi*, Venezia: Marsilio, 1976, 141-158.

746. ———. "'Nazioni Unite' (1942-1946): L'organo ufficiale della Mazzini Society." In Varsori, *L'antifascismo italiano* (1984), 295-330 (item 750).

747. Toselli, Tommaso. "Nel terzo anniversario della morte di Alberico Molinari." *La Parola del Popolo* (Chicago), *New Series*, no. 4 (October-December 1951): 19-20.

748. ———. *Un trentennio di attività anarchica (1914-1945)*. Cesena: Edizioni "L'Antistato," 1953.

749. ———, Maurizio Antonioli, Giampietro Berti, Santi Fedele and Pasquale Iuso, eds. *Dizionario biografico degli anarchici italiani*. 2 vols. Pisa: BFS edizioni, 2003.

750. Varsori, Antonio, ed. *L'antifascismo italiano negli Stati Uniti durante la seconda guerra mondiale*. Roma: Archivio Trimestrale, 1984.+

751. ———. "Sforza, la Mazzini Society e gli alleati (1940-1943)." In Varsori, *L'antifascismo italiano negli Stati Uniti* (1984), 129-154 (item 750).

752. Vecoli, Rudolph J. "Alberico Molinari. Il medico dei poveri." *La Parola del Popolo* 29, no. 147 (November-December 1978). +

753. ———. "'Free Country': The American Republic Viewed by the Italian Left, 1880-1920." In Marianne Debouzy, ed., *In the Shadow of the Statue of Liberty: Immigrants, Workers and Citizens in the American Republic*. Saint Denis: Presses Universitaires de Vincennes, 1988, 35 et seq.

754. ———. "'Primo Maggio' in the United States: An Invented Tradition of the Italian Anarchists." In Andrea Panaccione, ed., *May Day Celebration*. Venezia: Marsilio (Quaderni della Fondazione G. Brodolini), 1988.

755. ———, ed. *Italian American Radicalism: Old World Origins and New World Developments. Proceedings of the Fifth Annual Conference of the American Italian Historical Association held in Boston, November, 1972*. Staten Island: AIHA, 1973.

756. Velona, Fort. "Genesi del movimento socialista democratico e della 'Parola del Popolo.'" Clemente, *Cinquantesimo Anniversario 1908-1958. La Parola del Popolo* (1959): 19-33 (item 703).

757. Vezzosi, Elisabetta. *Il socialismo indifferente. Immigrati italiani e Socialist Party negli Stati Uniti del primo Novecento.* Roma: Edizioni Lavoro, 1991.

758. ———. "Le stanze della memoria. Il Primo Maggio dei radicali italiani negli Stati Uniti del primo Novecento." In G. Donno, ed., *Storie e immagini del Primo Maggio. Problemi della storiografia italiana e internazionale.* La-caita: Manduria-Bari-Roma, 1990, 481-495.

759. Zappia, Charles A. "Unionism and the Italian American Worker: The Politics of Anti-Communism in the International Ladies' Garment Workers' Union in New York City, 1900-1925." In Caporale, *Italian Americans through the Generations* (1986), 77-91 (item 500).

760. Zoccoli, Ettore. *I gruppi anarchici degli Stati Uniti e l'opera di Max Stirner.* Modena: Vincenti, 1901.

F ❧ WORKS ABOUT KEY AUTHORS AND SUBJECTS: CIAMBELLI, CORDIFERRO, GALLEANI, GIOVANNITTI, THE SACCO AND VANZETTI AFFAIR, AND TRESCA

Bernardino Ciambelli

761. Bernabei, Franca. "Little Italy's Eugène Sue: The Novels of Bernardino Ciambelli." In Boelhower, ed., *Adjusting Sites* (1999) (item 609).

762. Durante. "Bernardino Ciambelli." In *Italoamericana* (2005): 95-99, 133-134, 145-182, 233-234 (item 474).

See also Bosi, *Cinquant'anni di vita italiana in America* (1921), 408 (item 18) and Deschamps, "La letteratura d'appendice nei periodici italo-americani (1910-1935)" (item 620).

Riccardo Cordiferro

763. Aleandri, Emelise. "Riccardo Cordiferro." In Juliani, ed., *Italian Americans* (1989), 165-178 (item 527).

764. ———. "Cordiferro," in La Gumina, *The Italian-American Experience* (2000), 146-148 (item 484).

765. ———. "Italian-American Theatre." In Martelli, *Il sogno italo-americano* (1998) (item 487).

766. ———. "Riccardo Cordiferrro and the Origins of La Follia." *Italian Americana* 15, no. 1 (Winter 1997): 51-55.

See also Durante, "Riccardo Cordiferro: An Italian American Archetype," above, 18-29.

Luigi Galleani

767. Fedeli, Ugo. *Luigi Galleani: Quarant'anni di lotte rivoluzionarie (1891-1931)*. Cesena: Antistato, 1956.

768. Masini, Pier Carlo. "La giovinezza di Luigi Galleani." *Movimento Operaio* 3, no. 3 (May-June 1954): 445-458.

769. Molinari, Augusta. "Luigi Galleani: un anarchico italiano negli Stati Uniti." *Miscellanea Storica Ligure* XI (1974): 261-286.

770. Nejrotti, Mariella. "Le prime esperienze politiche di Luigi Galleani (1881-1891)." In *Anarchici e anarchia nel mondo contemporaneo* (1971): 208-216 (item 690).

771. Pernicone, Nunzio. "Luigi Galleani and Italian Anarchist Terrorism in the United States." *Studi Emigrazione/Etudes Migrations*, 30, no. 111 (September 1993): 469-489.

Arturo Giovannitti

772. Cavaioli, Frank and Jerre Mangione. "Arturo Giovannitti." In La Gumina, *The Italian-American Experience* (2000), 268-269 (item 484).

773. D'Attilio, Robert. "Arturo Giovannitti." In Buhle, *The American Radical* (1994), 135-142 (item 699).

774. De Ciampis, Mario. "Arturo M. Giovannitti." *Controcorrente* (Boston) 16, nos. 4-5, *New Series*, nos. 16-17 (January-February, March-April 1960).

775. Durante. "Arturo Giovannitti." In *Italoamericana* (2005), 574-575 (item 474).

776. Lalli, Renato. *Arturo Giovannitti. Poesia, cristisianesimo e socialismo tra le lotte operaie del primo Novecento americano*. Campobasso: Rufus, 1981.

777. Marazzi, Martino. "L'isola di Arturo: introduzione a Giovannitti." In Marazzi, *A occhi aperti* (2011), 153-168 (item 486).

778. ———. "Introduzione." In Marazzi, *Parole e sangue* (2005), 9-17 (item 390).

779. Pernicone, Nunzio. "Arturo Giovannitti's 'Son of the Abyss' and the Westmoreland Strike of 1910-1911." *Italian Americana*, 17, no. 2 (Summer 1999): 178-192.

780. Prezzolini, Giuseppe. "Elogio di un 'trapiantato' molisano bardo della libertà negli Stati Uniti." *Il Tempo* (May 10, 1963).

781. Sillanpaa, Wallace P. "The Poetry and Politics of Arturo Giovannitti." In Krase, *The Melting Pot and Beyond* (1987), 175-189 (item 528).

782. Tedeschini Lalli, Biancamaria. "La metapoesia di Arturo Giovannitti." *Letteratura d'America, Tuttamerica – L'America degli italiani* Year II, nos. 9-10 (Autumn 1981): 43-79.

783. Tusiani, Joseph. "La poesie di Arturo Giovannitti." *La Parola del Popolo* (November/December 1978).

784. ———. "La poesia inglese di Arturo Giovannitti," "Il primo processo celebre del secolo," "Arturo Giovannitti nel Bronx." In Marazzi, ed., *Parole e sangue* (2005), 339-354, 355-362, 363-376 (item 390).

785. Untermeyer, Louis. "Arturo Giovannitti." In *The New Era in American Poetry*. New York: Holt, 1919.

786. Zappulla, Giuseppe. "Arturo Giovannitti." *Italamerican* (February–May 1960).

The Sacco and Vanzetti Affair

787. Avrich, Paul. *Sacco and Vanzetti. The Anarchist Background*. Princeton: Princeton University Press, 1991.

788. Boston Public Library Staff. *Sacco-Vanzetti: Developments and Reconsiderations, 1979*. Boston: Trustees of the Public Library of the City of Boston, 1982.+

789. Botta, Luigi. *Sacco e Vanzetti: Giustiziata la verità*. Cavallermaggiore: Gribaudo, 1978.

790. Creagh, Ronald. *Sacco et Vanzetti*. Paris: La Découverte, 1984.

791. Dos Passos, John. *Facing the Chair: Story of the Americanization of Two Foreignborn Workmen*. Boston: Sacco-Vanzetti Defense Committee, 1927.+

792. Ehrmann, Herbert B. *The Case That Will Not Die: Commonwealth vs. Sacco and Vanzetti*. Boston: Little, Brown & Co., 1969.

793. Felix, David. *Protest: Sacco-Vanzetti and the Intellectuals*. Bloomington: Indiana University Press, 1965.

794. Feurlicht, Roberta Strauss. *Justice Crucified: The Story of Sacco and Vanzetti*. New York: McGraw-Hill, 1977.+

795. Frankfurter, Felix. *The Case of Sacco and Vanzetti. A Critical Analysis for Lawyers and Laymen*. Boston: Little, Brown & Co., 1927.+

796. Guadagni, Felice. *Il Caso Sacco-Vanzetti: Una mostruosità giudiziaria. Esposizione sintetica dei fatti più importanti inerenti al caso*. Boston: Comitato Centrale di Difesa, 1924.

797. Lyons, Eugene. *The Life and Death of Sacco and Vanzetti*. New York: Inter-

national Publishers, 1927. Trans., 1928, *Vita e morte di Sacco e Vanzetti*. New York: Il Martello Publishing Co. *Cat. 122a–b.*

798. Russell, Francis. *Tragedy in Dedham: The Story of the Sacco-Vanzetti Case.* New York: McGraw-Hill, 1962.

799. ———. *Sacco and Vanzetti: The Case Resolved.* New York: Harper & Row, 1924.

800. Vanzetti, Bartolomeo. *Autobiografia e lettere inedite*, ed. Alberto Gedda. Firenze: Vallecchi, 1977.

801. ———. "Bartolomeo Vanzetti (Note autobiografiche)." *L'Agitazione* (organ of the Defense Committee) (January and February 1921). Republished in *La Controcorrente* (Boston) 10, no. 2 (August 1948).

802. ———. *Non piangete la mia morte: Lettere ai familiari* (eds. Cesare Pillon and Vincenzina Vanzetti). Roma: Editori Riuniti, 1962.

803. ———. *Una vita proletaria. L'autobiografia, le lettere dal carcere e le ultime parole ai giudici*, introduction by Giuseppe Galzerano. Casalvelino Scalo: Galzerano, 1987.

See also items 428 (Sacco) and 431 (Schiavina).

Carlo Tresca

804. Arleo, Joseph. *The Grand Street Collector*. New York: Walker & Co., 1970.+

805. Bugiardini, Sergio. "Il Freelance della rivoluzione. Nota all'inedita autobiografia di Carlo Tresca." In "Esuli pensieri. Scritture migranti" (2005), 45-59 (item 632).

806. Cupelli, Alberto. "Trentesimo anniversario della uccisione di Carlo Tresca." *La Parola del Popolo* (Chicago) (March–April 1973).

807. Eastman, Max. *Heroes I Have Known: Twelve Who Lived Great Lives*. New York: Simon & Schuster, 1943.

808. ———. "Profile: Troublemaker." *The New Yorker* (September 15, 1934 (part I), 31-36 and September 22, 1934 (part II), 26-29).

809. Gallagher, Dorothy. *All the Right Enemies: The Life and Murder of Carlo Tresca*. New Brunswick: Rutgers University Press, 1988.+

810. Giovannitti, Arturo. "Omaggio a Carlo Tresca [1916]." Clemente, *Cinquantesimo Anniversario 1908-1958. La Parola del Popolo* (1959), 64-66 (item 703).

811. Gualtieri, Italia, ed. *Carlo Tresca. Vita e morte di un anarchico italiano in America*. Chieti-Villamagna: Tinari, 1999.

812. Marazzi, Martino. "L'Autobiography di Carlo Tresca." In *A occhi aperti* (2011), 249-267 (item 486).

813. Montana, Vanni. "L'assassinio di Carlo Tresca nel racconto di Vanni Montana." *La Parola del Popolo*, 29, Year 70. no. 147, November–December 1978: 47-51.

814. Pernicone, Nunzio. "Carlo Tresca: Life and Death of a Revolutionary." In Juliani, ed., *Italian Americans* (1989), 216-235 (item 527).

815. ———. *Carlo Tresca: Portrait of a Rebel*. New York: Palgrave Macmillan, 2005.+

816. ———, ed. *The Autobiography of Carlo Tresca*. New York: John D. Calandra Institute, City University of New York, 2003.+

817. Taddei, Ezio. *The Tresca Case*. New York: [n.p.], 1943.

818. Thomas, Norman. *Who Killed Carlo Tresca?* New York: Tresca Memorial Committee, 1945. *Cat. 125*.

819. ———. *Chi uccise Carlo Tresca?* New York: Tresca Memorial Committee, 1947. *Cat. 126*.

820. Vezzosi, Elisabetta. "Carlo Tresca tra mito e realtà a 50 anni dalla morte." In Gualtieri, ed., *Carlo Tresca* (1999), 13-25 (item 811).

Index

ABOUT THE AUTHOR

JAMES J. PERICONI, a Manhattan environmental lawyer by day, began collecting Italian-language American books and other printed materials in 2000. *Strangers in a Strange Land* was the catalogue for the original exhibition, at the Grolier Club of New York, Fall 2012, of this collection, on display at the Brooklyn College Library, Spring 2013, and at Westchester Community College in the Fall of 2013. He is bibliographic editor of the translation of Francesco Durante's monumental *Italoamericana: Storia e letteratura degli italiani negli Stati Uniti* (2005) for Fordham University Press (2014). He received his B.A., English Literature, Columbia College, 1970; M.A., English and Comparative Literature, University of Virginia, 1972; and his law degree, New York University, 1977.

VIA FOLIOS

A refereed book series dedicated to the culture of Italians and Italian Americans. For a complete list of our publications in this series and others, visit our website at www.bordigherapress.org.

DANIELA GIOSEFFI, *Escaping La Vita Della Cucina*, Vol. 85. Essays & Creative Writing. $22

MARIA FAMÀ, *Mystics in the Family*, Vol. 84. Poetry, $10

ROSSANA DEL ZIO, *From Bread and Tomatoes to Zuppa di Pesce "Ciambotto"*, Vol. 83. $15

LORENZO DELBOCA, *Polentoni*, Vol. 82. Italian Studies, $15

SAMUEL GHELLI, *A Reference Grammar*, Vol. 81. Italian Language. $36

ROSS TALARICO, *Sled Run*, Vol. 80. Fiction. $15

FRED MISURELLA, *Only Sons*, Vol. 79. Fiction. $15

FRANK LENTRICCHIA, *The Portable Lentricchia*, Vol. 78. Fiction. $16

RICHARD VETERE, *The Other Colors in a Snow Storm*, Vol. 77. Poetry. $10

GARIBALDI LAPOLLA, *Fire in the Flesh*, Vol. 76 Fiction & Criticism. $25

GEORGE GUIDA, *The Pope Stories*, Vol. 75 Prose. $15

ROBERT VISCUSI, *Ellis Island*, Vol. 74. Poetry. $28

ELENA GIANINI BELOTTI, *The Bitter Taste of Strangers Bread*, Vol. 73, Fiction, $24

PINO APRILE, *Terroni*, Vol. 72, Italian Studies, $20

EMANUEL DI PASQUALE, *Harvest*, Vol. 71, Poetry, $10

ROBERT ZWEIG, *Return to Naples*, Vol. 70, Memoir, $16

AIROS & CAPPELLI, *Guido*, Vol. 69, Italian/American Studies, $12

FRED GARDAPHÉ, *Moustache Pete is Dead! Long Live Moustache Pete!*, Vol. 67, Literature/Oral History, $12

PAOLO RUFFILLI, *Dark Room/Camera oscura*, Vol. 66, Poetry, $11

HELEN BAROLINI, *Crossing the Alps*, Vol. 65, Fiction, $14

COSMO FERRARA, *Profiles of Italian Americans*, Vol. 64, Italian Americana, $16

GIL FAGIANI, *Chianti in Connecticut*, Vol. 63, Poetry, $10

BASSETTI & D'ACQUINO, *Italic Lessons*, Vol. 62, Italian/American Studies, $10

CAVALIERI & PASCARELLI, Eds., *The Poet's Cookbook*, Vol. 61, Poetry/Recipes, $12

EMANUEL DI PASQUALE, *Siciliana*, Vol. 60, Poetry, $8

NATALIA COSTA, Ed., *Bufalini*, Vol. 59, Poetry. $18.

RICHARD VETERE, *Baroque*, Vol. 58, Fiction. $18.

LEWIS TURCO, *La Famiglia/The Family*, Vol. 57, Memoir, $15

NICK JAMES MILETI, *The Unscrupulous*, Vol. 56, Humanities, $20

BASSETTI, ACCOLLA, D'AQUINO, *Italic: An Encounter with Piero Bassetti*, Vol. 55, Essays, $8

GIOSE RIMANELLI, *The Three-legged One*, Vol. 54, Fiction, $15

CHARLES KLOPP, *Bele Antiche Stòrie*, Vol. 53, Criticism, $25

JOSEPH RICAPITO, *Second Wave*, Vol. 52, Poetry, $12

GARY MORMINO, *Italians in Florida*, Vol. 51, History, $15

GIANFRANCO ANGELUCCI, *Federico F.*, Vol. 50, Fiction, $15

ANTHONY VALERIO, *The Little Sailor*, Vol. 49, Memoir, $9

ROSS TALARICO, *The Reptilian Interludes*, Vol. 48, Poetry, $15

RACHEL GUIDO DE VRIES, *Teeny Tiny Tino's Fishing Story*, Vol. 47, Children's Literature, $6

EMANUEL DI PASQUALE, *Writing Anew*, Vol. 46, Poetry, $15

MARIA FAMÀ, *Looking For Cover*, Vol. 45, Poetry, $12

ANTHONY VALERIO, *Toni Cade Bambara's One Sicilian Night*, Vol. 44, Poetry, $10

EMANUEL CARNEVALI, Dennis Barone, Ed., *Furnished Rooms*, Vol. 43, Poetry, $14

BRENT ADKINS, et al., Ed., *Shifting Borders, Negotiating Places*, Vol. 42, Proceedings, $18

GEORGE GUIDA, *Low Italian*, Vol. 41, Poetry, $11

Bordighera Press is an imprint of Bordighera, Incorporated, an independently owned not-for-profit scholarly organization that has no legal affiliation with the University of Central Florida or with The John D. Calandra Italian American Institute, Queens College/CUNY.

www.ingramcontent.com/pod-product-compliance
Lightning Source LLC
Chambersburg PA
CBHW070912270326
41927CB00011B/2545